D1601280

THE CHRISTIAN YEAR

ANNULUS CHRISTIANUS

OFT

NIEVWE CATHOLYCKE

SERMOONEN

OP DE

Evangelien van alle de Sondaghen ende
Feestdaghen van het geheel Iaer.

DOOR DEN EERW. HEERE

Fr IOSEPHVS RIVIVS

Canonick van onse L. Vrouwe Kercke in de Abdye van
Tungerlo, der Ordre van Premonstreyt, ende hier
voortijts Pastoor van Druenen &c.

Argue, obsecra, increpa, in omni patientiâ &
doctrinâ. 2. ad Timoth. 4.

I.C.I.

t'ANTWERPEN,
By Hieronymus ende Ioan. Baptista Verdussen,
in de Cammerstraet in den gulden Leeuw.
Anno 1668.

THE CHRISTIAN YEAR
A BOOK OF 17TH CENTURY SERMONS
or
NEW CATHOLIC
SERMONS
ON THE
Gospels for all the Sundays &
Feast Days of the Entire Year

VOLUME I
ADVENT, CHRISTMAS, & EPIPHANY

JOSEPH RIVIUS O.PRAEM.
Canon Regular of the Norbertine Abbey of Tongerlo
and erstwhile Prior of that abbey
[first published 1668]

Translated by
Martin Roestenburg O.Praem.

AROUCA
PRESS

First published in Dutch in 1668
Copyright © Arouca Press 2021
Translation © Martin Roestenburg, O.Praem.

ISBN: 978-1-989905-94-4 (pbk)
ISBN: 978-1-989905-95-1 (hardcover)

Arouca Press
PO Box 55003
Bridgeport PO
Waterloo, ON N2J 3G0
Canada
www.aroucapress.com
Send inquiries to info@aroucapress.com

TABLE OF CONTENTS

TRANSLATOR'S NOTE

SOME YEARS AGO, BY A STROKE OF LUCK, I came into possession of a volume of the sermons of Joseph Rivius (1607–1666), erstwhile prior of the Premonstratensian St. Mary's Abbey at Tongerlo, Belgium. This stroke of luck may well have been an act of God because one day, as I was clearing out a pile of papers and books from a high shelf in the library of the Premonstratensian Generalate in Rome, a book fell on my head. Literally. It was old, leather-bound, slightly worm-eaten and printed in Gothic script. Upon examination I found it was a collection of sermons written in Dutch. Since I speak that language, I started laboriously translating one sermon, just for interest's sake, and as I became accustomed to the script, my affair with this book was born. One sermon led to another, and the rest is history, as they say.

The 1668 edition contains 113 sermons comprising those for the Sundays of the liturgical year, as well as some sermons for Saints' feast-days and one for the Dedication of a Church. Joseph Rivius was a faithful religious, a zealous prior, and a dedicated pastor. After his ordination in 1638 he was almost immediately thrust into parochial work, becoming pastor of the parishes of Drunen, Cuijk, and later Poppel in northern Flanders. He was elected abbot of Tongerlo but the King of Spain ousted him by placing his own favourite upon the abbatial throne. Rivius graciously ceded his rights and returned to parochial work. After having been a zealous pastor for a number of years, ailing health forced him to return to his abbey. A year later, in 1666, he departed this world. He wrote down the sermons he faithfully delivered each week to his parishioners, though he never saw them published. This work was left to his life-long friend and confrere Ludolphus van Craywinckel, himself a writer, who posthumously published the sermons as the volume we have today.

Rivius' "fire and brimstone" sermons had a strong effect on his "Catholic Listeners," as he affectionately called his congregation. Yet despite his punches, his sermons were profoundly scriptural. He based them on the "literal" meaning, and whilst first analysing the theme text, usually taken from the daily Gospel, he doesn't hesitate, however, to search out the "moral" or practical application of the text to his listeners. Some people have questioned, what is the point of translating old sermons, why bother with messages from the past? Yet I think if we want to move ahead with our faith, we also need to know what went before us. In these confusing, demoralising times where some in the Church seem to be trying their hardest to distance themselves from the past by creating a "parallel Church" where truth and Tradition are being assailed and threatened from both outside the Church and within her, it becomes all the more necessary to review our faith, and to be able to explain what we believe, and why. These sermons can help us in our quest. Written during a time when the Church was under siege from Protestantism, the sermons consolidated the Faith as handed down from Christ to the Apostles, and to us. They are clear examples of how we might strengthen our own faith in the face of adversity.

I therefore pray that by reading (or "listening") to this Norbertine preacher addressing his hearers almost four hundred years ago, we may come to the realisation, as I have, that the Faith of that age is recognizable as the Faith of the Church today. As someone once said, we are the sum total of what went before us. The message of Christ then is the same message of Christ now. The mystery of the Gospel remains relevant and awe-inspiring on the lips of a Flemish Norbertine canon, even though he is long gone. His message spurs us on to renew and strengthen our faith, to approach the Sacraments, to make acts of mortification and to do good works, for, as St Paul and St James tell us, our justification comes through faith and works. In this way, may we reach our true home in Heaven. May the Blessed Virgin Mary, Mother of God and Queen of Heaven, intercede for us.

[The Biblical Latin quotations are from the classical Vulgate. The English translations of Scripture are borrowed from the Douay-Rheims 1899 American version, except where for the sake of ease of reading or clarity I have used the 1989 New Revised Standard Version (Catholic Edition).]

TRANSLATOR'S INTRODUCTION

HISTORICAL BACKGROUND

In 1830 the country known as the Kingdom of the Netherlands was officially divided into two nations. That year, in a treaty signed by the five major European powers of the time, the new nation, Belgium, effectively became separated from the Netherlands and was assured its independence. The northern provinces were united under their king, William I of Orange-Nassau, and became known as the United Kingdom of the Netherlands. The provinces in the south became the Kingdom of Belgium, but, seeing that the newly independent nation had no royal house of its own, it chose as its first King of the Belgians a German, Prince Leopold of Saxe-Coburg-Saalfeld.

It was mentioned that the nation "officially" came to be divided, because in many ways a division between North and South had already existed for some centuries. Over the years each region experienced its own ebbs and flows, its own periods of greatness and decline. Even the capital would swing between Brussels in the South and Amsterdam in the North. The Burgundian Period (1384–1477) was the golden age for the Southern Netherlands. The court was moved to Brussels. The arts, sculpture, music, literature and architecture flourished as never before. It was the time of the van Eyck brothers, of Massijs, van der Weyden and Memling; the strains of Josquin des Prez, Ockeghem and Obrecht could be heard in the cathedrals to accompany heavenly Renaissance liturgies. Lay religious revival movements such as the Beguines and Beghards sprang up to give renewed impetus to the spiritual life. Industry flourished and Flemish cloth, lace and brocades were the envy of Europe. Commerce and trade flourished.

The Burgundian time came to an end with the rise of the Habsburg rulers. In 1519 Charles, the son of the Flemish Philip the Fair and his Spanish wife, Johanna the Mad, became Holy Roman Emperor. Under his rule the provinces of the Northern and Southern Netherlands were united for the first time. The economy made an enormous leap forward, commerce and industry increased, and Antwerp became a world city and leader in science and culture. One major event would bring all this to an abrupt end: the Protestant Reformation.

Some years earlier, in 1517, the German Augustinian friar Martin Luther launched a series of protests against the Church, which would give birth to the Reformation. Luther's writings would eventually lead to a split in Western Christianity, with the tragic consequences that followed. Lutheranism spread quickly from Germany to Scandinavia and into the Netherlands. Lutheranism appealed to the individualistic minds of the Dutch and the Flemings, and it soon took root among the populace, who saw it as a way of casting off the yoke of the Catholic Church. But Emperor Charles, who was a devout Catholic, sought to uphold the True Faith in his empire, and he quickly devised a means of eradicating the heretical Lutherans. This means came to be known as the Inquisition. Since Brussels was the capital at the time, the royal court was settled in the South, which left the North sparsely protected against the swarming Lutherans. Charles handed over succession to his son Philip, who became ruler of Spain and the Netherlands as King Philip II of Spain. Philip needed the revenues of wealthy Amsterdam in the North and lucrative Antwerp to the South, but as a fervent Catholic he was determined to stamp out heresy, and so he launched into his policy of religious persecution, starting in the North where by now many of the nobility had embraced Lutheranism.

The German-born Prince of Orange, William of Nassau, also called William the Silent because of his ability to keep his mouth shut when necessary, was born a Lutheran, but converted to Catholicism for political reasons. Prince William was a favourite at court, and in 1559 Philip made him governor of the province of Holland. Another favourite at the court, the young Flemish Count of Egmond, was likewise appointed Governor of Flanders and Artois. These two Catholic noblemen tried to persuade Philip to relent on persecuting the Lutherans, and, in particular, they sought to have the Inquisition disbanded. Philip resisted, but to add to his problems, a new strain of heresy was sweeping the country: Calvinism.

John Calvin was born a Catholic in 1509 in France. He started studying for the priesthood but changed his mind and took up legal studies at the Collège Royal in Paris, but soon had to flee that institution when he was denounced for his heretical views. While spending several years outrunning the ecclesiastical and civil authorities, he started composing a catechism and devised his own Eucharistic theology. Eventually he settled in Geneva, where he began a crusade preaching sermons, which won over many people. The teachings of Calvin spread like wildfire throughout Switzerland and France, and many people saw it as an opportunity to overthrow the Church of Rome; anything vaguely smacking of papism was considered evil and had to be wiped away. So began a period of iconoclasm, which resulted in many churches, monasteries and convents being ransacked and plundered. Many other churches were confiscated and taken over by the new religion, but not before being purged of papism and superstition by having their frescoed interiors whitewashed to reflect the new theology of purity and simplicity.

As statues in the churches were being smashed, and entire abbeys were being razed to the ground, many people feared a backlash for remaining Catholic and so they either apostatised or fled to the safety of the South. Even the Prince of Orange quietly escaped to his German estates at Nassau in expectation of quieter times, whilst the Count of Egmond loyally stayed at King Philip's side. Philip felt powerless in the face of so much needless destruction and had no choice but to send a large army of Spanish (Catholic) troops to the North to crush the heretics. And crush they did. Thousands were executed, including many noblemen. Among these was the Count of Egmond, himself no heretic, but he was punished for attempting to have the Inquisition disbanded. William of Orange also fell out of Philip's favour, which resulted in William raising an army to try to oust the hated Spaniards. His struggle sparked years of Dutch resistance in what would later be known as the Eighty Years' War against the Spanish invaders. William's band of men was no match for the professional Spanish soldiers, at least not on land. They took to sea and scraped together a kind of navy that made life difficult for the Spaniards by cutting off supplies and harassing them with sea raids. William reverted back to his birth-religion by rejoining the Protestant church, which move further strengthened Dutch resistance.

In 1575 fresh Spanish troops arrived in the South, and these managed to crush and defeat the Calvinists. Any resistance in the Catholic South eventually dwindled away. The Southern Netherlands under Spanish rule then came to be known as the Spanish Netherlands. The North battled on, managing to push the Spaniards southwards. In 1581, in the Union of Utrecht, they declared their independence from the Spanish South and King Philip II, thereby creating the Republic of the Seven United Provinces under Prince William of Orange. In 1609 a shaky truce was agreed upon, and the Habsburg ruler, now King Philip III, had to acknowledge the humiliating loss of the North by officially recognising the new Dutch Republic. From this time onwards the Dutch Northern and Flemish Southern Netherlands began their own independent histories.

The border between the Spanish-occupied Catholic South and the Dutch Protestant North became more or less the modern border between today's Belgium and the Netherlands. This border became, as it were, a buffer zone between two worlds. Despite their common origins and the many similarities between the two regions, especially in the light of culture, language and customs, the main difference was religion. Calvinism increasingly took hold on the Northern Netherlands, and in 1637, the last Catholic city and bastion of Catholicism, 's-Hertogenbosch, fell prey to the new religion. The many villages in the surrounding countryside of the province of Brabant (later split between North and South) became ensnared in the stranglehold of the new rulers. A short period of aggression against clergy and religious produced a number of Martyrs. We think here, for instance, of the nineteen priests and religious known as the Martyrs of Gorcum, who were hanged on 9 July 1572 in the town of Brielle by militant Dutch Calvinists; among them were two Norbertine Saints, the priests Adrian van Hilvarenbeek and James Lacops. The Catholic Mass was outlawed, and parish priests had to leave their parishes. Catholic schools were banned, and children had to attend Protestant schools. Tensions grew in families where some members had crossed over to the new religion. A great number of religious and priests in the North fled to the safety of the South. But many other pastors remained loyal to their flocks and chose to go into hiding to practice their ministry illegally, rather than let their sheep perish to the wolves. Those who could not go into hiding chose to work "at the coal face," as it were, in border villages and towns. There they tried their best to keep their flocks Catholic in the face of the threat of Protestantism. Because of the exodus to the South, there was a great scarcity of priests in the North. Catechism classes began being taught by lay people, many of them dedicated women. The lack of priests meant that many families could not attend Mass on Sundays, and so sermons were written down and gathered into books to be read out, often in homes within the family. In this way, the faithful would receive religious instruction whilst sanctifying the Sunday in their own way. The religious Orders, foremost among them the Norbertines and Jesuits, started sending priests to these border "mission territories." Many religious were appointed to parishes throughout the border areas. Some border villages swayed backwards and forwards between Catholicism and Protestantism. It is during this time and against this background that Joseph Rivius came to write his sermons.

LIFE OF JOSEPH RIVIUS

Petrus Rivius (van Rivieren in Dutch) was born in Leuven, in the Flemish-speaking part of modern-day Belgium, on 8 November 1607, the son of Gerardus van Rivieren, printer, and Joanna Boogaerts, housewife. They had another son, Joannes, who became an Augustinian and Doctor of Theology and who was appointed bishop of 's-Hertogenbosch in 1647 by King Phillip IV of Spain. Not much is known about Peter's early life. At some stage he studied medicine at Leuven, as his biographical details archived at the abbey of Tongerlo state: *promotus Lovanii studens medicinam.* On 19 December, 1628, the twenty-six year old Peter entered the illustrious Norbertine abbey of Tongerlo (founded 1128), where on 28 January 1629, he was clothed in the habit and entered the novitiate, taking the name Joseph. It was in the novitiate that he met Johannes Ludolphus van Craywinckel, and the two men were immediately united in the bonds of a life-long friendship. It was van Craywinckel who wrote the introduction to this *Book of Sermons*, in which he gives some insight into the life and character of his friend Joseph Rivius. He was also instrumental in having the work published. Van Craywinckel himself went on to become a noted writer and homilist.

Rivius took simple vows on 8 December 1630. In the abbey he held various functions: in 1636 he was appointed circator, chamberlain and instructor. He had a great devotion to the Mother of God, and next to praying the canonical hours he also daily prayed the Little Office of the Blessed Virgin Mary (the obligation for Premonstratensians to recite the Little Office in addition to the canonical hours was lifted in 1568 by Pope St Pius V), as well as a full fifteen-decade rosary. In 1639 he was appointed parish priest of Drunen and Cuijk, where he distinguished himself by his apostolic zeal and his thunderous exhortations. This appointment, given the Calvinist persecutions and difficulties of the times, must have been a challenging one. Ten years later, in 1649, he returned to his abbey, where he was appointed prior on 24 June, 1652. For "seven long years," as his friend van Craywinckel writes, he was an outstanding example to his confreres and a tireless worker. On 16 December, 1658, he took charge of St Valentine's parish in Poppel, where he showed himself to be an exemplary model for parish priests. The death of Abbot Augustine Wichmans on 11 February 1661 gave rise to an abbatial election in which the prior of Tongerlo, Siard de Smet, was elected the first candidate for the prelature, but he died not long after. A second election was called, wherein Joseph Rivius received the majority of votes, but his ascension to the abbatial throne was blocked by the Spanish King Philip IV, who appointed his own favourite, Albert Ursino, who at the time was parish priest of Rozendaal. Even though Ursino only attained sixth place as a candidate in the abbatial election, he was a *persona grata* at the Court and, as we said, a friend of the Spanish king. He was also well-known at the States of Holland, where he had once been delegated by the authorities to ensure the preservation of the Catholic Faith in the towns of dubious territory.[1] After the abbatial election, Joseph Rivius expressed his loyalty to Abbot Ursino, and graciously withdrew back to his parish at Poppel. Ursino's reign did not last long,

---

1 The details of the abbatial election are taken from Léon Goovaerts, *Écrivains, Artistes et Savants de l'Ordre de Prémontré*, vol.2: (Bruxelles, Schepens: Dictionnaire Bio-Bibliographique, 1899–1909), 96–97.

however, for he died just nine months after his abbatial blessing, on 23 February 1664. Rivius himself returned to Tongerlo 6 December, 1665, for health reasons and there he passed away the following year on 23 October, 1666, a few weeks short of his 60th birthday, in the 36th year of his profession and the 35th year of priesthood.

Rivius was an eloquent preacher and a skilled Latin writer and poet. After his untimely death, his friend Ludolphus van Craywinckel had the collection published in 1668 at Antwerp by H. and J. B. Verdussen under the title: *Annulus Christianus oft nieuwe catholycke Sermoonen op de Evangelien van alle de Sondaghen ende Feestdagen van het geheel Jaar* [*Annulus Christianus or New Catholic Sermons on the Gospels for All the Sundays and Feasts of the Entire Year*].

Rivius preached these sermons for the people he served in the parishes of Drunen, Cuijk (now in the Netherlands), and Poppel. He was well known to the noble family of van IJpelaer at Heusden, to whom he was going to dedicate his book in thanksgiving for the many benefits, support, and friendship he had received from them, but he died before he could do so. His friend and confrere, Ludolphus van Craywinckel, thereupon took it upon himself to have the work published. In fact, after the title-page, we find a letter written by van Craywinckel to Maria van IJpelaer, abbess of the Benedictine nuns' monastery of Munster Millen near Sint-Truiden, explaining that it was Rivius' intention to dedicate his book to the abbess as a token of his appreciation and thanks for the support and friendship she and her family had shown him. The noble family of van IJpelaer was well-known in the area, and it was widely believed that during the persecutions of the seventeenth century they had on one or more occasions given refuge to Jesuit priests.

Several reasons spurred van Craywinckel to publish the work. The first was obedience to his superior, who no doubt saw the value, both spiritual and economic, of having such work come to fruition. Secondly, to honour a promise to his deceased friend in having the work published, and finally, to fulfil a personal obligation towards the house of van IJpelaer, which in the past had been very generous and hospitable to the canons of Tongerlo, and which very likely had contributed financially to printing and publishing the work.

THE BOOK OF SERMONS

From the sixteenth century onwards, collections of sermons were bundled for various reasons: to edify the faithful, no doubt, or to preserve an author's snippets of wisdom for posterity, or as an aid to pastors preparing their own weekly sermons, and, especially in the case of the Roman Catholic Church, as a means to keep the Faith alive in areas where the Church was being persecuted, because the lack of priests and the prohibition of the Catholic Mass and Sacraments meant that Catholics could only sanctify the Lord's Day by reading the sermons at home, as we noted above.

Joseph Rivius' *Book of Sermons* was, as mentioned earlier, published by his close friend Ludolphus van Craywinckel after the author's death. Rivius never saw his book in print. How the sermons were preserved is a mystery. We do not know whether they were written out in long-hand, or in note form. Various anomalies attest to some attempts at editing. So, for instance, a direct comment such as "time is against me" or "the hour is almost up" is not something a preacher would normally include in his written sermon notes. It could also be that someone was taking down the sermons as they were being delivered, later collecting and bundling them.

As an introduction to the *Book of Sermons* there is, as we have mentioned, the flowery missive, or letter of thanks, by van Craywinckel to abbess Maria van IJpelaer, whose father seems to have financed the project. Then follows a letter of thanks to Jacobus Hroznata Crils, abbot of Tongerlo and van Craywinckel's superior, who gave permission for the printing of the work. Next comes a plaintive eulogy written by van Craywinckel in honour of his dead friend Rivius, which is followed by several approbations, the first by the Vicar General of the Order in Brabant, Libert, abbot of Park, and then an approbation by T. Voochts, the protonotary apostolic and censor. The final stamp of approval allowing distribution and sale of the book comes from the office of King Philip IV of Spain, who was, of course, at the time also king of the Spanish Netherlands.

The introduction is followed by 113 sermons, which the author divided into two sections, one for Sundays and major feasts and the other for Saints. We have divided the work into five volumes. Volumes

1–3 are headed "Sundays and Feasts for the Liturgical Year" and contains seventy-one sermons for every Sunday of the liturgical year. Volumes 4 and 5 have the title "Sermons for Feasts and the Proper of the Saints." They contain forty-two sermons for the major feasts of Our Lord and the Blessed Virgin, as well as feasts for Apostles and certain Saints.

I have attempted to address certain anomalies. The first of these is that neither the Sermons nor the Index contain dates. This is not such a problem for the temporal cycle, e.g., one knows that Christmas always falls on 25 December, or Epiphany on 6 January. But it becomes less clear for the sanctoral cycle, and so I have made a few adjustments. For instance, two feasts are out of order: the Immaculate Conception (8 December) has been placed before St Nicholas (6 December). Likewise, Blessed Herman-Joseph (8 May) is placed before St Mark (25 April). I have taken the liberty of restoring the proper order of these feasts. Interestingly, there are two sermons for 2 February, which correspond to the two names given to the same feast, though under different aspects: the Presentation of Our Lord (or Candlemas) and the Purification of the Blessed Virgin. These two feasts are ancient and have been fused into one and celebrated on the same day. Rivius has separated the two theological aspects of this feast into two separate sermons, which would possibly have been preached on the same day, one at the morning Mass, the other at afternoon devotions.

The collection of Sermons contains only one feast of St Peter's Chair. This ancient feast was traditionally celebrated on 18 January (St Peter's Chair at Rome) and again on 22 February (St Peter's Chair at Antioch). Given its placement in the list of feasts, I have assigned it the date of 22 February.

Another omission is a sermon for Passion Sunday, which feast fell on the Sunday before Palm Sunday, and which was certainly included in the Tridentine Roman Missal but is missing from the Book of Sermons. Curious, too, is the naming of the feast on 1 January, which is traditionally called the Circumcision of the Lord, or the Octave of Christmas, but which in the collection is simply given the secular name "New Year's Day."

Some readers may be unfamiliar with the feasts of Norbertine Saints such as Blessed (later Saint) Herman-Joseph and Blessed Godfrey. It must be remembered that the author was a Norbertine religious, who shared "his" Saints with parishioners in parishes that for many years had been staffed by Norbertine priests. The Norbertine Order had a great presence throughout the Netherlands, both North and South, at that time, as it still does today. The people would have been familiar with the white-habited priests who came to minister to them in their towns and villages, and these priests often fostered devotion to their own confreres who had been raised to the dignity of the altar. So, too, Rivius' spiritual father and Founder of the Order, St Norbert, would have been well-known to the "Catholic Listeners" of his time. St Norbert was formally canonised in 1582, just 25 years before our author's birth, and St Herman-Joseph was canonised in 1958 by Pope Pius XII.

As was the custom in those days, Rivius often delivered his sermons twice, first in the morning at Mass on Sundays, Feasts and Holy Days of Obligation, then later at evening devotions. It was customary for people to attend church twice on Sundays and certain Feasts. Often the preacher would prepare two different sermons each time, not wanting to subject those faithful who had attended morning Mass to the same sermon at evening devotions. Mass was always in the morning due to the Eucharistic fast which started the night before. In the afternoon there were devotions, which often included Benediction. The length of the sermons was usually one hour. We know this from such comments made by the author as "the hour has almost passed." He was aware of his time limit, and almost seems frustrated that he lacked time to elaborate on all his points. "Time is against me . . ." he remarks, but he is also aware that an hour is hard on his listeners. Elsewhere he almost apologetically adds ". . . I shall not keep you much longer." This is in stark contrast to modern times where even the Vicar of Christ has suggested that homilies should be no longer than eight minutes! An eight-minute sermon would likely have scandalised the "Catholic Listeners" of Rivius' time, who would have thought it decidedly un-Catholic.

The footnotes are entirely from the translator. For ease of reading, the original Latin scriptural quotes found in the text have been placed in the footnotes and replaced with their English equivalent. Similarly, patristic quotes in Latin have been placed in the footnotes and substituted by a translated version. Any scriptural citations have been added by the translator.

THEMES IN THE SERMONS

Each individual sermon is introduced by a verse from Scripture, in Latin, that is usually taken from the day's Gospel and which sets the theme for the sermon. The author develops this theme and uses various authorities to support it. Among these authorities the Bible holds primacy, followed by examples and references to Old Testament figures, or figures and anecdotes from the ancient world of the Greeks and Romans. Unlike many readers of today, the author assumes that at least some of his listeners would have had a basic education in the classics. To assist the modern reader, I have included at the end of the work some short biographical notes on the various historical figures and personalities mentioned in the text. Before continuing to the body of the sermon, the author first seeks the inspiration of the Holy Spirit through the intercession of the Holy Mother of God. He therefore invites the congregation to pray with him the *Ave Maria*.

In the fashion of the times, Rivius often draws his inspiration from the Fathers of the Church and turns to monastic writers such as St Bernard and St Thomas Aquinas, but he also makes use of contemporary theologians and historians of his day. He sometimes uses imaginary tales or examples, or stories about various characters, such as kings, army commanders, or travelling merchants. He also uses examples from nature, science, the cosmos, natural history, and stories about mythological animals, birds, etc. which would have fascinated and mesmerised his listeners, as well as having been an effective way to illustrate his point, and which give us a fascinating, and at times even humorous, glimpse into the quaintness and charm of the seventeenth century mindset. Use was also made of material produced by other writers. Unlike our modern times, authors then did not hesitate to "borrow" or appropriate texts from others, often translating whole slabs of text from other languages. So, for instance, we see that the Sermon for the Seventeenth Sunday after Pentecost bears a great similarity to a French work by the Jesuit Claude Maillard S. J. (*La Magdelaine Convertie*, published in 1646).

Rivius attempts to build up a relationship with his listeners by adopting a speaking voice, addressing them directly, and by asking rhetorical questions; at times he includes himself with his listeners in the first-person plural. At one point he uses a prop to illustrate a point he is trying to make. For instance, in the Sermon for the Passion of Our Lord, Part II, we read the directive *"here one shows an image of the scourged Christ."* One gets a clear mental image of Fr Rivius standing in the pulpit on Good Friday holding up an image of the scourged Christ to his faithful in order to move them to tears of compassion. His intention as a preacher was not so much to share knowledge with his listeners, but to move their wills and bring them to repentance and conversion of heart. Prayer especially is at the centre of his preaching. He will, at times, during his preaching launch into a prayer, a song of praise, or a personal dialogue with Our Lord, the Blessed Mother, or whichever Saint may be the subject of his sermon. Often his sermons end with a personal prayer of his own devising.

His moral instructions exhort his listeners to lead good Christian lives, to frequent Holy Mass and the Sacraments, especially Confession, to be good Catholics who need to work out their salvation and thus reach their ultimate goal, which is union with Almighty God in Heaven. Everything points to this union with God, to be in the Divine Presence, to experience the bliss of the Beatific Vision, to be happy forever in the glory of Heaven with the Saints and angels. The author is convinced that the only way to Heaven is within the Catholic Church, and he tries his hardest to convince Catholics of the truth of their Faith, that there is no other way that leads to Heaven except through membership in the Roman Catholic Church. His call echoes the famous adage of St Cyprian of Carthage (c.200–258) *extra Ecclesiam nulla salus* — outside the Church there is no salvation," and he exhorts Catholics not to leave the Church, not to be swayed by the new religion of the Calvinists, whose road will lead to perdition in the abyss of hell. For this reason, the Calvinists, whom he calls the "Reformed Brethren," at times do not escape his wrath and indignation, for he has seen too many of his faithful enticed by the new religion. We read, for instance, in the Sermon for New Year's Day:

> The Reformed Brothers, like birds of prey circling dead, stinking corpses, cannot abide the sweetness of the Name of Jesus, for they find pleasure in the stench of error and the filth of sin.... They are not in the least concerned for their immortal souls, even though a powerful and effective medicine can easily be found.

That medicine, according to the author, is calling upon the Holy Name of Jesus.

In a similar vein, we read on the First Sunday of Lent concerning the Eucharist:

> Finally, two more false witnesses have arisen, namely, Calvin and Luther, the former a Frenchman, the latter a High-German. Both have poured out terrible blasphemies against you (Christ). One says you are not truly present in the Most Holy Sacrament of the Altar, but only figuratively. The other says you are truly present, but together with the bread. In their belief they give false witness to your own words and they claim this Most Holy Sacrament to be a superstition, an impiety, sorcery and idolatry. These are without a doubt horrendous blasphemies.

Not only does our author consider the Reformers heretics because they preach a theology that contrasts, and even opposes, the Catholic position, but even more so are the Reformers considered traitors because they have turned their backs on the one, true Church founded by Jesus Christ. And so, in the sermon for the Nineteenth Sunday after Pentecost he laments:

> Christ shows His justice when He casts out of His heavenly glory into eternal damnation all those [...] who refused to believe and had not wanted to become members of the holy Catholic Church, [and] also all those who once had been in the Catholic Church and have left; they have now been deprived of their wedding robe, namely, of love and virtuous works.

HIS AUDIENCE

In today's post-conciliar climate of sanitised ecumenism, the author would have been severely condemned for being anti-ecumenical. But we must remember the background and times in which his words were written. We must also be aware of the composition of the congregation to whom he was preaching. The majority of the congregation would no doubt have consisted of people who were born, baptised, and raised as Catholics. He therefore calls them "Catholic Listeners." There may also have been Catholics present who had lapsed in the Faith, or even apostatised, and returned. There would have been people "off the street," Protestants even, who happened to be visiting the church as a priest was delivering his sermon. There would have been a number of poor or marginalised people who had no particular affiliation with the Church, but who occasionally felt drawn to ask for spiritual favours or assistance. There would have been travellers, merchants, people of every social class. Not to forget the Catholic diocesan "officials" who would sometimes turn up unexpectedly to listen to the sermon, thereby making sure that the priest himself was remaining loyal to Catholic doctrine and was not slipping into error, and who would report back to the bishop. These days we might call them "quality control" officers. And so, the pastor would have considered it his duty not only to preach the fullness of the truth of the Catholic Faith, but also to point out the errors of the new religion to those who most needed to hear it, that is, lapsed Catholics, former Protestants and even the Protestants themselves, for the sermon was often the only means whereby he could reach these people. We must also bear in mind that, even though the Low Countries at the time enjoyed one of the highest literacy rates in Europe, there was still much illiteracy, especially among the humbler classes. For many people, the spoken word, and hence sermons, was their only means of catechesis and the beginning of their faith.

During the mid-1600s when our author was most active, the Protestant Reformation was drawing to a close and reform had largely been accepted as an established fact. Despite the initial thrust of the Catholic Counter-Reformation after the Council of Trent (1545–1563), the schism caused by the Reformation was not going to heal quickly, if at all, and so the clergy of the time, especially in the Spanish Southern Netherlands, were resigned to the fact that there was no point in fighting the firmly-established Protestant church in the North, and that the best tactic to use was to affirm the truth of their Catholic Faith. Sermons started taking on a more didactic and apologetic nature. The people needed to know the teachings of the Catholic Church, what the Church taught and why, and the consequences of abandoning those teachings. If people were convinced of the truth, they would be less likely to wander and apostatise. Hear this dire warning from our author:

> Almighty God calls all people to the wedding feast of the Catholic Church ... but some refuse to come, such as, for example, the Jews, Turks and infidels. Some others, upon entering, have walked out again, such as the heretics; others have cut themselves off, such as the schismatics, and yet others have come and stayed at the wedding feast, but they were not properly dressed in the wedding robe of innocence and love, which should agree with their Catholic Faith; these people have become chopped up and ripped to pieces through impurity, gluttony and other kinds of wickedness [...] there are so many lukewarm, sluggish Catholic faithful who camouflage the name Catholic and the Catholic Faith with the garment of immodest and heathen practices, thus making themselves unworthy to remain in the Church of God, and consequently deserve to be expelled from His glory [...] neither the non-believers nor the heretics nor those in a state of mortal sin will find access to the Kingdom of God. Faith, love, and the virtuous life will be our entrance ticket (Sermon for the Nineteenth Sunday after Pentecost).

RIVIUS' THEOLOGY

As a true shepherd who cared for his sheep, Joseph Rivius' sole desire was that his sheep would be saved and not be left to the wolves to be torn asunder. One great threat was that his sheep would stray outside the flock of the Catholic Church to the religion of the Calvinists. But there were other threats to their salvation. Sin, the world, the flesh and the devil, obstinacy, tepidity in the Faith, giving in to temptation, living a life of vice, and so on, were equally destructive to a soul seeking salvation. Rivius was well aware that man is a creature flawed by original sin, and his sermons reflect his concern that man should repent of his sins and return to God, the merciful, loving Father who welcomes the sinner. Whilst it is true that God punishes wickedness, nonetheless, mercy and justice go hand-in-hand, and God is ever patient with the sinner and accepts all who return to Him in repentance. God promises eternal life to the believer, and we need to conform ourselves to Him in whose image we are made, so that we may merit returning to our natural home, our eternal glory, in Heaven. Therefore, in this life we must avoid anything that may hinder us reaching our eternal goal. We must become holy by rejecting the Evil One, by keeping God's commandments, by fleeing fleeting, mundane things, by seeking the end for which we are made. Furthermore, we must above all avoid mortal sin, which blinds our reason and kills the life of the soul; mortal sin separates us from God and damns us to hell if we are unfortunate enough to die with mortal sin on our soul. To keep us on track and to help us reach our heavenly goal, use must be made of the many aids God has given us, such as the holy Sacraments, and especially Penance. We must nurture the practice of repentance and contrition and go to Confession; we must imitate the Blessed Virgin and read the lives of the Saints, who constantly pray for us from Heaven, and we should imitate their virtues; we should frequently meditate on Christ's Passion and suffering, His sacred wounds and holy Cross, and the meaning of the Redemption; but most importantly, we must believe, we must have faith in what Christ and His holy Catholic Church teaches us, for it is only through faith and good works that we can hope to reach Heaven, as St James tells us: "For just as the body without the spirit is dead, so faith without works is also dead" (Jas 2:26).

For Rivius, the Apostle's words held particular significance, for they solidified the Catholic theology of justification, which states that one is justified by both faith and good works. The Lutheran and Reformed theology, on the other hand, states that man could be saved by faith alone, *sola fide*, and this became a central rallying cry of the sixteenth century Reformers. Rivius weighs in on this by repeatedly propagating the Catholic position, exhorting his congregation that salvation can only be obtained through faith *and* good works. So he clearly states in the Sermon for the Sixth Sunday after Easter:

> Listen, the teaching that will get us to the glory of Heaven is made up of two ladders, both of which are necessary to our Catholic Faith, namely, faith and good works [...] the Prophet Ezekiel attributes the decay and destruction of Sodom to the negligence of its citizens in practicing works of mercy.

The merit earned by performing good works can also be applied to our fellow Catholics suffering in Purgatory:

> The prayers, alms and good works offered up by the faithful who are in the world are immensely profitable when applied to the departed souls, both to alleviate their pain and to shorten their time; this is a sure and true article of Faith (Sermon for All Souls' Day).

Rivius' fiery words were not just reserved for obstinate Catholics and sinners who refused to repent, or for the Reformers who were leading his flock astray, but priests, too, would sometimes have to hear some uncomfortable truths about their behaviour and way of life, words that are relevant also in our own time:

> So then, if the officials do not give sound advice, and if priests live without fear of the Lord, then it is no wonder that the entire community can become immoderate and coarse [...] these are the kind of things that made Christ our Saviour weep bitter tears, even though in His omnipotence He had already foreseen them (Sermon for the Ninth Sunday after Pentecost).

A bitter pill, too, for those priests who have a taste for wealth:

> The clergy should therefore take note not to hoard the income Almighty God has provided for them, nor to store up treasures, but they should generously distribute what they earn to the poor. [...] Therefore, the clergy should learn from this that the Church's income is the price of the Son of God's Precious Blood, and consequently it should not be locked away in chests but liberally distributed to the poor

and needy through acts of charity and mercy (Sermon for the Fourth Sunday of Lent).

Time will tell whether Rivius will ever be regarded as a great preacher, but he was certainly a good communicator. Through his preaching he tried to convince his audience of the truth of Scripture and the Tradition of the Roman Catholic Church. He was convinced that there was an ultimate truth to be revealed, and that truth was God's Eternal Word contained in Sacred Scripture. The many scriptural citations he uses to support his arguments are evidence of this. Truth, too, was to be found in the Tradition of the Church Christ founded, which was for Rivius the One, Holy, Catholic, and Apostolic Church founded upon St Peter. Despite the occasional "fire and brimstone," his sermons could also show tenderness and a genuine concern for the well-being and salvation of his flock. And we, the "Catholic Listeners" who read across the centuries do not feel excluded. The Christian message then is the same as today—believe, repent, live good Christian lives in order to reach salvation in the glory of Heaven, our true home. In the letter written to Abbess Maria when presenting this book of Sermons, van Craywinckel wrote, "I hope these sermons may serve Your Reverence and your holy community as a key with which to unlock Heaven, thus being able to enter in." This, too, the author would no doubt also wish for you, the readers, his beloved "Catholic Listeners."

Summary of the Sermons
ADVENT TO EPIPHANY

FIRST SUNDAY OF ADVENT

Signs in the heavens — the Day of Judgment — God is Judge of the living and the dead — people will be publicly sentenced to Heaven or hell — God's verdict is final — God's mercy and justice — sinners will be punished — Mary Queen of Heaven advocates for sinners — the splendour of the Saints, our helpers.

SECOND SUNDAY OF ADVENT

John the Baptist — how can evil triumph over good? — everything happens according to God's plan, even evil — John sends his disciples to Jesus — Jesus is the Saviour, we must witness Him in our lives — sin blinds and cripples Christians — sin kills the soul — many are blind to God's judgement — Jesus the heavenly Physician.

THIRD SUNDAY OF ADVENT

John the Precursor — we turn from Jesus towards worldly things, from God to changeable goods — in ignorance the Jews turn from Jesus to John — all is vanity — flee the world and its temptations, for all will pass away.

FOURTH SUNDAY OF ADVENT

Division creates chaos — during the reign of Augustus, the Word comes to John — wicked rulers rule Palestine — the Jews trample underfoot their service to God — the fullness of time — God sends prophets to help people — God sends holy men in His Church to fight heretics, such as Norbert, Dominic, etc. — man is made in God's image — God became man so we may more easily love Him — go to Confession, purify yourselves — level the mountains of pride.

THE SOLEMNITY OF CHRISTMAS — FIRST SERMON

The humility of Christ to be born a Child — the Child shall slay His enemies, the pride of Eglon and the devil — sinners should stay away from the stable — do not be duplicitous — He is the King of peace — Christ is born for us, even though we deserve punishment for our sins — the miraculous fountain of oil in Rome — the balsam of Engaddi — come to Bethlehem.

THE SOLEMNITY OF CHRISTMAS — SECOND SERMON

Christ's birth is astonishing — who can believe that God was born a child? — the prophets' predictions are fulfilled — Mary, Joseph, and the Incarnation — Mary bore Christ without pain — St Gertrude the Great was puzzled by term "first-born" — Christ the Child in the manger is omniscient — Christ was born to free us from sin — come to the stable.

THE FEAST OF SAINT STEPHEN, MARTYR

Nothing is greater than giving one's life for one's friends — the horrors of martyrdom — St Paul — the Reformed Brethren get upset when challenged — Stephen's life and martyrdom — Jacob's ladder — Jerome and Eustochia — the glories of Heaven — explanation on how we can see the distant God — loving one's enemies — Cicero and Caesar — Aristides — mercy and forgiveness.

THE FEAST OF SAINT JOHN THE EVANGELIST

John is like an eagle — John the disciple of grace — the Lord's beloved — are we disciples of Christ or the world? — signs of Christ's love for John — his special graces — boiled in oil at the Latin Gate — John's virtues and perfections.

THE FEAST OF THE HOLY INNOCENTS

Man's inordinate, evil desire to dominate — man's power over others — Herod fears the birth of a new king — the Holy Innocents are "flowers of the Martyrs" — turn from sin, remain faithful to God — we will be judged in measure according to our sins.

ON THE SUNDAY NEAREST CHRISTMAS

God gives joy together with sadness — the astonishment of Joseph and Mary — the prophets are astonished — man's dignity is raised through the Incarnation — the devil is jealous of Christ and rouses the Jews against Him — some Catholics contradict the teachings of Christ and His Church — the false doctrines of heretics — sin also comes from within the Church — are we children of God or the world? — receive the Sacraments worthily.

NEW YEAR'S DAY

Keeping silence in contemplation best praises God — the "seat of truth" — Jehovah, the Holy Name — the Reformed Brethren are like birds of prey — invoke the sweet name of Jesus — circumcise your senses, especially the tongue — strip off the old Adam, put on the new.

THE FEAST OF THE THREE KINGS — EPIPHANY

Christ's birth was announced by a star — God orders Heaven to adore His Son — the obstinate Jews refuse Christ — come to the stable — kings bring gifts, we bring ourselves — instead of gold we bring sin — turn from sin, come to Bethlehem.

THE FIRST SUNDAY AFTER EPIPHANY

Young Tobias does not return home — his distraught parents — distraught too are Mary and Joseph upon losing Jesus — their joy upon His return — Jesus was born a normal child, though full of wisdom — Mary and Joseph seek the Child — we separate ourselves from Jesus through mortal sin — Jesus was obedient to Mary and Joseph — children should be obedient to their parents — be about your Father's business.

ON THE SECOND SUNDAY AFTER EPIPHANY

Christ uses various means to reveal His glory, even the extraordinary — Christ is present at the wedding of Cana to show His approval of marriage — some heretics denounce marriage — husbands must love their wives — have children to fill the earth with devout people — receive Jesus and Mary into your homes — Mary's concern for us — the Reformed Brethren deny invoking Mary or the Saints — the sweet honey of truth — the testimony of the Saints — Mary our advocate — Jesus and Mary are models for a bride and groom.

ON THE THIRD SUNDAY AFTER EPIPHANY

We must show mercy and compassion — the two properties of love: joy and compassion — the centurion's love and faith — the unbelieving Jews — God tests us — God accepts all who return to Him — Confession — why are we so lukewarm in the Faith? — we are sinners, like many-hued birds — do not provoke God's wrath — beware of being damned to hell.

ON THE FOURTH SUNDAY AFTER EPIPHANY

Caesar in the storm — Christ stills the seas — God's command contains the sea — God sets a limit around the sea, and around our vices — all creatures must obey God, including us — even the dumb beasts obey Him — all things seek the end for which they were created — nothing is more harmful than following one's own will — stubbornness — our purpose on earth — let not the devil deceive you as he deceived our first parents — submit to God's law, or fear punishment.

ON THE FIFTH SUNDAY AFTER EPIPHANY

Christ explains the parable to His disciples — the Trinity as applied to the parable — the good seed indicates righteous people: the bad seed indicates the Reformed Brethren — Luther and Calvin blasphemed — the devil sows bad seeds of heresy — sin bites us, like the Italian viper — be vigilant like the gazelle — God's patience with the sinner — on the Last Day the Reformed Brethren and the bad Catholics will be shackled by their own sins — there is still time to repent.

ON THE SIXTH SUNDAY AFTER EPIPHANY

Great things are contained in small origins — all things are passing — the Catholic Church represents the Kingdom of

Heaven — the Church's humble beginnings — growth and expansion of the Church — the Apostles are princes of the Church — the Kingdom of Heaven is within you — our hearts must be receptive by living as good Catholics — heretics do not understand the humbleness of our Sacraments — do not follow the deceptive world — be like pungent mustard — be not surprised by death.

Crest of Abbess Maria van IJpelaer OSB

Missive To the Very Reverend
and Noble Mistress, the Lady
Maria van IJpelaer
Abbess
of the noble convent of
Munster Milen
of the Order of St. *Benedict*, etc.,
situated in the Land of *Luik* near the town of *Sint-Truiden*.

Reverend Lady,

Pope Gregory the Great once wrote a letter to King Ethelbert of England, sending with it a small yet valuable gift, namely, some filings rasped from the chains with which the Apostle Paul had been bound, and soldered into the ring of a small silver key. His Holiness included these words, *Parva xenia transmisi, quae vobis parva non erunt, quia ex benedictione Beati Petri Apostoli suscepta* — "I have sent a small gift, which I hope Your Majesty will not consider small, because it comes with the blessing of the holy Apostle Peter."

I, too, approach Your Reverence with a gift, which, though small, may nonetheless, I hope, be pleasing to Your Reverence, because it is presented to Your Reverence with great affection, and it is made by a good friend. It is the Sermons of the Saints whom the holy Church celebrates throughout the year. It contains some filings of beautiful doctrines and their sublime virtues. I hope these sermons may serve Your Reverence and your holy community as a key with which to unlock Heaven, thus being able to enter in. They originate, not from the blessings of Saint Peter, but from the talented pen of the Reverend Peter Joseph Rivius, Norbertine canon of Tongerlo, in his time a parish priest of Drunen and Cuijk, where he wrote these sermons, preached them and admonished his subjects to observe them.

I believe he may have been fairly well known to Your Reverence and to Your Reverence's noble family at Heusden, from whom he received many favours; he therefore decided, as a token of appreciation and thanks, to dedicate this, his work, to Your Reverence, but alas! being surprised by death, he was not able to accomplish this himself. I, then, as guardian of this orphan, and as an exceptional friend of the deceased, have taken this task upon myself, partly upon order of my Superior, partly in order to fulfil the wish and desire of the deceased, and also to discharge my obligation to the noble House of IJpelaer. For I still often think about the generosity and friendship shown towards me by that House, when in 1635 during my younger years I was sent by my Superior to Drunen to stay with the parish priest, the Rev. Melchior Waterfort, as his vicar or associate. There I saw for myself how hospitable the Lord, your father, was towards religious persons, especially to religious from the monastery of Tongerlo (just as I personally experienced the zeal with which he won many heretics from their erroneous ways back to the true Roman Catholic Religion by means of his admonitions and alms-giving, and also how kind he was to the poor, how diligent he was to the Divine Services, travelling every Sunday and feast-day, despite rain or storm, to Drunen, which is one mile from Heusden, to offer Holy Mass, and how reverently he celebrated the Sacraments, of which he often partook with great fervour, thereby edifying everyone by his good example).

Just as Abraham, who received the angels in person, was also greatly blessed by God in his seed, so I strongly hope that he, both in his soul on high, as well as in his children here below, is able to enjoy divine blessings from the Lord, and since children always take after their parents, as the old proverb tells us, "As the old birds sang, so the young ones chirp," and again, "like father, like son," so I am not surprised that in Your Reverence's youth you were so virtuous, so God-fearing, so edifying and friendly to all and sundry. Even though Your Reverence wore a secular habit, according to your rank and state, in order to satisfy Your Reverence's parents, nonetheless Your Reverence internally wore a spiritual one to please your heavenly Bridegroom, and from that time on you already had the desire to bid farewell to the world, and to depart for the spiritual life.

In addition, it is quite right that Your Reverence bears on your escutcheon the pelts of that purest of creatures, the ermine, which would rather die than besmirch its fine, white pelt. In a similar fashion, from an early age Your Reverence had also wanted to flee the impure world, and like Lot fleeing from the fires of Sodom to Mount Segor, so you betook yourself to the holy Order of the Patriarch Benedict in order to preserve your purity, immaculate and undefiled, like the ermine, knowing full well that in that place there were fewer occasions to sully your purity, and greater means to maintain it. So the mellifluous Bernard teaches us with these sweet words, *In religious life man lives more purely, falls more rarely, rises more speedily, walks more cautiously, is bedewed with grace more frequently, rests more securely, dies more confidently, is cleansed more quickly, and rewarded more abundantly.* The two crosses on Your Reverence's escutcheon signifies the double cross which Your Reverence wears, one internally, the other externally, the one in your heart, the other on your body and governance. The first is your constant meditation on the Passion of Christ, the compassion with your bleeding Bridegroom Jesus; the second is knowing that the stricter one maintains the discipline of the cloister, the quicker will grow the difficulties of its subjects, who themselves have caused a good deal of crosses for the Superiors, who can never satisfy everyone's wishes. As a Superior once said, "no one knows what burdens lie hidden under this excellent habit." But Your Reverence does know, as Bernard says, that the crosses that strike hard on the outside, God anoints and sweetens on the inside by His grace, solace, and knowledge. No one is free from crosses, as the lives of the Saints well testify, for they all cry out with Teresa, *we either suffer or die.* For there is nothing more blessed than to carry one's cross. See Abel struggling with Cain, Moses with Pharaoh, David with Saul, Susanna with the elders, Joseph with his brothers, Daniel with the courtiers who were crueller than lions, Christ with the Jews, Mary with the Cross, the Martyrs with the tyrants — all of them call out, *si tollis crucem, tollis lucem,* that is,

The Cross gives Whatever shines;
Whoever removes the Cross, Removes the light.

This alludes to that small wooden cross attached to a supporting cork which floats on top of the oil in a lamp, through the centre of which runs a burning wick; if this cross is missing, the wick will fall into the oil, and the flame will go out.

But Your Reverence is not made of a cross, whose *hope*, according to Your Reverence's motto is always *in God*, who is faithful and never lets anyone suffer beyond his strength but uses ordeals for one's benefit; after suffering He gives eternal joy, after yearning, pleasure, after darkness, light, after virtue, joy, and after languishing and death, the inheritance of everlasting bliss.

All this I wish Your Reverence from the depths of my heart, praying that Almighty God may deign to keep Your Reverence, and in all times and at all times to bless you with both temporal and eternal prosperity. I remain, Reverend Lady,

> Your Reverence's humble servant in Christ.
> Frater *Ioannes Ludolphus van Craywinckel*,
> Norbertine Canon of *Tongerlo*
> Parish-priest of *Oelegem*

To the Very Reverend Lord
Lord Jacobus Hroznata Cril
Abbot of the Illustrious Abbey of *Tongerlo*
of the Premonstratensian Order.
Lord of *Tongerlo, Kalmthout, Essen, Huijbergen*
Lord in *Ravels, Werbeek, Zondereigen, Hooidonk*, etc.

Very Reverend Father,

Among all the creatures with which Almighty God's providence has enriched and adorned this world, I have found three unlike any other, which are wholly and substantially different from each other, both in their being as in their usefulness. For some creatures are useful and profitable whilst alive, but not when dead. Others are profitable when dead, but not when alive; and then there is a third type which is profitable both dead and alive.

Among the first type we count falcons and greyhounds, which, whilst alive, are useful in bird hunting, here catching a couple of partridges, or there with its claws catching a hare in its nest, which it deposits before the feet of the gamekeeper; these creatures, so useful in life, are cast on the dung-heap when they die.

Of the second type is the pig, who neither generates nor produces much that is profitable when alive, having its snout constantly in a trough of husks and swill; but when this greedy creature's throat is slit with the butcher's knife, man will feast on sausages and tripe, lardy cakes and roast ribs, and bacon pancakes and hams once more appear on the table; how much more useful is the pig dead than when alive.

The third type includes oxen, cows and sheep, for while they live, they can be harnessed to pull wagons, or plough the land; they also give butter, milk, cheese and wool. After death they supply fine roast meats, beef stews, great slabs of salted meat, threaded and marbled through with prized healthy fat.

Now of these three types of creatures, when taken in an ethical sense and applied to man, the first is illustrated by those people who in their lives draw on pensions, or those who go off with their rapier on some modest employment; they are profitable in life, but not profitable after death.

The second type is illustrated by those stubborn skinflints who, when asked to draw one farthing out of their pockets, act as if they were asked to extract a rib from their chest, always being dissatisfied, that is, until their mouths fill with soil, and then they will see how dear Nephew and Niece, after having buried them in the cemetery, will grabble at their coins, quarrelling to control them, for as the saying goes, "squander behind the coffin dost wander."

Do I hear someone asking me who I thought might be profitable both in life as well as in death? Well, I would answer that they are the humble parents, the hard-working fathers and conscientious mothers, who go about from early morning until late at night, like honey-sucking bees, or industrious ants, earning by the sweat of their brow not only their children's daily bread, but also managing each year to save a pretty penny or two, which their sons or daughters sooner or later would be able to claim as part of their inheritance.

I have to admit, that there is wisdom in the pen of those who first discovered this and left it for our edification, for they knew how to hit the nail on the head, so to speak. Therefore, if I might raise the standard somewhat, that third type of person I would like to raise from the corporal plane to the spiritual; among them we count those people who during their lives had provided excellent and seasoned teachings, and challenging, well-planned, and coherent sermons, and who laboured with devotion and perspiration for the salvation of the people. Furthermore, after their death, through their learned books, they continue to edify and enlighten, teach and convert their entire Fatherland. Among these persons there stands out the Reverend Lord *Joseph Rivius*, of happy memory, canon of the most-illustrious Abbey of Tongerlo. In regard to his great harvest of souls, Drunen will bear testimony, and Poppel will tell us about that swollen *River* of erudition, zeal and godliness, which flowed and meandered out far and wide, taking in on both sides the young as well as the old. If he had to admonish his listeners, he would sweeten his wormwood in the friendliest way; if he had to provoke or bring sense to his listeners, he did so with an abundance of powerful words and persistent reasoning. In the manner he fulfilled his office, so he cared for his sheep, like another Jacob, perspiring in the heat of summer and with chattering teeth in the cold of winter, always moving about, ever watchful, knowing well that "sleepy shepherds help fatten the wolves."

What can I say about his profound devotion to the Queen of Angels, and the steadfastness of his daily prayers to her? For, apart from his canonical hours as well as the Little Office of the Blessed Virgin Mary, he also said each day a fifteen-decade rosary whilst meditating upon the holy mysteries contained therein. It is no wonder, then, that he bore the name of St Joseph, thereby taking on the role of the well-beloved spouse. He knew all too well that Mary was contained in the thirst for the spring of living water, that she was in the hunger for that manna which the angels sent down from Heaven, that during a storm she was in the compass with which to navigate to safety, in poverty she was in the treasury of divine riches; there he slaked his thirst, there he found his safe haven, there he sang praises for the graces he received.

I do not want to praise the seven years he served as Prior, always being polite and friendly. I shall also keep silent about the time when, on 11 February 1661, the Rev. Prelate Augustinus Wichmans passed away, and there was an abbatial election; since he won the most votes, the religious wanted to place the mitre on his worthy head, but why did this joyous event not come about? Following like the Wise Man when they asked him, "why are you not a king?", I believe Rivius answered, "I would prefer if they asked: Why are you not a king, than that they asked, Why are you a king?"

This very reverend Joseph, then, who should have earned a long and fruitful old age, departed from us prematurely last year on 23rd of October 1666, in his 60th year, the 36th year of his profession, and the 35th year of his priesthood. God grant eternal rest to his soul. Yet even though death has claimed him, he lives on in his children, that is, the learned books which he has left behind; these fatherless orphans and wandering, abandoned children I have taken to myself as their guardian, and being a loyal friend of their deceased father, I now humbly present them to Your Reverence in the hope that they may be raised to their proper state of perfection, so that their father might be honoured and praised by his fine and excellent children. Just as the Patriarch Jacob took the children of Joseph, Ephraim, and Manasseh to himself, and blessed them and cared for them, so I hope and pray that Your Reverence shall not withhold Your Reverence's paternal blessing upon these spiritual children of our beloved Joseph, and that you may take them to yourself. Thus sheltering under Your Reverence's wings, and being protected from wicked tongues and defamation, they may reach a perfect old age, to the greater glory of God and the salvation of souls.

Meanwhile, I thank Your Reverence for the dues and honour given to our deceased lord Rivius, my best friend in Christ, and I shall always remain bound to pray to Almighty God that He will bless Your Reverence at all times with both temporal and eternal blessings, prosperity and glory. I remain, Very Reverend Father,

Your Reverence's most humble Son
Frater *Ioannes Ludolphus van Craywinckel*
Religious of *Tongerlo*.

Eulogy

I wonder, should I let the whole world know
Of Rivius's death, with either a River of tears in flow:
    Else with a River of eloquence wise
    His virtue holding aloft 'pon his demise?
O love, give me counsel, come instruct me,
Should this man be mourned or praisèd be?
      To praise him or mourn him, what matters it now?
      For both sorrow and praise from love's source do flow.
He who through God's Word sought amply to praise Him,
Is himself worthy to receive from us honour and praising;
    And we, after his death, the praises do sing
    Of him whose heart to God honour did bring.
And as we behold our 'flection in a River
So Rivius reflects our image as in a mirror.
    For every Sermon, placed here by Lord Rivius
    Shall be as a mirror, reflecting virtue to us.
His Preachings admonish, provoke, and arouse
The sinner who reads them to tears and vows,
    And once contrite, is now that sinful heart
    Washed clean and sees stain and filth depart.
In a righteous person they cause such commotion
That man just melts in tears of devotion.
    And so, he, 'pon this River of tears and wailing,
    'long the River that gladdens to God's City goes sailing.
And just as earth's Rivers do flow and wind
To strengthen and adorn land, town and such kind
    And just as their abundant wetness does flow
    'pon the land, great fruitfulness to bestow
So was Lord Rivius the glory of the Catholic
But for some others, the scourge of the heretic.
    Near Den Bosch, where the Beggars their swords did sway,
    So he over the churches of Drunen and Poppel held reign,

And there, by whom did God's service so greatly grow
But by him, who on that Land his water let flow?
    Yet now, as the world's spin never stops, never quiets,
    So our Lord Rivius on that fair River expiréd.
Those pious shoulders, which to Our Dear Lord
Did carry the heavy burden of souls, and hearts out-poured,
    Have now 'pon his brothers' shoulders been laid
    And carried midst weeping and wailing to the grave.
He who loved his cell as 'twere his court
And seven long years as Prior did report,
    Now has a cell of seven double boards
    And in a grave long seven feet is stored.
Heliogabalus long lies with his bones
In a fine sepulchre of pearls and jewelled stones;
    Cerastes' body in a crystal case was hung,
    But the grave of Rivius in a pool of tears was sunk.
Alas! my eyes with grief and tears o'erflow'd
For Pale Death now those sweet eyes e'er has closed
    Of such a man, who in regard I've held high
    And loved and honoured as the apple of my eye.
He was my strength, in grief my comforter and aider
When I with him here lived, a novice in the cloister:
    Though a novice too was he, his virtue made time hasten
    In years he was but young, tho' in holiness he was sure brazen.
In honour of his virtue I have penned this humble Ode,
So that forever through his book he may find his abode;
    So, too, I hope, that he in Christ forever may abide,
    Who in the Book of Life his name may evermore inscribe.
Like all the brooks, and all the Rivers tame
Which flow back to the sea from whence they came,
    Lord Rivius now before God has arrived
    From Whom his noble soul had first derived.
He has, I hope, betrod that Realm of sanctity,
There for evermore and for all eternity
    To praise God and His Saints with mirth
    As he had done whilst here on earth.
He now abides with God on high, in light and glory,
And lives forever forth on earth dear in our mem'ry.
    Through this his book in which he penned God's praise,
    And gives new life to God's vast throng of Saints,

In this book Life's waters' thirst he does slake
Just as a River for no reason weaves and snakes;
   And for no other reason did he himself put out
   'Cept that God be his reward, both in season and out.
So may the Lord Almighty, when in Him I come to rest,
slake my thirst from the sweet stream which flows from Heaven's best:
   For He Himself has promised from His heav'nly throne on high
   That giving just one cup of water will itself receive its prize.
Please God, when flees my soul from my corrupting flesh
Then Rivius I hope to find in Heaven's pastures fresh;
   For dear Rivius has not really departed,
   He just somewhat ahead of us has started.
O Reader! To you and I His grace God wants to give
So that by this book's wisdom we may decide to live;
   Thus may Lord Rivius enjoy the benefits of his labour:
   The salvation of poor souls, of you and me and neighbour.
And so, to you the readers of this book, I pray,
To ever keep in mind the Lord Rivius on the way,
   And pray that God grant His eternal light
   To those who through this book are roused and edified.

Ex amore et dolore posuit

Frater *Joannes Ludolphus van Craywinckel,*
Norbertine canon of *Tongerlo* and parish priest of *Oelegem.*

Duo Chronica

I.

PRODIT HÆC POSTHVMA PROLES
PATRIS IOSEPHI RIVII.

2.

HEV TVNGERLOÆ ANNO PRÆCEDENTI MORTVI.

AUTHORISATION

The Sermons on the Gospels for all Sundays and Feast days of the entire year, entitled *The Christian Year*, preached by the Rev. Joseph Rivius, Canon of the church of Our Lady of Tongerlo, of the Order of Prémontré, may be published in print. Issued at Park, the 15th of December, 1654.

> *Libert*, Abbot of *Park*
> *Vicar General of the above-mentioned*
> *Order in* Brabant, *etc.*

AUTHORISATION

I have inspected and read two sections of a Book entitled *The Christian Year*, or *Sermons on the Gospels for all Sundays and Feast days of the entire year*, preached by the Rev. *Joseph Rivius*, Canon of the church of Our Lady of Tongerlo, of the Order of Prémontré, formerly parish priest at Drunen, and I found that it contains nothing that is contrary to the general Apostolic doctrine of Rome: but it does contain many sweet, learned discourses that

18

may benefit both those who preach the Word of God, as well as those who try to attain Christian perfection. Issued at Antwerp, the 21ˢᵗ of July 1654.

Theod. Vooghts, S. T. Licent.
Protonotary Apostolic, Canon and Archpriest of
Antwerp
Censor of Books

PRIVILEGE

Philip, by the grace of God King of Castille, Leon, Aragon, the Two Sicilies, Portugal, Navarre, etc. has consented that the Lord Rivius may print and sell a certain book titled *The Christian Year, or, Sermons on the Gospels for all Sundays and Feast days*, manufactured by the Rev. *Joseph Rivius*. All other printers and booksellers are forbidden and interdicted from copying the same, under pain of punishment, etc.

SIGNED,
Loyens

THE CHRISTIAN YEAR
A BOOK OF 17TH CENTURY SERMONS
or
NEW CATHOLIC
SERMONS
ON THE
Gospels for all the Sundays &
Feast Days of the Entire Year

VOLUME I
ADVENT, CHRISTMAS, & EPIPHANY

On the First Sunday of Advent

Erunt signa in sole, et luna, et stellis — "There will be signs in the sun, the moon, and the stars" (Lk 21:25).

ATHOLIC LISTENERS, WHILE Christ our Saviour was on this earth ministering to the people, He taught many beautiful divine doctrines and performed many sublime works; in doing so He mainly focused His attention on man's justification on the day of the Last Judgement, when He will take up the task of coming to judge the world in righteousness. This will truly be a frightening and terrifying task, one that will be accompanied by strange signs in the heavens above and on the earth below. For as Almighty God told Moses, "I will do signs such as were never seen upon the earth, nor in any nation: that this people may see the terrible work of the Lord which I will do" (Ex 34:10). Furthermore, to the Prophet Habakkuk He said, "Wonder, and be astonished: for a work is done in your days, which no man will believe when it shall be told" (Hab 1:5). Similarly, in the Prophet Joel we read, "And I will show wonders in Heaven, and on earth, blood and fire and vapour of smoke. The sun shall be turned into darkness, and the moon into blood: before the great and dreadful day of the Lord comes" (Joel 2:30–31). That day will be great, terrifying, brilliant and revealing. The learned Tertullian speaks of this passage in chapter twenty-two of his book 'On the Resurrection of the Flesh' and not without good reason, for the Day of Judgement will be a horrific event for all people and especially sinners; it shall be brilliant, glorious, and revealing because the Lord Jesus shall freely reveal Himself, and all eyes shall behold Him as the Judge of both the living and the dead. Moreover, this task of the Lord will be terrifying and dreadful because all kinds of people

23

will hear their sentence read out in public; they will be sentenced either to eternal happiness or to eternal misery. Our Lord commanded His Apostles, and subsequently all the pastors of the holy Catholic Church, that they should proclaim this message to all the people of the world. As St Peter says, "And He commanded us to preach to the people, and to testify that it is He who was appointed by God to be judge of the living and of the dead" (Acts 10:42). St Gregory tells us that "the truly learned preacher is one who knows how to say something new about the sweetness of the Kingdom of God; this also goes for the preacher who can use old news about the eternal flames of hell to move those souls who remain unimpressed by the promise of eternal reward to become frightened by the prospect of eternal suffering."[1] The Prophets and the Apostles were therefore sent by Almighty God to preach and announce retribution and eternal reward to the righteous and those people God had chosen, and the unhappy news of eternal punishment to reprobates and the godless. Thus we hear the Prophet Isaiah announcing that he had been sent to proclaim the year of the Lord's favour, of retribution and eternal reward to the righteous and chosen ones, and the day of vengeance to the unrighteous and reprobates (see Is 61). In today's Gospel Our Saviour, being the true Son of God, foretells these signs. In times of old, the Wise Man spoke these words concerning Him, "He knows signs and wonders before they are done, and the events of times and ages" (Wis 8:8), and especially those of the last day on which "there will be signs in the sun, the moon, and the stars." Before I explain this further, let us first pray for the grace of the Holy Spirit, through the intercession of the Blessed Virgin Mary, to whom we present the angelic salutation,

Ave Maria

IN TIMES PAST, ALMIGHTY GOD WANTED TO CONVERT Pharaoh and his Egyptian subjects from their sins and wicked ways by striking fear into them. He therefore showed them strange signs and wonders in the heavens and on the earth, to which King David testifies, "He sent forth signs and wonders in your midst, O Egypt: upon Pharaoh and upon all his servants" (Ps 134:9). God did not want

---

1   St Gregory the Great, *Homilies on the Gospels*, Homily 11.

24

to conquer them unexpectedly, hoping that the strange signs He had sent as a rebuke might convert them to the Lord. Christ our Saviour tells us in today's Gospel that on the Day of Judgement wondrous signs will appear throughout the whole world, signs not so much of vengeance but more of clemency, and that by heeding these fearful and menacing signs we might be spared, rather than becoming lost for all eternity. In the words of St Chrysostom, "If we remain firm and steadfast in heeding His threats, we avoid punishment. Then His words will not frighten us, nor will His deeds."[2] These signs shall be seen in the sun, the moon and the stars. The word 'sun' represents our blessed Lord Jesus Christ, who sits on the judgement seat with great power and majesty. For just as the sun's clarity and radiance overshadows the other planets, so shall Christ's sublime brilliance overshadow the brightest lights in the heavens with the rays of His divine light, as St Augustine tells us. And just as the sun cannot be corrupted or influenced or changed in any way, so Christ our Saviour on the day of that righteous and judicious judgement shall not be able to be swayed or bought in the least, neither by gifts nor by prayers. But the Glory of Israel will not recant or change His mind, as the Prophet Samuel writes (see 1 Sam 15:29). The wise Solomon says, "For jealousy arouses a husband's fury, and he shows no restraint when he takes revenge. He will accept no compensation, and refuses a bribe no matter how great" (Prov 6:34–35). Thus shall the wise Judge, like the sun, remain uncorrupted in righteousness, and no one shall be able to deceive or bribe Him, but He shall judge each man according to his deeds. St Gregory of Nyssa states this quite clearly, "Just as an expertly made mirror will show whether the image of a face is happy, sad, ugly or beautiful, and no one can accuse the mirror's nature of reflecting the images in it, so too the just judgement of God shall reflect our affections and it shall incur a retribution equal to our deeds."[3] Thus the

---

2　*Quo firmi ac stabiles evitemus minas, poenam minatur, et terret verbo, quo minus opere terreat.* St John Chrysostom, On Penance, Homily 5.

3　*Quemadmodum exactum perfectumque speculum, tales ostendit vultuum effigies, quales ipsi vultus fuerint, aut laetos, aut tristes, deformes, vel pulchros; neque speculi naturam aliquis culpare poterit: ita justum Dei judicium, nostris affectionibus assimulatur; qualia a nobis commissa fuerint, tales nobis de suo praebens retributiones.* St Gregory of Nyssa, On the Beatitudes, Homily 5.

Day of Judgement shall truly reflect as in a clear mirror the hearts and deeds of men, and they shall be rewarded according to their works, according to whether they be good or wicked. Even though sinners are fond of the darkness, and adulterers love the dark night, and thieves and murderers welcome the sun's absence and gloomy places, nevertheless, the sun will one day return, and they will have to appear before the judgement seat of God where their scandalous behaviour shall be revealed by the light of the Sun. "You did it in secret" Almighty God said through the mouth of the Prophet Nathan to King David, after David had committed adultery, "but I will do this in the sight of the sun" (2 Sam 12:12). St Gregory asks, "What does he mean by 'the sight of the sun', except the knowledge of manifest vision?"[4] Conversely, the righteous and chosen people may rejoice, for even though in the world they had been obscured, rejected, and spurned, yet shall they stand in the presence of this Sun before the throne in sight of the Lamb, as St John the Evangelist writes, "clothed with white robes and with palms in their hands" (Rev 7:9). These are signs of their victory; they shall be counted among the children of God and will appear with Him in glory.

Today's Gospel, then, talks about the Sun of Righteousness, and that there will be signs in the sun. What signs? St John speaks of these signs in the Book of Revelation, "When he had opened the sixth seal, the sun became black as sackcloth" (Rev 6:12). Many holy Fathers of the Church interpret this passage to mean the Day of Judgement on which the sun, which is the blessed Jesus Christ, shall become like sackcloth. First of all, to be clothed and covered with sackcloth is a sign of mourning and repentance for what we have done. Christ our Saviour, then, will appear on that last day as if clothed with sackcloth, for having seen the wickedness of humanity and its grave sins and ingratitude, He foresaw its eternal damnation. On the one hand, man's sins provoked His anger, but on the other hand He sorrowed for the eternal loss that awaited man, and He was no doubt filled with remorse, for He had created man and redeemed him, and had led man to know Him. In ages past, during the time of Noah when the wickedness of man was great upon the earth, many people drowned

---

4   *Quid per conspectum solis, nisi cognitionem insinuat manifestae visionis?* St Gregory the Great, Morals on the Book of Job, Book 34, ch 26.

in the flood God sent because of their sins, and He cried out with remorse in His heart, "I am sorry that I made them" (Gn 6:7). At the end of the world He shall appear as in sackcloth, sorrowing in His heart, because man, whom He made in His own image, shall be banished forever from His Kingdom. Secondly, sackcloth can have the meaning of abstaining from the flesh and sin, according to Origen in his Homily Thirteen *On Exodus*, or it can mean weeping and doing penance for one's sins, according to St Gregory in his Book 23, *On Morals*, chapter twelve. That the sun will become like sackcloth means nothing more than that man must see in this new sign a warning that he must avoid the wrath of God in order to be spared. Therefore, he must take up penitential practices, abstain from sins of the flesh and avoid the occasions of sin.

Catholic Listeners, behold the Lord's mercy and the patience of Jesus Christ, who, despite being saddened by godless sinners, is yet mindful of His mercy, and He warns them by signs of His wrath that they should flee from sin and escape the threat of His torments. But just as Pharaoh and the Egyptian people gave no credence to the signs Almighty God sent them at the hands of Moses and Aaron, thereby hardening their hearts and perishing, so the wicked will give no credence to the signs and wonders in the sun and the heavens at the coming judgement of the Son of God; nor shall they convert themselves or do penance. Instead, they shall jeer and scoff and belittle these celestial signs, as the Angelic Doctor, St Thomas, describes.[5] These people will remain obstinate and stubborn against the light and they shall persist in their wickedness, says St Paul in his letter to the Thessalonians, "They will say 'There is peace and security,' then sudden destruction will come upon them" (1 Thes 5:3). For the Sun of Righteousness will consume them by the heat of His wrath and they shall be delivered unto the everlasting fires, as the Prophet Isaiah says, "that He may perform His work, which work is strange to Him" (Is 28:21). The work of vengeance over sinners and the work of righteousness and judgement is work proper to Jesus Christ our Saviour, who acts by the power given Him by His heavenly Father, "The Father has given all judgement to the Son" (Jn 5:22). Nonetheless,

---

5   See St Thomas Aquinas, *Summa Theologiae*, Suppl. III, Q 73, A 1, ad. 1.

this work is strange to Him because whilst the works of mercy are more proper to Him, "O God, whose nature is always to have mercy and to spare,"[6] He was provoked and incited to anger through the sins of the godless. "He shall be angry as when the sun stood still in the valley of Gibeon (cf. Josh 10)." He shall change His works of mercy into those of wrath and punishment, being provoked to do so by the sins of mankind.

Everyone will know the story of Joshua. While he was busy fighting the armies of the five kings around the city of Gibeon, he chased his enemies in hot pursuit; the sun stood still in the heavens until he had avenged his enemies and obtained victory. This is an image of what will happen on the Day of Judgement, for when the true Joshua takes revenge on his enemies, the sinners, the sun, which usually stays its course and brings much goodness to all kinds of people, will on that day stand still in the heavens, and no amount of cries for mercy or clemency will move Him, but He shall stand still and unmoved in an act of vengeance and righteous judgement. The enemies of Jesus Christ will then take flight to the mountains and will try to hide in caves to escape the Lord's wrath, as St John the Evangelist says, "And the kings of the earth, and the princes, and the strong, and the rich, hid themselves in the dens and in the rocks of mountains. And they said to the mountains and the rocks, Fall upon us, and hide us from the face of Him that sits upon the throne and from the wrath of the Lamb" (Rev 6:15–16). So then, give heed to these words and listen carefully to their mysteries: they speak of the wrath of the Lamb. They say that the Judge sits on the judgement seat, angry and wrathful, and yet these words profess Him to be a lamb. Seeing that on that last day Christ our Saviour shall fill sinners with dread, yet shall He be kind to the righteous, with reason He shall be likened to both an angry lion and a meek lamb. Listen carefully to what will happen to the Saints and chosen ones on that day when the Sun of Righteousness will consume and devour the reprobates with the fire of His wrath; we shall see that their fate will be as St John the Evangelist describes, "Neither shall the sun fall on them, nor any heat. For the Lamb, which is in the midst of the throne, shall

---

6 *Deus cui proprium est misereri semper et parcere.* From the Litany of the Saints.

rule them, and shall lead them to the fountains of the waters of life"
(Rev 7:16–17). The Sun of Righteousness shall not harm them, for
the Lamb, which sits on the judgement seat, despite pouring wrath
and rage on the godless, shall treat the Saints and chosen ones with
kindness and gentleness. He will rule them, and satisfy them and fill
them, and lead them to the fountains of living water gushing forth
from God's Paradise. May it be so, O Jesus! May the Saints and
righteous become inebriated by the superabundance of your house,
and may they be quenched with the flood of your delights, for with
you is found the fountain of life.

On that Day of Judgement, not only will strange signs be seen in
the sun but also in the moon. I think the moon here represents the
Blessed Virgin Mary. First, because in Sacred Scripture the moon is
called the Queen of Heaven, as in the Prophet Jeremiah (see Jer 7:44).
Who could this Queen of Heaven be if not the most-holy Virgin, the
Queen of Angels, the Mother of the Supreme King and the Comforter of the world? In the Song of Songs she is called "fair as the
moon" (Song 6:10). But to tell the truth, she is much more beautiful
than the moon, and purer and more brilliant. She illuminates the
murkiness of our lives and directs poor sinners to the path of truth
and the haven of salvation, and through her intercession we enjoy
an abundance of divine graces. St Ambrose tells us that the moon is
gentle and has an abundance of dew, and is not the Blessed Virgin,
this Mother of Mercy, gentle, and does she not pour out an abundance
of heavenly dew? See how she has brought us the Son of God from
Heaven to earth as a saving dew, of which the Prophet Isaiah writes,
"Drop down dew, you heavens, from above, and let the clouds rain
the just" (Is 45:8). In other words, 'drop down dew from above, you
heavens, and give us Jesus our Saviour.' Furthermore, as the moon is
the mother of the dew, so is the Blessed Virgin Mary the Mother of
grace and mercy and a heavenly dew for our souls; because all the
grace we receive from Almighty God comes through Mary. This is
why the Mellifluous Doctor St Bernard openly declared, "We should
have nothing which has not passed through the hands of Mary."[7] The

---

7 *Nihil nos Deus habere voluit, quod per Mariae manus non transiret.* St Bernard
of Clairvaux, On the Vigil of the Nativity of the Lord, Sermon 3.

words of the Prophet Isaiah may also fittingly be applied to her, "For your dew is the dew of the light," or as the Septuagint translates it, "The dew which is from you is health for them" (Is 26:19).[8] It is like this: the grace that is given through the Blessed Virgin Mary is life and health to Christian souls and is like medication for our lives and our eternal immortality.

Therefore, this Queen of Heaven, this full moon, this Mother of grace and mercy, now gives her light to mankind, and she will never refuse us the dew of mercy and loving kindness. She is always ready to help sinners, advocating for them before her beloved Son, so that He might grant them forgiveness of their sins. But on that terrible Day of Judgement, "there will be signs in the moon." What signs? "The moon will not give her light and will be turned to blood." What a miracle! What a terrifying event! Mary, the Mother of mercy and Queen of compassion, who shows loving kindness towards sinners, who brought salvation to the world, who illuminated everyone and supports the suffering, who brings health to our sick souls and diverts God's wrath away from us, shall not give her light on the Day of Judgement, but she shall hide her light and be turned into blood. As the astronomers have observed, the further the moon goes from the sun, and the more she aligns herself with it, the more light she gives us, but the closer she comes to the sun, the more she seems to hide her light and distances herself from us. So, too, Catholic Listeners, the further Mary the Queen of Heaven moves away from her Son, so to speak, on the Day of Judgement, the closer she moves towards us to turn His wrath from us, and to pray for us; she will illuminate us with her light and support us with heavenly benefits. But on that last day she shall also be further away from sinners and closer to the throne of her Son the Divine Judge, and she shall join herself to the Sun of Righteousness. "His throne shall endure before me like the sun, and be established forever like the moon" (Ps 88:36, 37).

Thus Jesus and Mary, the Sun of Righteousness and the Full Moon, shall unite against the sinners of the world; they shall speak out their wrath against them and shatter them into pieces like clay jars, and they will be damned for all eternity. Surely then "the moon shall not give

8 *Ros lucis, ros tuus,* or in the Septuagint *Ros qui a te, sanitas.*

her light," and she will hide her mercy and loving kindness from the reprobates and godless so that they will perish forever, together with the world. Of course, we remember the words of the wise Solomon, "From the moon comes the sign for the festival days," that is, the day of the Blessed Virgin Mary, which was the feast day of our redemption, the day of conversion and justification, which day caused great rejoicing among the angels in Heaven. But the wise Solomon adds to this, "A light that wanes when it completes its course" (Sir 43:7). Thus the Moon is an all-beautiful light which will diminish at the end of the world, hiding her light from the wretched; she will not be seen again, even though she will appear on the last day, "having turned to blood." She will convert her mercy and kindness into anger and wrath against godless sinners, and seek revenge upon them from her Son, crying out to Him from her throne in a voice much louder than the blood of Abel. Notice that Queen Esther's demand for vengeance over the wicked Haman was heard by King Ahasuerus, who then had him hanged from a gibbet; so, too, shall our blessed Queen conceal her light from sinners before Christ, the King of Righteousness, demanding of Him vengeance against the world and the Prince of the world, so that he might be destroyed and forever disappear from God's sight. Hear what the Prophet Habakkuk says, "The sun and moon stood still in their place" (Hab 3:11). With this he means to say that the Sun of Righteousness will not be moved or swayed to have pity on humanity, but He will stand still so that He may judge with wrath. The moon, too, that is, the Blessed Virgin Mary, shall not be moved to show any mercy to the wretched, but she, too, will stand still and will see the vengeance over the wicked, and she will wash her pure hands in their bloody depravity. It will be a time for avenging the wicked, and she will present to mankind all the benevolence she had brought into the world, and to sinners she will call to mind all the prayers she had answered for health of mind and body; all the mercy and loving kindness she had shown them will work against them and will lead to an even greater damnation. Perhaps the Blessed Virgin will speak to her Son the words the Prophet Jeremiah spoke long ago, "Remember that I stood before you and spoke in their behalf to turn your wrath away from them. Therefore, hand them over to the power of the sword" (Jer 18:20, 21). Deliver them over to the devil where they may experience eternal torments. Perhaps now the Divine Majesty will have expelled the sinners by hundredfold, where they will be drawn down to the eternal fires of hell. And so, this time the kind Queen, who is called the Mother of mercy and advocate of sinners, did not appear before God to speak in their behalf to divert the anger of His wrath; the obstinate and wicked sinners, who daily become even more wicked, will without a doubt witness and observe that on the Day of Judgement she will not only appear as their enemy, but above all she will demand that every benefit they had been granted would be used against them in their judgement and damnation. Thus shall be kindled the fiery wrath of the Lord and of His Mother, our Queen. Therefore, let us fear the wrath of the Lamb, and the wrathful countenance of the most-holy Dove, who, even though she is now without gall, yet will she vex her enemies. They will perish, but she will remain together with the sun and before the moon, forever and ever.

Finally, on that last day not only will signs be seen in the sun and the moon, that is, in Jesus and Mary, but also in the stars, in holy and righteous people. For in the Kingdom of Heaven the Saints are not all equal in glory, just as the lights in the sky are not all equal in brilliance. As St Paul the Apostle tells us, the sun has one kind of splendour, the moon another, and the stars another. The sun's splendour comes from Christ, from whom all the other lights receive their light; the moon's splendour comes from Mary, the Queen of Heaven, and the splendour of the stars comes from the Saints, among whom is much diversity, for as one star differs from another in glory, so the Saints differ from one another in merit in the heavenly glory. But what signs shall be seen in the stars? Here we must turn to the holy Prophets, and especially the Prophet Joel who says, "The stars shall withdraw their shining" (Joel 2:10), and the Prophet Isaiah continues, "The stars shall not display their light" (Is 13:10).

The light of the Saints, Catholic Listeners, is the help they give us, and the teachings with which they instruct us, the counsel, good example, and prayers with which they illuminate all those belonging to the holy Catholic Church, and who would have fallen into error and darkness without the light of Jesus and His Saints. This is why the Prophet Daniel says, "And they that instruct many to justice, shall shine as stars for all eternity" (Dn 12:3). Currently they light up our night as stars in the firmament of the heavens; they instruct us with the light of the teaching they have left us; they move us by their good examples and they do not cease to obtain for us many heavenly benefits through their prayers. But on that last day when Christ, the Sun of Righteousness, shall appear to judge the world with wrath, the stars shall withdraw their light from worldly and unbelieving people. They will not appear in the firmament of Heaven to shine on sinners or to speak on their behalf. Yes, all the Saints will appear with the Righteous Judge to avenge the sins of His enemies. And just as the Lord who lives in the heavens shall laugh and deride them and shall speak to them in anger, as King David says in the second Psalm, so will the Saints laugh the sinners to scorn upon seeing their punishments, using the words written in the Book of Deuteronomy, "Where are their gods, in whom they trusted? Let them arise and help you, and protect you in your distress" (Dt 32:37,38). Where are your gods and idols in whom you trusted, which have separated you from the living and true God? Where is the world you served, and the flesh you caressed with impurity? Where are the riches you worshipped as an idol and the pleasures on which you set your heart? Will they now appear and arise to help and comfort you and drag you out of this helpless situation and extreme misery?

These are the signs, Catholic Listeners, that on the Day of Judgement will be seen in the sun, the moon, and the stars, that is, in Jesus, Mary and the Saints. Woe to us if we do not heed these signs and take them to heart. The sun in the sign of Leo can cause the world extreme and unbearable heat, and Jesus, who will be enraged like a lion on that last day will damn the wicked to the unbearable flames. On the last days of the month the moon sheds her light until the last quarter; Mary will pray for us and grant her help until the final Day of Judgement; the stars will not be favourable to us when they stand in opposition to the moon. While this time of mercy still lasts, let us work at turning these lights of Heaven to our favour and advantage, so that we may one day shine in the heavens, together with the Saints, for all eternity. Who lives, etc.

On the Second Sunday of Advent

Cum audisset Ioannes in vinculis opera Christi; mittens duos de discipulis suis, ait illi: Tu es qui venturus es, an alium expectamus? — "When John heard in prison of Christ's doings, he sent two of his disciples and said to him: Are you the one who is to come, or are we to wait for another?" (Mt 11:2–3).

CATHOLIC LISTENERS, IN ANCIENT times the heathens of Arcadia worshipped the goddess Venus, and they honoured her with the title, or should I say, with the scandalous name, Dea manchinatrix, which means "Schemer of sly tricks and lustful ways." So, when John the Baptist frankly reprimanded Herod's licentious behaviour by telling the King, "It is not lawful for you to take your brother's wife" (Mk 6:18), this Venus planted lustful thoughts in the head of Herodias, who then had John chained and thrown into a dungeon; thoughts which would only be quenched by his blood and the taking of his life. Here the words of the Wise Man ring true, "There is no anger above the anger of a woman" (Sir 25:23). When we hear in today's Gospel how John, the herald of the truth, had been clapped in chains, we must remember that this resulted from a sly act by lustful, immoral people, who, when they have the upper hand, can throw into chains and imprison anyone who dares rebuke them. Did this not also happen to Joseph when he refused to give in to the impure seductions of Potiphar's wife? And did not Susanna also undergo a similar fate when she refused to give heed to the impure desires of the two elders? As you have heard, the same occurred to John the Baptist because he boldly rebuked the lustfulness of Herod and Herodias. O defilement! you are a hellish fire. Your chimney is the impure and unchaste soul; your embers are desires and wicked ploys; your flames, arrogance and haughtiness; your smoke, blood and cruelty; your ashes, a bad name and reputation, and your end will be the eternal flames of hell. Nevertheless, when we see John bound in heavy chains and languishing in the dungeon and Herod and Herodias in their palace, burning with passion and desires, would we not say with the Prophet Jeremiah, "You will be in the right, O Lord, when I lay charges against you; but let me put my case to you. Why does the way of the wicked prosper? Why do all who are treacherous thrive?" (Jer 12:1). See, the Bridegroom's friend, the herald of Heaven, the Precursor of Christ, the mirror of virtue and the most perfect among the children of man, is cast into a dungeon, clapped in chains, and scandalously tortured by an adulterer and a godless man, just to satisfy the desires of a trollop. Could it be that sin can triumph over virtue, or wantonness over chastity, or impurity over innocence, or a godless man and a loose woman over the godliness of an earthly angel? This is a question which many a mind has tried to understand. As King David said, "I studied that I might know this thing, it is a labour in my sight" (Ps 72:16). If we were only to observe this from the outside with a human eye, we would almost start to doubt divine prudence and righteousness if the godless were to get the upper hand over the righteous, and if the cruelty of a wicked judge were to gain over the innocence of the Precursor of Christ. But if we delved a bit deeper and reflected quietly on this, we would find that all this occurs according to a particular order and plan which Almighty God has put in place for the great advantage and glory of His chosen ones. The destiny of a just man is that in this present life evil comes his way in order to train and test him, so that he may increase in virtue, and in the next life he will be raised to Heaven on high, as St Paul tells us, "No man should be shaken by these tribulations. You yourselves know that this is what we are destined for" (1 Thes 3:3). St Augustine follows St Paul's reasoning when he writes in his commentary on the psalms, "when you see the wicked man flourishing and the good man labouring hard, you might be inclined to say, O God, is this your justice, that the wicked prosper and the good are burdened? How will He answer you? Will He not say, 'Is this your faith? Did I ever promise you, or did you become a Christian, that you would prosper in this present life?' Indeed, from the very beginning of the world Almighty God has put His own to the test. In the Old Testament we see how the first righteous man, Abel, who was persecuted and murdered by Cain, was held up as a model for all righteous people. The old Tertullian says it well, 'From the beginning, indeed, righteousness suffers violence. Forthwith, as soon as God has begun to be worshipped, religion has got ill-will for her portion.'[1] When Our Saviour established the New Covenant, He presented John the Baptist as an example to all righteous people of how to earn the reward and crown of Heaven by living a perfect life of endurance and penance. We must not, therefore, become discouraged when hearing of John's imprisonment, but let us remember that everything St Paul wrote about in this Sunday's Epistle has been written for our instruction, so that through patient and unhurried reading of the Scriptures we might find hope and comfort. Even if we have to suffer somewhat in this life, we shall rejoice in the next. Before drawing out more instructions from today's Gospel, let us first pray for the grace of the Holy Spirit through the intercession of the Blessed Virgin Mary by presenting to her the angelic salutation,

Ave Maria

THE HOLY FATHERS ARE NOT UNANIMOUS IN THEIR views on why John the Baptist, chained and imprisoned, sent out his disciples to encounter Our Saviour. According to both St Hilary and St Chrysostom the cause was this: John noticed that his disciples were starting to honour him above Christ, thereby distancing themselves from Our Saviour, because the fame of John's miracles and wondrous works was increasing daily. "John's disciples were starting to turn from Jesus, and they always had jealous feeling towards Him. And it is plain, from what they said to their master: See, He is baptizing and everyone is coming to Him."[2] So, like a good master not seeking his own benefit and glory, he corrects and instructs them by

---

1   *A primordio justitia vim patitur: statim ut coli coepit Deus, religio invidiam fortita est.* Tertullian, Against the Gnostics, ch. 8.
2   *Alieniores erant discipuli eius, et invidiae cuiusdam stimulis semper agitabantur, magistrum suum pluris esse cupientes; ecce hic baptizat, et omnes veniunt ad eum.* St John Chrysostom, On St Matthew's Gospel, Homily 36 on Chapter 11.

showing that Jesus is the promised Messiah and the true Saviour of the world, and that John was only His messenger and precursor. "I am not the Christ, but I have been sent to go before Him" (Jn 3:28). Nonetheless, despite trying to reason with them and showing them proof for his argument, he could not sway them, and they ascribed his reprimands to his humility, and they were still not persuaded by Christ's miracles. And so John took the opportunity to send two of them to Jesus, saying, 'you tell me so many things about Jesus and His miracles, yet you refuse to believe that He is the promised Saviour of the world; go now to Him and ask Him in my name whether He is the promised Messiah, or should we look for another? For I myself have no doubt that He will prove to you with words and deeds that of which I cannot seem to convince you.'

Indeed, an attentive father spends his whole life caring for his children, personally guiding them towards goodness and on occasion reprimanding them, but on his deathbed he has to hand over this care to a child guardian or trusted friend. Similarly, John, while he lived, at times had to reprimand his disciples, instructing them about the various qualities of Jesus Christ and the things he had witnessed. But now he was chained up in prison and his death was imminent, so he sent to Christ those he could not personally instruct, knowing that he could then die in peace in the knowledge that his disciples' faith in Christ would now be perfected. The disciples set off and they heard Our Saviour preaching and they witnessed His many wonders, and they relayed their message, "Are you the one who is to come, or are we to wait for another?" The Lord knew they had been sent by John for their own instruction, and He answered them, "Go and relate to John what you have heard and seen. The blind see, the lame walk, the lepers are cleansed, the dead rise again" (Mt 11:4–5). To prove that He was indeed the Saviour of the world, He performed many more miracles, more by deed than by word, as He was accustomed to do. So, for example when the Jews used many and lengthy words to question the woman caught in adultery so that they could stone her, He just told her to keep quiet and started writing in the dust with His finger, "He that is without sin among you, let him cast the first stone" (Jn 8:7). Similarly, when He was asked whether it was lawful to pay taxes to Caesar, He asked for a coin, and after examining it He told them, "Render to Caesar the things that are Caesar's, and to God the things that are God's" (Mk 12:17). So too, in today's Gospel He responded to the question posed by John's disciples by miracles and wondrous works. We are here reminded of the Lord's words found in St John the Evangelist, "The works that I do in the name of my Father, they give testimony of me" (Jn 10:25). He also gave a frank answer to the question of the Jews, "How long will you keep us in suspense? If you are the Christ, tell us plainly" (Jn 10:24). St Ambrose also gives us these words appropriate to the subject, "Jesus makes Himself known through His works, but by His works as the Son of God, He reveals the Father. I see Jesus, when I read how He smeared mud on the eyes of a blind man and restored his sight, and I am reminded how He fashioned the first man out of clay, pouring life into his spirit and giving him light so he may see. I see Jesus when I hear how He forgives sins, for no one can forgive sins except God alone."[3]

Today Christ shows us through His wondrous works that He is the promised Messiah and the Saviour of the world, and so all those who through the Sacrament of Baptism have been gathered together to fight under the banner of Christ must demonstrate by virtues and virtuous works that they truly are Christian people; they do this by showing mercy and humility, by being meek and frugal, by obedience and purity and other virtues, to show to the world that we have within us the grace and the spirit of Jesus Christ. Otherwise, as St Augustine warns us, "If you do differently and profess something else, if you are faithful in name only but demonstrate the opposite through your deeds, you run the risk of being discovered and surprised."[4] Therefore, how can one bear a name that leads to life when one performs deeds that lead to sin and death? How can one bear the

---

3 *In operibus, Iesus videtur: in operibus Filii et Pater cernitur. Video Iesu, quando lego quia caeco linivit oculos luto et redidit visum. Ipsum enim recognosco qui de luto finxit hominem et ei vivendi spiritum et videndi lumen infudit. Video Iesum quando peccata condonat: nemo potest peccata dimittere, nisi solus Deus.* St Ambrose, Commentary on St Luke's Gospel, Book 1, ch. 8.

4 *Detegeris et deprehenderis; quando aliud agis, et aliud profiteris; fidelis in nomine, aliud demonstrans in opere.* St Augustine, Treatise to Catechumens on the Creed, Book 4, ch. 1.

name of Christian if one's life is worse than an unbeliever or a pagan? Indeed, all labourers show their skill through their handiwork or art; a cobbler demonstrates his skill by the shoes he makes; likewise, a tailor by his clothes, an artist by his paintings and a goldsmith by the gold and silver vessels he makes. And what does the Christian show? Is it not virtuous to be God-fearing, obedient, sober, pure, and devout? Did you not renounce the devil and the world with all its pomps, and did you not promise to follow the grace and Spirit of Jesus Christ? So why then do you follow impurity and drunkenness, pride and injustice and other evils that are contrary to your profession? Therefore, be careful that on the Day of Judgement you shall not be recognised just for your name but also for your deeds, just as today Christ was recognised as the Saviour of the world by His works, namely, that "the blind see, the lame walk, lepers are cleansed, the dead rise again" (Mt 11:5). O Jesus! in times past you showed the dignity of your Divine Majesty through your wondrous works; in your mercy show us today your divine power, for the world is like a hostel full of blind, crippled, diseased and dead people, not in their bodies, but even worse, in their spirits and souls. Let us examine these blind people. What do you think? Who are they? Are they not the people who have eyes yet do not see where they are going, as St Gregory says, "For 'the blind' is he that as yet sees not where he is going, but 'the lame' is he who has not the power to go there where he sees."[5] To tell the truth, the majority of worldly people know how to root about in the dirt to obtain temporary and perishable things, but they are completely in the dark and blind as moles when it comes to knowing about things pertaining to Heaven and their eternal salvation. What joy can they have if they cannot see the light of Heaven because they have forgotten about eternal glory and the judgement of God? They are so blind that they do not even notice the wretched state of their lives. O desirable avarice! how many people do you strike blind so that they notice only money and goods, never giving a thought to their eternal good, thereby losing it as if it were of little value and no worth. O immodesty! how many people's eyes have you ruined,

---

5 *Coecus quippe est, qui adhuc quo pergat non videt.* St Gregory the Great, Morals on the Book of Job, Book 19, ch. 39.

just as the eyes of Tobias were ruined when birds' droppings fell in them, and he could no longer see the light of day. And you people who hate and are jealous, does not your hatred and jealousy poison your eyes too? "Whoever hates his brother walks in darkness" says St John (1 Jn 2:11). For even if you are not completely blind, nonetheless your eyes will at least have become dim, just as the eyes of the priest Eli had become so dim that he could only see the lamp of God with great difficulty (see 1 Sam 3:2). Unfortunately, the number of blind Catholic Christians is not small. Some have been blind from birth, that is, they have never known how to do something good; others have seen and have even at times practised virtuous deeds, but later they went blind because of their wicked desires and disordered passions. Thus they have cast aside that light which they would be hard-pressed to acquire later. That is why St Paul the Apostle says, "For it is impossible to restore again to repentance those who have once been enlightened, and have tasted the heavenly gift, and have shared in the Holy Spirit, and have tasted the goodness of the word of God and the powers of the age to come, and then have fallen away" (Heb 6:4). It is impossible, says St Paul; with this he means to say, it is extremely difficult for those people who had once been enlightened by the grace of God, and who had cast aside and spurned this grace, again to be able to obtain the same. Even so, nothing is impossible for Almighty God, Catholic Listeners, nor for the Supreme Physician. Therefore, the blind and the confused must come to Jesus, who in today's Gospel gives witness of His powers and abilities when He says that He makes the blind see. But the greatest difficulty is that many people do not recognize, or want to admit, that they are blind. How many blind people are there who claim they can see, yet do not realise, or do not want to admit, that they are ill? Thus they cannot be helped, and they continue to wander about to their eternal loss, not knowing that if only they admitted their wretched state they could be dragged out of it. If only they could say together with St Augustine, "Alas, the times when I did not know you! Alas, my past ignorance when I did not know you, O Lord!"[6]

---

6 *Vae tempori illi quando non cognoscebam te! vae praeteritae ignorantiae meae quando non cognoscebam te Domine.* St Augustine, Soliloquies, Book 1.

Not only is the world full of blind people, but also cripples and the lame. These are those who do not tread the path of virtue nor follow the path of God's commandments or that of His holy Catholic Church, but with one foot they seem to wander on the right path while with the other foot they tread the path of wickedness. Similarly, they are lame who have one leg longer than the other. Then there are people whose spiritual legs or the legs of their soul, so to speak, which are the intellect and mind, are not of even length and quality. So the intellect indicates the virtues and the commandments of God, but the will zealously discards them, and so they limp towards the soul, to her great shame and detriment. Concerning this we can heed the words the Prophet Elijah spoken long ago to the Israelites, "How long will you go limping with two different opinions? If the Lord is God, follow him; but if Baal, then follow him" (1 Kings 18:21). Neither is the number small of these crippled and lame Catholics, these Christians who hang onto God with one side but onto the devil with the other. Here they go off to God's house to pray, yet there they visit the bawdy house of the devil to get drunk and practise immorality. In church they appear as angels through their exterior piety, yet in the tavern they become like possessed people, using bad language and cursing and swearing. Almighty God speaks of these through the mouth of King David, "The children that are strangers have lied to me, strange children have faded away, and have halted from their paths" (Ps 17:46). These strange children, in respect to Almighty God, are those who serve Him with hypocritical and imperfect hearts, nor do they follow their heavenly Father or His divine will; even though they have been called to the True Faith by His grace and He directed their feet on the right path to salvation, they have nonetheless easily turned off that path. They are children, even though they have received the promise of an eternal inheritance. Yet they have become strange children because they have reneged on the promise they made to God. For seeing that they renounced the devil at their baptism, and solemnly promised to forever adhere to Almighty God, one might truly say that they have become lame by forsaking God and turning to the devil and his empty works. We see how the Patriarch Jacob went lame after he had wrestled with the angel. This was to indicate that one part of his children would stay on the right path, that is, they would come to know the Messiah who is the Saviour of the world, and they would follow in His footsteps and observe His commandments. The other part of his children would go lame, that is, they would deny and leave Christ, as St Augustine wisely commented upon in his book *The City of God*, "Jacob was at one and the same time blessed and lame, blessed in those among that people who believed in Christ, and lame in the unbelieving. For the breadth of the thigh is the multitude of the family. For there are many of that race of whom it was said, 'And they have halted in their paths.'"[7] Thus there are among Catholic Christians those who live according to the children of Jacob, some going straight on the path of God's commandments, while others go lame by rejecting God's laws, to their detriment. In times long past the Prophet Isaiah prophesied that when the Messiah comes "the lame man would leap like the deer" (Is 35:6), and this has been fulfilled in today's Gospel, where Christ makes cripples walk again, and so they need to approach Him to gain health and strength. He will not order them to engage in burdensome or difficult remedies, but as long as they trust in His power with firm faith and are mindful that He has come into the world for the salvation of man, then, with just one word, He will give them the strength they need to walk strong and upright on the path of divine law. See then how the lame man, who was lying at the Beautiful Gate of the Temple in Jerusalem, after seeing the Apostle Peter, stood up on his feet and began to walk; so, too, those who look on Jesus, and with firm hope beg His help and grace, will leap up, praising Almighty God and blessing Him because He has restored their feet and made them like the feet of a deer, as the Prophet Habakkuk says in chapter three, "He will make my feet like the feet of a hart," so that they may wander the path of God's law and that of His holy Catholic Church.

Furthermore, Our Saviour also showed the dignity of His Divine Majesty when in today's Gospel He healed the leper for no other reason than to invite all the lepers of the world to be cleansed and

---

7 *Iacob rectus fuit in electis, claudus in reprobis: femoris latitudo; generis est multitudo: plures quippe in ea stirpe sunt, de quibus dicitur, claudicaverunt a semitis suis.* St Augustine, The City of God, Book 16, ch. 39.

healed by approaching Him. Do you want to know who are these lepers? They are those people who infect others through the leprosy of their foul sins; or who incite others to commit sins of impurity through their unchaste words; or those who through gossip and false accusations make their listeners party to their wickedness, and finally, there are those who cause others to sin through giving bad advice. You can therefore easily see that there are various kinds of leprosy by which one person can infect another. But the Divine Physician, our Blessed Lord Jesus Christ, gives us a clear witness of His knowledge and experience by being able to cleanse them all, when in today's Gospel He says that the lepers are cleansed. We think here of the story when the Emperor Constantine, after he had contracted leprosy, had been ordered by his physicians to take a bath of warm blood of infants and children as a cure for his bodily disease. Our Lord Jesus Christ has a much better and more powerful bath for curing spiritual leprosy as well, namely, that of His most Precious Blood, which has the undisputed power to heal all leprous wounds and to make the soul as pure and innocent as a child's through His divine grace. Come then, you lepers, to the Divine Physician and tell Him with sorrowful hearts and deep humility, "Lord, if it be your will, you can make me clean." And no doubt He will answer straight away, "I will it, be cleansed." It could happen that someone might not find the courage to come into the presence of the Divine Physician, in which case you can approach His priests and servants, who will have sympathy with you, if you truly wanted to avail of the remedy which He instituted for cleansing the leprosy of sin. It was to the priest that He sent the lepers who so humbly called out to Him in these few words, "Jesus, Master, have pity on us" (Lk 17:13), and He answered them, "Go, and show yourselves to the priest," and while they went on their way they were purified and healed, just as spiritual lepers can be healed if with true contrition they show their leprosy to a priest, who is the servant of God. If they make a sincere confession to him, the leprosy of sin will disappear from their souls and the purity and grace of God will again enter in.

Finally, if we take a look through the hospital of the world we will notice not only the blind, cripples and lepers but also the dead. Who are these? They are those people who live in a state of mortal sin and are happy lying there, notwithstanding that they know they are hideous in God's sight, and Heaven's. Why do you think mortal sin is called just that, a sin which is mortal, deadly? For no other reason than that it causes the death of the soul. "Sin is the death of the soul" says St Bernard.[8] Most appropriately then should we count among the dead, or those who lie in the shadow of death, those people who persevere in the state of mortal sin. That is why the Prophet Baruch cried out, "How is it, Israel, that you are in the land of your foes, grown old in a foreign land, defiled with the dead, counted among those destined for Hades?" (Bar 3:10–11). In other words, what he was saying is, think, and think again about the miserable state of sin in which you find yourself. That is the reason you are now lying in a grave, foul and soiled, trampled by your enemies and very close to the gates of hell. Catholic Listeners, this will overcome all those who remain in mortal sin. For just as there is death of the body, so there is death of the soul. The body dies when it is deprived of life, and the soul dies when it is deprived of God's grace, which is the true life of the soul. As St Gregory says, "Just as exterior death separates the soul from the body, so interior death separates the soul from God."[9] This death by sin is called the first death, for following this comes the second death of damnation, which robs a person of eternal life. This first death, which is caused by mortal sin, leads to the second death, and a person in this state may be reckoned among those descending to the depths of hell, unless he manages to regain the life of grace by doing penance. Alas! it is a sorry fact that there are many who carry about in their living bodies souls that are dead or dying. Of course, the stench of death is not noticeable to others around them, but to Almighty God and His angels this stench is quite unbearable. Even though a corpse has hands and feet, a tongue, a mouth, and eyes, yet it cannot feel, or walk, see or speak, so those people whose souls are dead can still perform good works like other people, despite being robbed of the interior life of grace. Yet they earn no merit, they

---

8 *Peccatum mors est animae.* St Bernard, On the Song of Songs, Sermon 15.
9 *Sicut mors exterior ad anima dividit carnem, ita mors interior a Deo separat animam.* St Gregory the Great, op. cit., Book 9, ch. 46.

only appear to be meritorious, and so it can truly be said of them that they perform dead works without merit. Despite all this, man does not seem to hold in high regard the life of the soul given by the grace of God, which His only Son obtained for us by pouring out His Precious Blood on our behalf! In fact, they think so little of it that they easily dismiss it for a small gain, a paltry delight, or some filthy pleasure. The children of men are so unhappy that they would easily exchange the life of the children of God (which finds its origin in the Divine Life and thus leads to the joys of eternal life) for a life wasted on trifles and trinkets. And so, in their unhappiness they continue to scorn and neglect the spiritual life, even though they can easily win it back, choosing instead to stay for days, months and even years in the tomb of their stinking sins.

Seeing then that no one actively chooses eternal damnation with its gnashing of teeth in the flames of hell, listen now to these glad tidings those of you who continue to lie in the death of sin, yet who still desire to live for all eternity. Look towards the heavenly Physician who does not want the death of the sinner and who can make the blind see, the lame walk and lepers clean. In today's Gospel He tells us that He can also raise the dead to life. He had raised a young man from death to life in front of the gate of the city of Nain just by touching the funeral stretcher; He took someone's daughter by the hand, and healed many others by just a word, and today He uses His servant to call to those who lie in the death of sin, "Awake, sleeper, arise from the dead; and Christ will be your light" (Eph 5:14). Christ is prepared to raise up everyone who wants to live a life of truth. He calls so that they will rise from the grave of sin and be obedient to the voice of life. Listen to Him, for from the tender mercy of God He has visited us from on high. He came to be a light to those sitting in the shadow of death, and to guide their feet on the path of true peace.

O Jesus! heavenly Physician so long awaited, the world is full of people who are blind, crippled, diseased, and dead. Display the depths of your love and mercy over sickness and infirmity. You are the true Light that illuminates all men. Give light to the blind, that they may see what can harm them, and embrace what will save them. You are the way; give strength to the lame, that they may walk the path of

45

your divine laws. You are the Sun of Righteousness in which not the slightest impurity can be traced; cleanse the diseased from every stain of sin, so that they may ever enjoy your peace and friendship. For, "Whoever loves purity of heart shall have the King for his friend" (Ps 22:11). And finally, you are the life. Pour the life of your divine grace into the souls of those who have died because of sin, so that they may say together with St Paul the Apostle, "It is no longer I who live, but it is Christ who lives in me" (Gal 2:20). He will give me a share in eternal life, in the glory of Heaven. Who lives, etc.

On the Third Sunday of Advent

Miserunt Iudaei ab Ierosolymis, Sacerdotes, et Levitas ad Ioannem, ut interrogarent eum: Tu quis est? — "The Jews sent from Jerusalem priests and Levites to John to ask him: 'Who are you?'" (Jn 1:19).

ATHOLIC LISTENERS, LAST SUN-day we heard how John the Baptist, who was chained up in the dungeon, had heard of the wondrous works of our Saviour Jesus Christ, and how he sent two disciples to Jesus to ask Him "Are you he who is to come, or shall we look for another?" (Mt 11:3). John himself did not doubt that Jesus was the true Light who had come into the world to illuminate all men, for he had given clear witness to Christ, but this question was intended to strengthen the ignorance and weak, fragile faith of his disciples, so that they would recognise in the Person of Jesus the dignity of the Messiah. Today the Jews of the royal priestly city of Jerusalem sent out envoys to John the Baptist, not just any common or insignificant envoys, but the most reliable and worthy among the priests and Levites, to ask him if he were the Christ, that is, the Messiah, promised in the Law. "Who are you?" (Jn 1:19). These envoys were sent either to find out the truth, or to see whether there was any question of deceit, hatred or envy. They saw his simple clothing, how he abstained from food and his holiness of life; he seemed more like a common man than a prophet. Many were aware that he had been conceived to barren parents, and that he had been promised by an angel and sanctified in his mother's womb, and that he descended from a noble, priestly race. They heard that after his birth many people had asked, "What then will this child be?" (Lk 1:66). Furthermore, there was great expectation that

47

the arrival of the Messiah was imminent, for the royal sceptre of Judah had fallen to the foreigner Herod Antipas, as the Prophet Jacob had foretold long ago about the time of the Messiah's coming, "The sceptre shall not depart from Judah, nor the ruler's staff from between his feet, until he comes to whom it belongs, and to him shall be the obedience of the peoples" (Gn 49:10). These signs, and others besides, would make the people wonder whether John could be the Messiah promised in the Law, or not. That is why these envoys, these priests and Levites, asked him whether he was the Messiah. "Who are you?" St Chrysostom says that this question was asked out of envy because they wanted John to accept the fair title of Messiah so they could trap him. In this way was revealed the wicked nature of those priests, who also wickedly opposed Our Saviour. Nevertheless, these priests and Levites were sent out as envoys by the great Council, according to the opinion of the Cardinal,[1] and they asked John "Who are you?" Was he Christ the Messiah, the Saviour of the world? He answered them, No. And seeing that he had preached the Word of God with a loud voice, and courageously punished and chastised the people for their sins, they then asked him whether he was perhaps Elijah. Again he answered, No. They then asked him "Are you a prophet?" The Angelic Doctor, St Thomas, when commenting on this passage, writes that some people were of the opinion that he was perhaps the Prophet Elisha because he had baptised with water, just as the Prophet Elisha had ordered the Prince of Syria, Naaman, to wash in the River Jordan so that he would be cured of his leprosy (see 2 Kings 5). Again, he answered that he was no prophet. But they insisted on hearing from his own mouth who he might be, and so he told them, "I am a voice crying in the wilderness." This, then, was John's statement and answer. Tertullian comments on this in his writings, "He formed, as it were, the boundary between the Old Covenant of Judaism and the New Covenant of Christianity."[2] In order to glean more teachings from today's Gospel for our general edification, let us first pray for the grace of

1 Cesare Cardinal Baronius. See *Annales Ecclesiastici*, Tome 1, Annus Christi 31, xxi.
2 *Quasi limes constitutus est inter vetera et nova, ad quem desineret Iudaismus, et inciperet Christianismus.* Tertullian, Against Marcion, Book 4.

the Holy Spirit through the intercession of the Blessed Virgin Mary by presenting to her the angelic salutation,

Ave Maria

MAN SEEMS TO HAVE BEEN BORN WITH AN INNATE sense of wanting to be honoured and praised, and there is nothing that flatters the heart more than status, honour, and dignity. Contrary to this, there is nothing that offends us more than being oppressed, spurned, disdained, and humiliated. And so we might wonder whether John the Baptist, when seeing the arrival of the important priests and Levites who were sent to him as ambassadors and envoys in the name of the Council of the Jews, might not have been tempted when asked by them, "Who are you?" not to tell the truth, thereby reaping for himself the honour and dignity of the Messiah, the Saviour of the world. But seeing that Almighty God always strengthens humility with His grace, as Sacred Scripture tells us, "He gives grace to the humble" (Jas 4:6), he confessed the truth like a reed shaken in the wind of earthly honour, as St Augustine writes, "It is not the grain that the wind carries away, nor the solidly rooted tree that the storm blows down."[3] So he confessed and clearly professed that he was not the Christ. He noticed that the brilliance of his God-fearing life gave joy to the Jews, and the words of his preaching softened their hearts to do penance. "And the people asked him, saying, What then shall we do?" (Lk 3:10). Nonetheless, he was mindful of his office and of the Person whose Precursor he was, and so he made Christ known not only by his voice and preaching, but also by pointing Him out with his own hand, "Behold the Lamb of God, behold Him who takes away the sins of the world." (Jn 1:29). Another way of saying this is, "You Jews, priests and Levites, why do you come to me? Why blind your eyes by staring at the brilliance of my life, or why deafen your ears listening to my preaching, why look upon me as the Saviour of the world? I am not the Light, but merely a herald of that Light; I am not the Physician who can heal you, but I merely point out your

---

3 *Triticum non rapit ventum nec arborem solida radice fundatam, procella subvertit.* Augustine appears to be quoting from St Cyprian of Carthage, *De Catholicae Ecclesiae,* 73.

ailments; I am not the Bridegroom, but only His best man; I am not the Word but I am the voice of the Eternal Word, so that through the example of my life and the sound of my voice and preaching, you may come to know the Eternal Word, the Saviour of the world."

Now here is a strange matter. Jesus was in the middle of the land of Palestine, as in the middle of a circle. He was like a burning lamp, and like the sun He cast His light throughout the Jewish world. Yet they passed Him by, they ignored the heat and rays of this Divine Sun, preferring to rejoice in John's light, "You were willing to rejoice for a while in his light" (Jn 5:35). They had by-passed the Eternal Word, theirs ears were not attentive to the voice of His calling. This error, which Jews committed a long time ago, still takes place in the hearts of Christians today, when they forsake the Eternal Word, choosing instead to listen with pleasure to words that pass away. They forsake Jesus and cling with pleasure to temporal creatures. All creatures are merely voices that call to us in the deserts of this world. They tell us that Almighty God is the Lord, that He is the all-powerful Creator of all creatures, that He is wise, and fair, merciful and forgiving, and worthy of all praise, service and love. St Augustine testifies to this when he writes, "All places and all things proclaim to you their Creator; and the species of creatures are nothing more than voices praising their Creator."[4] It is truly so, for beauty, honour, riches and wealth are nothing more than voices of the Divine Word, who speaks to us in the words of the Wise Man, "By me kings reign and princes rule; with me are riches and glory, glorious riches and justice" (Prov 8:15, 16, 18). Alas! we tend to follow the example of the Jews in today's Gospel, we run to these voices, eagerly grasping them and putting them to use; but in doing so we pass by the Divine Word, Jesus, and we forsake Him. To us, then, can easily be applied the lament of the weeping Jeremiah, where he comments on the Person of Our Saviour, "What wrong did your ancestors find in me that they went far from me, and went after worthless things, and became worthless themselves?" (Jer 2:5). O man, what bitterness did you find in Jesus that you have left Him, and have gone after worthless things? Is He

---

4   *Undique tibi omnia resonant Conditorem. Et ipsae species creaturarum voces sunt quaedam Creatorem laudantium.* St Augustine, Exposition on Psalm 26.

not your forgiving Lord and merciful Saviour who desires not your loss but rather that you prosper and are saved? Should you not seek Him who obtains for you temporal goods in this world and eternal goods in Heaven? Do you not realise that riches and wealth are temporal things, and status and honour will pass away, like all the other creatures who are only voices that will fade away? For just as melodious music will for a short time gladden the ear, but ultimately disappears, so, too, the sweet possessions of the world's creatures will not last long, but they will pass away like a puff of smoke. On the other hand, the Eternal Word of the Father, Jesus Christ our Lord, will last for all eternity; He has an abundance of everlasting goods and He satisfies His followers with eternal pleasures; indeed, every sweetness to be found among creatures comes from Him, for He is the fountain and source of all delights. Nonetheless, if you lustfully choose to drink the murky waters from the cistern, how much harder will you need to strive to obtain the pure waters of the living fountain? Hear how Almighty God rebuked the Jews of old through the mouth of the Prophet Jeremiah, for they had committed two sins, "For my people have committed two evils: they have forsaken me, the fountain of living water, and dug out cisterns for themselves, cracked cisterns that can hold no water" (Jer 2:13). Here he is telling us that we have forsaken God, the fountain of all sweetness, and turned to the cracked cisterns of the world that cannot hold sweet water. This is what the school masters teach, namely, that every mortal sin is a turning away from God, and a turning towards worldly creatures. In other words, the person who sins mortally turns away from God, the fountain of all good, and turns towards the created things of this world, which are like cracked cisterns and broken wells. St Thomas, the Angelic Doctor, tells us, "Now sin comprises two things. First, there is the turning away from the immutable good, which is infinite, wherefore, in this respect, sin is infinite. Secondly, there is the inordinate turning to mutable good. In this respect sin is finite, both because the mutable good itself is finite, and because the movement of turning towards it is finite, since the acts of a creature cannot be infinite."[5] Thus speaks the Angelic Doctor, St Thomas.

---

5   *In peccato duo sunt, quorum unum est aversio ab incommutabili bono quod est*

Observe that one can direct the course of a ship just by agitating a magnetic sundial, which points not to the sun, but to a pole or a small star; likewise, ignorance turned the minds of the Jews away from the Sun of Righteousness and directed them towards the light of a small star, namely, to John, so that they might recognise him as the true Messiah. So, too, do our hearts move us to desire the temporal and perishable things with which they are concerned. In so doing, they turn away from following God, our brilliant Sun, choosing instead to follow some small, twinkling stars of the dark, worldly night, namely, temporal and perishable creatures. We read in Sacred Scripture that the fair Absalom tried to assume the authority and kingdom of his father King David "by drawing to himself the hearts of the men of Israel," or as the Hebrew text has it, "He stole their hearts" (2 Sam 15). Thus the world and its creatures attracts and steals people's hearts so that they forsake God and cling to temporal things. Continuing in the same scriptural passage we read how a messenger came to David, saying, "The hearts of all the Israelites are following Absalom" (2 Sam 15:13). So, too, do the majority of people follow the world together with its perishable things, its wealth, honour, and pleasure, and they leave Jesus, the true David.

What advice should we heed not to follow the fair Absalom, that is, the deceptive world that only looks at the beauty of an exterior façade? Listen then, Catholic Listeners, how the Jews in today's Gospel sent out important envoys to ask John who he was. "Who are you?" Therefore, we too should send out envoys, not vile reprobates who fool us into asking the world who it might be, but noble, wise envoys who will instruct us in the honest truth. Observe around you the sensual lust for pleasure and passion, and the desire for wealth and goods; see, too, their vile assistants and disloyal servants. If you sent them out to enquire about money and goods, pleasure and lust or status and honour, or if you were to ask them, "Who are you?", that is, what quality and condition they are, they will answer you that the lusts of the flesh are pleasurable, that an abundance of wealth

---

infinitum: unde ex hac parte peccatum est infinitum. Aliud quod in peccato est, est inordinata conversio ad commutabile bonum. Et ex hac parte, peccatum est finitum. St Thomas Aquinas, *Summa Theologiae*, I–II, Q 87, A 4, ad. 3.

brings ease of life, and status and honour gives rise to prestige and reputation. But if you were to send out noble and wise envoys, namely, the intellect and faith, they will remind you of the words of the wise Solomon, "Vanity of vanities, and all is vanity" (Eccl 1:2). It is indeed so. Because all the wealth and riches, honours and pleasures you might hope to receive from the world in exchange for your hard work, even when legitimate, are but transient, false and temporal. St Augustine asks, "What is joy in the world? Rejoicing in iniquity, rejoicing in infamy, rejoicing in what is vile? These are all the things the world rejoices in. What the world relishes is villainy that no one punishes. Let people indulge in dissolute living, in fornication, let them drown themselves in drink, befoul themselves with infamy and suffer no harm. There you have the joy of the world!"[6]

St Gregory reports in his *Dialogues* [7] that St Benedict once saw the whole world in the form of a fiery globe, together with its pleasures and desires, its wealth and honours. He would think well of us, were we to have the light of this holy man. For in various passages of the Scriptures, the Holy Spirit compares this present life's prosperity to a dream or deep sleep, as He speaks through the mouth of King David, "All the foolish of heart were troubled. They have slept their sleep; and all the men of riches have found nothing in their hands" (Ps 75:6). The people given over to the world, he says, are those who have toiled and sweated all their lives without right thought or discernment; on the day when the Lord comes to lead them from the day of this life to the night of death, they are surprised to find their hands empty of all those things of which they had dreamed. St Augustine comments on this line of thought, "All the happiness that people experience in this world is no more but a dream of those who sleep; just as a poor person in a dream considers himself rich because he sees a great treasure, but upon waking finds himself poor again, so will those people who rejoice in the vanities of this world

---

6   *In saeculo gaudium quod est? Gaudere de iniquitate, gaudere de turpitudine, gaudere de deformitate? De his omnibus gaudet saeculum. Saeculi laetitia est impunita nequitia, luxurientur homines, fornicentur homines, ebriositate ingurgitentur, turpitudine foedentur, nihil mali patiantur; videte saeculi gaudium.* St Augustine, On the Words of the Apostle, Sermon 171 on Philippians ch.4.
7   St Gregory the Great, Dialogues, Book 2, ch. 35.

find that their joy will be as in a dream; upon waking they will find that everything was only a passing dream, as Scripture says, 'like a dream of someone awaking from sleep.'"[8]

Furthermore, the wealth, honours, and pleasures of the world have one great shortcoming, namely, that they will plant in our hearts a sense of discontentment, as it were, for we know deep down that they cannot satisfy us. St Augustine writes about this in his Commentary on Psalm 84, "We will find that all those things in the world we thought would give us contentment will ultimately disappear."[9] And he is correct, for as the Wise Man says, "A covetous man shall not be satisfied with money" (Eccl 5:9). We also read about Our Saviour telling the Samaritan woman, "Whoever drinks of this water shall thirst again; but whoever drinks of the water that I shall give, shall not thirst forever" (Jn 4:13). The reason for this is that everything in this world is made of matter, whereas our soul is spiritual, and it has been created in God's image; thus the soul cannot be happy unless it beholds the Divine Being in whose image it has been formed. Since the things of this world are transitory and our soul is immortal, it therefore follows that worldly things are finite, whilst our soul was created to enjoy the eternal good. St Bernard puts this well when he says that "money no more lessens the hunger of the mind than air does that of the body. If then you should happen to see a starved man with mouth opened in the wind drinking in the air with puffed-out cheeks as if to satisfy his hunger thereby, would you not think him mad?" He goes on, "But it is no less foolish to imagine that the soul can be satisfied with worldly things, which only inflate it without feeding it."[10] A noteworthy example of this can be found in the person of King Solomon, who, after he had expended all his power and

---

8 *Omnes istae felicitates, quae videntur saeculi, somnia sunt dormientum quomodo qui videt thesaurum in somnis, dormiens dives est, sed evigilabit et pauper erit: sic omnia ista vana huius saeculi, de quibus homines gaudent, in somno gaudent; evigilabunt et invenient somnia illa fuisse, et transisse, sicut dicit Scriptura, velut somnium surgentis.* St Augustine, Exposition on Psalm 131.

9 *Quidquid hic nobis providerimus ad refectionem, illuc rursus inveniemus defectionem.* St Augustine, Exposition on Psalm 84.

10 *Sic non minoris insaniae est, si spiritum rationalem, rebus putes quibuscumque corporalibus, non magis inflari, quam satiari.* St Bernard, Treatise On Loving God, ch. 7.

means, recalls how he searched for earthly things that would cheer his heart; he had built great houses and palaces, surrounded himself with courtiers and concubines, gathered to himself silver and gold and many treasures, and gave in to his heart's desire. As he himself said, "Whatever my eyes desired I did not keep from them; I kept my heart from no pleasure, for my heart found pleasure in everything" (Eccl 2:10). Yet he found that all these things that normally should have given him happiness, in so far as they were capable of giving happiness, instead gave him nothing but misery and depression of spirit. Thus, the truth, as well as his own experience, obliged him to pronounce those famous words we have heard so often but have so seldom put into practise, "Vanity of vanities, and all is vanity" (Eccl 1:2). Yes, everything is vanity, apart from "loving God and serving Him alone," as the contemplative Thomas à Kempis writes.[11]

Therefore, Catholic Listeners, we must disregard the created things of this world, which are but fleeting voices, and embrace the Word of the Father, Jesus Christ, who formed and redeemed us. And because He formed us, we owe Him our service; and because He redeemed us, we owe Him our love. For even though all creatures belong to Him, "The earth is the Lord's and the fullness thereof" (1 Cor 10:26). We nonetheless belong to Him in a particular manner for He created us in His own image and likeness, not only to raise us in dignity above all His other creatures, but also to show us the special ownership He has over us by making us His heirs, as He once long ago told the people of Israel, "Out of all the nations you will be my treasured possession" (Ex 19:5). And so it is. Therefore, we should listen to the words of St Laurence Justinian, "Natural reason cries out in each one of us, that we are subject to the One from whom we have our being."[12] In other words, through natural lights, or right reason, man perceives that he owes obedience, honour and love to the One from whom he has his being. Or, as St Bernard puts it, "There is no excuse for any infidel, even, if he does not love the Lord his God with his whole heart, with his whole soul, and with all his strength. For, that innate

---

11 *Amare Deum et illi soli servire.* Thomas à Kempis, The Imitation of Christ, Book I, ch. I.

12 *Clamat innata ratio ut quisque se illi subiiciat, a quo habet ut sit.* St Laurence Justinian, Treatise on Obedience, ch. 5.

sense of justice which reason is not ignorant of, cries out to him from within that he is bound with his whole self to love Him to whom, he is not unaware, he owes all that he is."[13] And so, righteousness, which gives him right reason and clear knowledge, cries out to the ears of his heart that he should love God above all else and dedicate himself to His service. Since all of us have received our being from the Lord our God and have become Christians through His grace and mercy, we have become more enlightened and better instructed than the heathens. We therefore have stronger bonds with the Divine Majesty, which also places upon us greater obligations to love, honour and serve Him, according to the demands of those bonds and the tenets of our Faith.

What is more, our obligations are based not only on the fact that He created us, but because we were ransomed and redeemed by Him, for as St Paul says, "You are not your own, for you were bought at great price" (1 Cor 6:19–20). When someone buys something, the thing he purchased becomes his possession in a greater degree than if he was given it, or if he had found it. Seeing, then, that Christ our Saviour has bought us, there is no doubt that we belong to Him, especially since He bought us at great price. Hear how St Peter explains this text, "You were not redeemed with corruptible things as gold or silver, but with the precious Blood of Christ, as of an unblemished lamb" (1 Pet 1:18–19). Know that Jesus has purchased us with the labours of His life, with the pains of His holy death and with every drop of His Precious Blood, which contains an endless stream of delights, far more than we could ever be worthy of. So He has bought us at a price that cannot be valued. This moved St Bernard to write, "Truly I ought to love the one through whom I have my being, my life, my understanding. Lord Jesus, whoever refuses to live for you is clearly worthy of death."[14] To whom would a man give the service

---

13   *Inexcusabilis est omnis etiam infidelis, si non diligit Dominum Deum suum toto corde, tota anima, tota virtute sua. Clamat nempe intus ei innata, et non ignota ratione iustitia, quia ex toto se illum diligere debeat, cui se totum debere non ignorat.* St Bernard, Treatise On Loving God, ch. 2.

14   *Valde mihi omnino amandus est, per quem sum vivo et sapio. Dignus plane est morte, qui tibi, Domine Iesu, recusat vivere.* St Bernard, On the Song of Songs, Sermon 20.

of his life other than to the One who died for him, so that he might have the hope of attaining true life? We who have been created by Almighty God and redeemed by the Precious Blood of His Son must distance ourselves from the world and kindle within us a desire to seek Jesus and to follow Him, resolving thereby to persevere in His service. In this we can follow the example of St Epipodius who suffered persecution under the Emperor Antoninus Verus. According to Surinus, in order to strengthen himself to persevere and remain courageous while suffering pains and torments, Epipodius cried out, "I confess that Jesus Christ is God, together with the Father and the Holy Spirit. It is but reasonable that I should resign my soul to Him who has created me and redeemed me."[15]

Finally then, Catholic Listeners, I say together with St Paul, "Those who use the world should act as if they did not use it; for the world in its present form is passing away" (1 Cor 7:31). Indeed, this present world is passing away all too quickly, as St Ambrose tells us, "Those who seek the sun must come out of the shadows, and let those avoid smoke who want to follow the light."[16] In honour of Jesus Christ, let us have nothing to do with the material things of this world, as well as honour, status, desire, and pleasure, for He will grant us much more in return, as He promised in His own words in St Matthew's Gospel, "Everyone who has left houses or fields, for my name's sake, will receive a hundredfold, and will inherit eternal life" (Mt 19:29). Who lives, etc.

---

15 *Christum cum Patre ac Spiritu S. Deum esse confiteor, dignumque est, ut illi animam meam refundam, qui mihi et Creator est, et Redemptor.* Laurentius Surius, Lives of the Saints, Life of St Epipodius, 22 April.

16 *Relinquamus umbram qui solem quaerimus, deferamus fumum, qui lucem sequimur.* St Ambrose, Flight from the World.

On the Fourth Sunday of Advent

Anno quintodecimo Imperii Tiberii Caesaris, procu-
rante Pontio Pilato Iudaeam, tetracha autem Galileae
Herode, Philippo autem fratre eius tetrarcha Itureae,
sub Principibus Sacerdotum, Anna et Caipha; factum
est verbum Domini, super Ioannem Zachariae filium —
"In the fifteenth year of the reign of Emperor Tiberius, when Pontius Pilate was governor of Judea, and
Herod was tetrarch of Galilee, and his brother Philip
tetrarch of the region of Ituraea, during the high
priesthood of Annas and Caiaphas, the word of God
came to John, the son of Zechariah" (Lk 3:1–2).

CATHOLIC LISTENERS, AT THE
beginning of today's Gospel St Luke the Evangelist
elaborates for us the various circumstances and
events occurring in the Jewish kingdom during the
fifteenth year of the reign of the Emperor Tiberius,
and he even lists the names and functions of the spiritual and secular
leaders. He does this not only to indicate the demise of the old world,
but also to show the new Kingdom with the coming of Our Saviour,
Jesus Christ. St Luke mentions three secular rulers who ruled over
various parts of Palestine and Syria after the death of King Herod,
who was the one who murdered the innocent children. This Herod
was the last king of the Jews. After his death the Emperor Augustus
divided the kingdom into quarters as a way of diminishing the power
of the Jewish rulers. The young Herod Antipas, who was the son of
the afore-mentioned King Herod, was the one who was involved in
the death of John the Baptist; at the time he ruled over the tetrarchy
of Galilee, that is, one quarter of the kingdom. Herod's brother, Philip,

whose wife Herodias lived in adultery with the young Herod, ruled over the tetrarchy of Trachonitis, which lay in Syria between Mount Lebanon, the Sea of Tiberias[1] and Iturea. Lysanias, a virtually unknown foreigner, ruled the tetrachy of Abilene, likewise in the environs of Mount Lebanon, as Josephus tells us in his Antiquities of the Jews.[2] Thus the land of the Jews, which was formerly ruled by one king, now came to be governed by numerous lords and monarchs. This verifies Our Lord's prophecy in St Luke's Gospel, "Every kingdom divided against itself shall be brought to desolation, and house upon house shall fall" (Lk 11:17). The division of the Jewish kingdom among various secular rulers was not the only reason for its destruction, but the other reason must surely also be the division of the High Priesthood, for in those days there were two High Priests, namely, Annas and Caiaphas, his son-in-law. Notwithstanding that Almighty God had given a perpetual ordinance that the High Priest of the Jews should reign for the term of his life, nonetheless, when the land of the Jews fell into the hands of the heathens, with God's permission, the kings and governors changed the criteria of the High Priest and sold his office to the highest bidder, or to whoever was most in favour. Among these were Annas and Caiaphas, who served the High Priesthood, alternating years between them. This office was often renewed, sometimes even annually, as Josephus writes. Sacred Scripture also mentions Caiaphas being High Priest that year. Therefore, while the world, and particularly the land of the Jews, was being ruled in this manner, it appeared that the long-promised time of Our Saviour's coming was at hand, "The Word of the Lord came upon John, the son of Zechariah." Since his youth, John had lived in the wilderness, and through the inspiration of the Holy Spirit he was led to the River Jordan near the place where they could easily cross by boat, and he lived in the environs of the river, preaching a baptism of repentance for the forgiveness of sins. He reprimanded the people and made them see the errors of their ways, so that through sincere contrition and a firm purpose of amendment and acts of penance they would turn from their sins and prepare a place in their hearts for Christ, whose

---

1 Also known as Lake Tiberias, Lake Genessaret or the Sea of Galilee.
2 Josephus, *Antiquities of the Jews*, Book 19, ch. 4.

coming was very near. Hear the words of the Prophet Isaiah, "The voice of one crying in the desert: Prepare the way of the Lord, make straight in the wilderness the paths of our God. Every valley shall be exalted, and every mountain and hill shall be made low, and the crooked shall become straight, and the rough ways plain" (Is 40:3–4). Thus may the Messiah enter in without by-passes or obstacles; thus may He come to the people without let or hindrance, helping them with His forgiveness and mercy. In order to glean more teachings from today's Gospel for our general education, let us first pray for the grace of the Holy Spirit through the intercession of the Blessed Virgin Mary by presenting to her the angelic salutation,

Ave Maria

ALMIGHTY GOD (WHOSE NATURE IS GOODNESS, WHOSE will is power and might, and whose deeds are pure mercy, as St Leo tells us)[3] did not randomly guide the pen of St Luke the Evangelist so that he would record for us such particulars as the time and year, and even during whose reign John the Baptist had left the wilderness where he had lived from his youth, and from whence he had come to live among the people, to whom he came to announce the reconciling year of the Lord, all the while preaching repentance and contrition. No, Almighty God intended the Evangelist to record all these different particulars so that people would have clear knowledge of God's divine wisdom and prudence (see Eph 1:8), as well as the care He takes in ordering all things, and His great faithfulness in providing whatever is necessary. It is not surprising that under those godless rulers and self-interested priests the people, who came from different classes and backgrounds, would grow into a nation that was spiteful, vainglorious, avaricious, unjust and many other wicked things. For as the Wise Man said, "As the people's judges are, so will their officials be, and as the ruler of a city is, so also are all of its inhabitants" (Sir 10:2). What kind of ruler, then, was the Emperor Tiberias, who used his position to sniff out the affection of his subjects? He was a loyal servant of the gods and one who bestowed divine honours on demons; and if we are to believe the words of Suetonius and Tacitus, he was

---

3 St Leo the Great, On the Nativity of Christ, Sermon 22.

to have been a bloodthirsty, vindictive man. Herod the Younger was no better, for Sacred Scripture tells us that he quite openly flaunted his incestuous way of life and his adultery with Herodias, the wife of his brother Philip. Pilate was a judge who sold verdicts and sentences for money; he gladly condemned innocent people to death, as he did with Our Saviour, and with great cruelty he did much injustice and injury to many people, as Philo writes.[4] Annas and Caiaphas were spiritual rulers of the Jewish Republic, but they had bought their High Priesthood with gifts and money. St Augustine claims that they took turns to rule on alternate years,[5] although others say they were co-rulers, which would have been in direct defiance of the divine law. However it may be, the only thing these godless and unjust rulers, these fine priests and spiritual leaders could sow among the people was wickedness, injustice, disdain, and loathing for both human as well as divine laws and commandments.

Nor is it surprising that through their wickedness all virtue had disappeared from the world, the service of God had been trampled underfoot by the Jews, and fraternal charity had grown cold. These injustices brought upon them such punishments as thunder and lighting and plagues and destruction, as we saw happening in ancient times with the cities of Sodom and Gomorrah, which had sinned gravely. Nonetheless, the Word of the Lord came upon John the Baptist, that he might preach forgiveness of sins and, in the words of Scripture, make known to the people that "the clouds will rain down justice, and the earth will open and sprout forth the Saviour of the world" (Is 45:8). On this topic St Bernard writes, "It was evening, and the day was far spent; the sun of justice had well-nigh set, and but a faint ray of his light and heat remained on earth. The light of divine knowledge was very small, and as iniquity abounded, the fervour of charity had grown cold. No angel appeared, no prophet spoke; both hopelessly baffled by the exceeding obduracy and obstinacy of mankind. Then it was when the Son of God said: Behold I come."[6]

---

4   See Philo Judaeus, *De legatione ad Caium.*
5   See St Augustine, Tract 113, On the Gospel of John.
6   *Vere advesperascebat et inclinata erat iam dies; recesserat paulo minus Sol iusti-tiae, ita ut exiguus nimis splendor eius, et calor, esset in terris Nam et lux divinae notitiae parva admodum erat, et abundante iniquitate, fervor refrixerat charitatis :*

So then, just when the night of sin had eclipsed the light of grace, and the darkness of ignorance had extinguished the light of faith, and when the hearts of mankind had grown cold through lack of charity, when the angels had gone into hiding and the Prophets had stilled their tongues, in short, when the world itself was descending into the abyss because of its grave sins, to Heaven's great surprise and earth's delight and hell's horror, the Son of God said "Behold I come." I, who am immortal, come as a mortal; I, who can undergo no suffering, come as one suffering in order to offer my life on the gibbet of the Cross as a pleasing sacrifice for the reconciliation of the human race. O infinite goodness! O endless mercy! If you were to ask the reason for this endless mercy, St Paul will tell you in his Letter to the Ephesians, where he writes about God's abundant goodness, wisdom and providence, "He has made known to us the mystery of His will, according to His good pleasure that He set forth in Christ, as a plan for the fullness of time" (Eph 1:9–10). What fullness of time? By this he means that God will show us His grace and mercy when the measure of sin has reached its limit.

King David confirms this when, in the spirit of prophecy, he anticipates the favourable time of God's mercy, "It is time, O Lord, to act, for they have broken your law" (Ps 118:126). It is time, O God, for you to pour your mercy upon the earth, seeing that the ungrateful and reprobate people have trampled your law underfoot and have lost respect for you. He was saying in other words, 'See, O Lord! now is the right time to show your goodness to mankind, even though they have sinned and done wicked things.' St Augustine offers an explanation of King David's words "It is time, O Lord, to act, for they have broken your law" when he writes, "Now what is this, save the grace which was revealed in Christ at its own time?"[7] St Ambrose is of like mind when he comments on the same psalm, "When the Holy Spirit made the Prophet see the transgressions of his people, and all their extravagance, their self-indulgence, deceit, fraudulence, greed and

---

iam non apparebat angelus, non loquebatur propheta; cessabant velut desperatione victi, prae nimia utique duritia hominum, et obstinatione. At ego ait Filius Dei, tunc dixi, Ecce venio. St Bernard of Clairvaux, Sermons for Advent, Sermon 1.
7 *Hoc facendi tempus, quid est, nisi gratia, quae fuit in Christo, suo tempore revelata.* St Augustine, Exposition on Psalm 118, 125.

drunkenness, he then ran to Christ, almost as if wanting to intercede on our behalf, and he told Him: It is time, O Lord, for you to ascend the Cross to die a bitter death."[8]

Through the grace of the Divine Majesty, whose deeds are merciful, today the Word of the Lord descended upon John the Baptist in the wilderness, that is, he was summoned to leave his hidden life in the wilderness and go out to precede Christ Jesus, who until now was hidden in mortal flesh and was living a hidden life, to announce that He was the Son of God and the Saviour of the world. Thus mankind would echo the words long ago spoken by the Prophet Isaiah, "Truly, you are a God who hides himself, O God of Israel, the Saviour" (Is 45:15). Truly, you are a God of goodness and saving help in time of need, who takes away our sins on the day of tribulation. It is truly so, for we see in the Old Testament that when wicked kings had the upper hand, God sent them prophets, according to the demands of the matter and the time, to punish and admonish them, and to teach them how to live a virtuous life. But when the world had come to an end, so to speak, He sent them the greatest of all the Prophets, John the Baptist. John himself followed the precepts of God and he accepted his office to preach the Word of God, and, in the words of the Prophet Isaiah, "to bind up the broken-hearted, to proclaim liberty to the captives, to comfort all who mourn, to give them a garland instead of ashes, the oil of gladness instead of mourning and the mantle of praise instead of a faint spirit" (see Is 61:1–3). Catholic Listeners, even though our merciful Saviour triumphantly ascended into Heaven after His glorious Resurrection, in subsequent years He did not stop caring for His holy Catholic Church. Since the degenerate and unfettered ways of the people had made it necessary, He sent out apostolic men and preachers who were inflamed with His Divine Spirit to take up the prophetic office and to continue the work of John the Baptist, so that they might stand up to the godless tyrants and kings, thus denouncing sin and preventing errors and heresies. Therefore, after the time of the Apostles and during the years of

---

8 *Cum videret in Spiritu Sancto Propheta praevaricationes populi luxuriam, delicias, dolos, fraudes, avaritiam, temulentiam; quasi pro nobis interveniens currit ad Christum.* St Ambrose, Exposition on Psalm 118, Sermon 16.

persecution, God sent the glorious Martyrs so that by their words and example they might lead and strengthen the faithful to be able to withstand the unbelievers. And so they gave witness to the truth of the Catholic religion by heroically shedding their blood and very lives. In addition to this, the Word and the Spirit of the Lord had so enkindled them that no one was able to withstand the wisdom and intelligence that spoke through them. Moreover, during the time when heresies were emerging, God raised up learned men and excellent Doctors of the Church such as Jerome who expelled the heresy of Vigilantius, and Augustine who crushed the heretic Pelagius, and many others who strengthened the faith of doubters through their faith, teaching, and exemplary holy lives. But when the drowsiness and lethargy of man once again let the weeds of sin and corruption sprout throughout the Lord's vineyard, God, who alone is unchangeable, let His Word descend upon excellent and holy persons, here upon a Norbert and Bernard, there upon a Dominic and Francis, again there on an Ignatius and a Francis Xavier, and many other apostolic men and founders of religious Orders, so they would, by themselves or by their spiritual champions, build a dam and form an embankment against the flood of wickedness, both spiritual as well as secular; thus they would obstruct and rein in evil by their God-fearing holy lives, by their strictness of speech and good example, by their disciplined and impeccable lives. God Himself will accomplish all this until the end of the world comes, when we shall see the return of the Prophets Enoch and Elijah, the former to invite the Jews, the latter to invite the remaining heathen to improve their lives and to move them to do penance for their sins, to abhor their wicked ways and to love God.

Similarly, the Word of the Lord descended upon John the Baptist so that he would preach repentance to the Jews and prepare their hearts so that they would approach God with sincere, pure love, so that they could receive the Saviour of the world. We, too, are warned through the words of today's Gospel to prepare the way of the Lord by laying low the mountains and hills of sin, by making the crooked straight and the rough places plain, so that with a pure conscience and sincere love we may receive Him who was born into the world and became man for us, so that, by casting aside sin we may love Him before all things.

For He humbled Himself out of pure love for us and for our salvation. Among the various reasons that moved the Son of God to take on our human nature was also this one, namely, that He would forever unite mankind to Himself, so that man would love Him, and from then onwards there would be no excuse for not learning to practise the love of God. For this reason, God has always and above all things desired and demanded man's heart and his love, as the Wise Man says in that famous passage from Proverbs, "My son, give me your heart" (Prov 23:26). In order to move and encourage man, God used every competent means at His disposal. In the first place, God knew well that goodness has the power to kindle love and affection in man, and so He provided man with goodness, and raised him above all other creatures. As St Gregory the Great writes, "In man is combined various qualities of all creatures. Being he has in common with stones, life he has in common with trees, feeling in common with beasts, understanding in common with angels."9 Almighty God gifted man with all these perfections and benevolences so that he would all the more come to recognise and love his Lord and Benefactor. Furthermore, as the teachings of the philosophers and experience itself has taught us, an image of someone can stir up and generate love. That is why God created man in His own image and likeness, as we read in Sacred Scripture, "God created man in His own image and likeness" (Gn 1:27). Notice that Scripture does not say that God made man in man's own image, as you do when commissioning an artist to paint a portrait, but God Himself created man in God's own image and likeness, so that man would become inflamed to love the One who had formed and created him. Therefore, if a painting or a statue representing a king could speak, or could love someone, who more would it love than the king? And if the king had fashioned it with his own hands, would he then not love it in return? Without a doubt then, if it could be forced to love someone else to the detriment of the king, then it would answer, "Who else do you want me to love, apart from the one in whose image I have been made, and who made me with his own hands, and who

---

9 *Omnis autem creaturae aliquid habet homo. Habet namque commune esse cum lapidibus, vivere cum arboribus, sentire cum animalibus, intelligere cum angelis.* St Gregory, Homilies on the Gospel, Homily 29.

is a king and an important person?" Man, therefore, who is made in God's image, not by a strange hand, but by the divine hand, is bound to flee from excessive love for creatures, which only leads to wickedness and sin, and to unite himself with a pure conscience to God's love.

Even so, God saw that, despite the benevolences He had given, He could not entirely win over man's heart to burn for love of Him alone, despite man's heart having a great capacity to do so; with great insincerity had man turned his love towards temporal things. Therefore, to reach His goal, so to speak, God used the most powerful means His eternal wisdom and omnipotence could muster, which great approaching event we are about to celebrate, namely, when He came down to earth "and became man." By entering into this great but humbling work of love, God hoped to win the love and affection of mankind. "The main purpose for Christ coming into the world was that man might learn how much God loves him; and that he might learn this to the intent that he might be kindled to love the One by whom he was first loved," says St Augustine.[10] Indeed, the main reason man was prevented from loving God was because God was invisible in a natural sense, and He could not be experienced by our bodily senses, being a pure spirit. For even though on the one hand man was bound to love Him through his intellect, on the other hand this posed an enormous obstacle, because in this present life, man's mind can only understand what is taken in through the senses; similarly, the will can only love whatever the mind presents to it. Hence Almighty God wanted to remove this obstacle in order to make it easier for man to love his Lord and God, and so He took on our human nature and was born into the world. Being in human form, He could now be seen with the eyes and heard with the ears and touched with the hands. Through this divine invention He made Himself capable of being loved as a man who was visibly and noticeably born into the world.

Many years ago at the beginning of the Catholic Church, during the persecution of Catholic Christians by tyrants, the authorities

---

10 *Maxime propterea Christus advenit, ut cognosceret homo quantum eum diligat Deus, et ideo cognosceret, ut in eius amorem, a quo prior dilectus est, inardesceret.* St Augustine, On Catechizing the Uninstructed, ch. 4, 8.

had let out cruel beasts, tigers, bears and lions, to tear apart and kill the Martyrs. But often those beasts just stood there in all calmness, immobile and gentle, without harming the Christians. The cruel executioners noticed this, and do you know what they did then? In order to spur on the cruelty of the beasts, and to remove the last shred of respect or decency from the Christians, they dressed the holy Martyrs in the hides and skins of dead animals, which deceived the beasts and aroused their imagination. They then pounced on the Martyrs, ripping them apart and devouring them. In the same way, Catholic Listeners, the Divine Majesty saw that mankind could not approach God or adhere to Him who is pure spirit, for man can only understand or love things that are visible, tangible or physical. And so He put on a body and was born into the world so that man would unite himself to God in love, and would have no further excuse for not loving Him.

There is something that lends even more support to the above reason, and that is this: even though God could assume any other bodily nature, He chose our human one, because "the Word was made flesh and dwelt among us" (Jn 1:14). The Catholic Church has always understood these words to contain a most wondrous mystery that points to the Holy Sacrifice of the Mass, which we honour on bended knees as a sign of thanksgiving, mutual love, and reverence. There is a reason for this, because Almighty God could easily have made Himself visible by taking on some other physical nature, given the weakness of our minds and the fragility of our wills. For example, He could have put Himself in the sun and spun over our heads, securing our salvation by pouring out over us the sunbeams of His grace. Nonetheless, He did not elect to do it that way, choosing instead, in His goodness and mercy, to assume our human nature. This led St Augustine to pronounce these remarkable words, "To heal souls God adopts all kinds of means suitable to the times which are ordered by His marvellous wisdom. But in no way did He show greater loving-kindness in His dealings with the human race for its good, than when the Wisdom of God, his only Son, coeternal and consubstantial with the Father, deigned to assume human nature. For thus he showed to carnal people, given over to bodily sense and unable with the mind to behold the truth, how lofty a place among creatures belonged our human nature, in that he appeared to men not merely visibly — for he could have done that in some ethereal body adapted to our weak powers of vision — but as a true man."[11] This happened for only one reason, says St Augustine, which is that when God appeared in the likeness of men, He might be more easily loved by them.[12] It is said that Alexander the Great (and according to some, also Emperor Charles V when he was approaching Africa) would dress himself in the Persian style in order to win over the hearts of the Persians with greater force, thereby subduing both theirs wills and their land. Similarly, the Son of God, in order that He might all the more be loved by men, put on the garment of their humanity, and became one of their equals. As St Paul the Apostle says, "Being born in human likeness, and being found in human form" (Phil 2:7).

This mystery full of love and mercy, Catholic Listeners, is what we will be celebrating in the coming solemnity. Therefore, according to the words of John the Baptist in today's Gospel, "Prepare the way of the Lord, make straight His paths" and purify your soul and cleanse your conscience through perfect contrition and a sincere confession. Even though your eyes may have rested on inappropriate persons with whom you live in impurity, or even though your ears may have been too attentive to tales, thus leading others to spread gossip or insult, and even though your own tongue has been too loose in speaking wickedness or evil of others, and even though your hands and the other members of your body have led you to injustices, which brought about damage to your soul and disdain from God, you can still sweep the dust from your conscience and put on the bridal gown of God's love. Flatten the mountains of pride and fill in the valleys of laziness and pettiness when you hear that God our Saviour is showing His

---

11   *Cum omnibus modis medeatur Deus animis pro temporum oportunitatibus, quae mira sapientia eius ordinantur; nullo modo beneficentius consuluit generi humano, quam cum ipsa Sapientia Dei, id est, unicus filius consubstantialis Patri et coeternus totum suscepit hominem. Ita enim demonstravit carnalibus corporeisque sensibus deditis, quam excelsum locum inter creaturas habeat humana natura, quod non solum visibiliter (nam et id poterat in aliquo aethereo corpore, ad nostrorum aspectuum tolerantiam temperato) sed etiam hominibus, in vero homine apparuit.* St Augustine, On True Religion, ch. 16, 30.

12   *Ut familiarius diligeretur ad homine Deus, in similitudinem hominis Deus apparuit.* St Augustine, Enchiridion, ch. 26.

grace to every person throughout the world, so that by spurning god-less and mundane desires all people may live on this earth in sobriety, righteousness and devotion; sobriety to themselves, righteousness to their neighbour, and devotion to God. Thus may they await in blessed hope the grace of God in this world, and the enjoyment of His glory in the next. Who lives, etc.

On the Solemnity of Christmas—I

Verbum caro factum est, et habitavit in nobis — "And the Word became flesh, and dwelt amongst us" (Lk 1:14).

ODAY IS THE JOYFUL DAY, CATH-olic Listeners, longed for by the ancient Fathers, Patriarchs, and Prophets, on which the Son of God was born to bring peace to the world, freedom to prisoners, liberty to captives, healing to the sick, and comfort to those who mourn, as the Patriarch Abraham foretold. His spirit rejoiced, as Our Lord tells us, "Abraham your father rejoiced that he might see my day: he saw it, and was glad" (Jn 8:56). In a sermon preached on this very feast day, Pope St Leo raised up the people's hearts to spiritual gladness, because each and every one has an equal right to rejoice on this day. "All men have an equal share in the great cause of our joy. Rejoice, O you who are holy, for you draw nearer to your crown! Rejoice, O you who are sinful, your Saviour offers you pardon! Rejoice also, O Gentiles, God calls you to life!"[1] For when the fullness of time had come, the Divine Majesty led the Bridegroom of the Catholic Church to His throne to assume our human nature. O happy day! O day of rejoicing and gladness! Indeed, the Catholic Church, which is the Bride of this heavenly Bridegroom, could never have satisfied her love, nor her eyes, if the Word had not become flesh and dwelt among us. For just as no one can gaze at the brilliance of the sun unless it is wrapped in a cloud, so the Son of God, whose divinity no eye can see nor mind can understand, was born into the

---

[1] *Una cunctis laetitiae communis est ratio: exsultet sanctus, quia appropinquat ad palmam; gaudeat peccator, quia invitatur ad veniam: animetur Gentilis, quia vocatur ad vitam.* St Leo the Great, Sermons on the Nativity of the Lord, Sermon 1.

world in a human nature and veiled by a cloud, as it were, so that He could more easily reveal Himself to man. What does this feast demand of us, Catholic Listeners, except that we dispose ourselves to observe this great mystery with thanksgiving, casting our eyes upon such a great vision. First, though, let us take off our shoes of worldly desires, so that together with the innocent shepherds we might humbly and simply approach our God who is sheltering in our nature; we come to Him as if approaching a precious pearl or a hidden treasure, or a grain of wheat or a mustard seed. For here we have a precious pearl, but it lies in a dirty stable; here is a hidden treasure, but He is wrapped in old cloths and dirty rags; here is a superb grain of wheat, but it is cast into a dark place; here is a mustard seed, the smallest of all seeds, as a symbol of humility, which in itself contains wondrous strength because before long it will be greater than all the other herbs, and within the intricacy of its branches it creates pleasant shade for the Catholic Church; thus the birds of the air, which are all the righteous and God-fearing souls, will find a home among its branches. Miracle of miracles! Here we see the Lord uttering His Word over the earth, as St Paul tells us in Romans, chapter nine. There we see a conception without the help of man, a delivery without blemish, a birth without stain of sin. Let us then worship this Child Jesus with great humility, and with devout attention observe the manner, time, and place of His birth, so that we might follow the example of love, poverty and humility of the One who is born. In order to benefit all the more from our work, let us first pray for the grace of the Holy Spirit through the intercession of the Blessed Virgin Mary who bore this Child, by presenting to her the angelic salutation,

Ave Maria

JUST AS THE SUN REVEALS ITSELF THROUGH ITS RAYS, and fire betrays itself through its heat, so the Son of God's majesty is revealed through His wondrous birth into the world. Let us then discover how He was born in Bethlehem on this day. Here we are not dealing with the birth of a common man, nor of a David, who was the holiest among the kings; nor of a Solomon, who was the wisest of all the princes; nor of a Samson, the strongest among the judges, nor of a John the Baptist, of whom Truth Himself testified that there was no one greater among those born of woman, even though in fact He is a David in holiness, a Solomon in wisdom, a Samson in strength, and a John in innocence. What we are dealing with is the birth of the Son of the Most High, the mediator between God and man, of the blessed Jesus Christ who is begotten of the heavenly Father as a tree is begotten from a root, or heat from fire, or a river from a spring of water. See then, the One who existed in eternity long before the Morning Star, is born in time. He who is begotten of the heavenly Father before all ages is now born of the Blessed Virgin Mary. Never before have we heard of such a thing. The brilliance of the eternal light has been born, a mirror without spot, an image of God's goodness, a figure of His being, but although He is endowed with the dust of our mortality, He is not accepted by man. The King of Kings, whom no eye has ever seen, is born; He takes on the form of a servant and lets Himself be seen and touched by human hands. The Creator of the entire world, whose wisdom knows no bounds, is born. He will allow Himself to be called a carpenter's Son, and He shall grow in years and in wisdom.

Today He lies in a manger in a stable, crying and blubbing. What do you think, Catholic Listeners, was this not an example of deep humility and unheard-of submissiveness? Nonetheless, He submitted to this freely, He was not coerced. Even though He is in the form of this tender Child, which lies crying amidst the hay and the straw, His power and dominion over the world are not compromised. Even though this Child is so small, it is actually a giant, for as King David says, "He goes out from the highest Heaven" (Ps 18:7). He is like a mighty giant with a sword girded to his thigh, because the Son of God has taken on our fragile nature to fight an exceptional battle with the devil, the prince of this world. See this wondrous way of speaking which brings together two natures in the one Person of the Son of God. He is a Child and He is a giant, He lies in a crib and He thunders in the heavens, He is swaddled in rags and He governs the world, He is fragile and weak and He is well-armed to do battle.

The pagan poets and philosophers of old claimed that Hercules, while still a young child, used to tame cruel beasts and hideous monsters. But this was the stuff of fables and stories. Our own Hercules, the blessed Child Jesus, overcame the serpents of hell while still lying in the cradle. He did not have to wait until He was old, for His power is always the same. As the Prophet Isaiah said, "For before the child knows how to call his father and his mother, the wealth of Damascus and the spoil of Samaria shall be taken away before the king of the Assyrians" (Is 8:4). Indeed, the hellish powers will fall down throughout the entire earth, and the dominion of the devil shall be wiped away through the word and command of a little Child. It is true that the devil's strength was great throughout the world, for as St John the Evangelist says, "Woe to the earth and the sea, because the devil has come down to you with great wrath" (Rev 12:12). But then a voice was heard in Heaven, "Now is come salvation and strength and the kingdom of our God and the power of His Christ" (Rev 12:10). Indeed, this tender Child Jesus can cast out the power of devils and subdue and crush them, even though His dominion has not yet been laid upon His shoulders by carrying the wood of the Cross, and despite Him not yet having suffered a bitter death. King David, then, speaks the truth when he says of this blessed Child, "A thousand shall fall at your side, and ten thousand at your right hand, but it shall not reach you" (Ps 90:7). While still in the crib the Child says, "I will pursue my enemies and overtake them, and I will not turn again until they are consumed" (Ps 17:38).

Have you ever heard anyone mention how Gideon smashed the clay jars, or how Sangar slew his enemies with a plough share, or of Samson's donkey jawbone, or Ehud's double-bladed dagger, or how David slew the giant Goliath with a stone? These are all types and examples of what would be accomplished through the tender Child Jesus. Indeed, the hidden torches inside the clay jars frightened the Midianites, who were the people of Israel's enemy, and they took flight, and they were routed (see Judg 7). See how the blessed womb of Mary is often described as being like an earthen vessel in which was hidden the brilliant torch, the tender flesh, the fragile Body of Jesus Christ. The lamp of His Divine Godhead is lit with a fire that is all-consuming and all-devouring, "For our God is a consuming fire. Like a light inside a clay jar, He is divinity wrapped in flesh," says St.

73

Gregory.[2] Indeed, this is what wounds and destroys the enemy of the human race, namely, both the weakness and the strength of Jesus Christ. For what does a plough share mean in the hand of Sangar, or a donkey's jawbone in the hand of Samson? They are but poor cast-off instruments, yet they caused terror and fear among the Philistines, just as through the submissiveness of Our Saviour our decaying world was raised up and He became victorious over His enemies.

Allow me now to use one figure to illustrate all the others. I focus my remarks upon Eglon, king of the Moabites, who was puffed up not only with obesity but also with pride and despotism, while the people of Israel served under his tyranny for eighteen years. It was he whom Ehud murdered with great finesse (cf. Judg 3.) This makes me think about the tyrant of the human race, the devil, who spread his domain over the people. He, too, was puffed up at having won over so many thousands of souls, but Our Saviour freed us and snatched us from his grip. This can be even more clearly seen when we compare them with each other. For example, we see how the Judge Ehud concealed a double-edged short-sword under his garments, and under the cover of our human nature lies hidden the Word of God, which cuts sharper than any double-edged sword, "It penetrates like a double-edged sword," says St Paul. Sacred Scripture tells us that Ehud used both his left as well as his right hand, "who could use both hands as we do our right."[3] See then the blessed Child Jesus who, as both God and man, is armed against the devil. In similar fashion, just as the glorious Ehud had secured the desired freedom for his Israelite companions, so Jesus Our Saviour has released our souls from the devil's slavery. The fact that the giant Goliath was defeated by a catapulted stone should make us mindful of Christ who is the stone cut from the mountain, but not by human hands, which fell and crushed the power of the demon Zebulun.[4]

---

2 *Deus noster ignis consumens est. Lumen vero in testa, est divinitas in carne.* St Gregory the Great, Homilies on the Gospel, Homily 30.

3 *Utraque manu pro dextra utebatur.* Although the Septuagint suggests Ehud was ambidextrous, he appeared to be left-handed, since he bound the dagger to his right thigh so as to be easily drawn out by the left hand. See Judges 3:15.

4 See Dan 2:34. This seems to refer to the destruction of the 'evil' Land of Zebulun which had been plunged into darkness and distress, not only by apostatising

Turning back to the birth of the Child Jesus and His Blessed Mother, a wondrous exchange occurred between the Son and His Mother, between the Creator and the created. God gave of His divinity and the Mother gave of her humanity, and these two were united into one Person. Even so, Catholic Listeners, we must be careful not to speak indiscreetly or be quick to judge, lest we say something disrespectful against the second Adam who put on our human nature. He became like us in all things, except that He was without sin. His blessed Body was formed out of flesh and blood, but undefiled and without a trace of stain. Today He is born of a Virgin, but neither He nor she was born into sin. Today He is wrapped in swaddling clothes and laid in a manger on hay and straw; nonetheless, the angels honoured Him with a heavenly hymn, "Gloria in excelsis Deo." He is worshipped by shepherds, "Let us go over to Bethlehem, and let us see this word that is come to pass, which the Lord has shown us" (Lk 2:15.) But the godless fear Him, "And Herod the King hearing this, was troubled, and all Jerusalem with him" (Mt 2:3). Yes, the One who lies in this dirty, dark stable has come into the world as the true light, "which enlightens every man that comes into this world" (Jn 1:19). The One who lies here silently is the Word of the eternal Wisdom. He is your Counsellor, O man! so that you will not err in your deeds and works. He is Emmanuel, so that you will not be timid in times of adversity. He is strong and mighty so that you will not be overcome in battle. He is the Father of the age to come, so that you will not set your hearts on the temporal things of this world, and finally, He is the Prince of Peace, so that you may always live in solidarity with God and your neighbour. The birth of Jesus Christ is indeed a joyous occasion. He is not born for the disobedient angels who forfeited their own glory, but for us poor, rejected people who once were subjected to eternal damnation; we are indeed far from having merited this joyous birth, for although we have all sinned through the first Adam, we have become justified through the second. We are all children of wrath, children who have provoked the divine anger, and thus have become deserving of eternal

---

to false gods and idols, but also through the deportation of the inhabitants by Tiglath-pilizer. See 2 Kings 15:29.

punishment. Therefore, we should openly admit that we were once enemies of God and therefore undeserving of His love. Nonetheless, because of His great love for us, the Father of mercy and the God of consolation sent us not a man, for man had sinned, and not an angel, for angels could not save us, but His only-begotten Son, who would become for us the Saviour and Redeemer of the whole world, despite our eternal guilt. O wondrous mercy of God! What sublime counsel and unutterable love the Holy Trinity has for us! Is anyone able to ponder this great event half-heartedly, or even to forget it entirely? O man, you are arrogant, pompous, and proud; you are nothing more than dust, yet do you not feel ashamed when you hear that the Word became flesh, that the Second Person of the Trinity became man? Indeed, those proud people who look down on others should take note that, unless they humble themselves by becoming like a small child and temper their pride in the sight of the Most High and the Child Jesus, they shall not enter the Kingdom of Heaven. Do you not think there is something mysterious about the words of St John the Evangelist when he said, "And the Word became flesh"? Note that he did not say, "And the Word became a soul," for the flesh has no comparison with God, whereas the soul has at least some. By this he wanted to make known the Son of God's great humility and love; no greater distance exists between the one and the other, between the highest and the lowest, between mortality and immortality, between God and man. Because of His great and extraordinary love for us, God came down from highest Heaven to earth in order to become man, appearing as an innocent Child wrapped in swaddling clothes and lying in a manger. Was there a better way for Him to teach us or show us His endless love? Even though His love and humility are great, they are permanently connected to each other. That is why, when we observe His love, we will always see His humility and subservience, for humility comes from love. Love among people can also bring forth evil and wretched deeds, as Seneca says, "To be in love and at the same time to be wise, is scarcely given to even God Himself."[5] Our amazement at this is lessened when we observe God's

---

5 *Amare simul et sapere, vix Deo conceditur.* The original quotation from the *Sententiae* of Publilius Syrus reads "*amare simul et sapere, vix Jove conceditur.*"

wondrous deeds, and in particular when we contemplate the Divine Majesty's love for us in wanting to put on our feeble human nature. How blessed are you, O human nature, which the Divine Majesty loved so much that He honoured you by marrying you to His only Son. For just as poor, simple Ruth could rejoice in her marriage to the wealthy Boaz, so may human nature rejoice in the fact that, despite being weak and fragile, it has through Christ's becoming man been joined in marriage to the Son of God. Therefore, the heavenly Bridegroom shows the effect of that marriage by being born this day in a stable in the town of Bethlehem, which stable even to this day is held in high honour and renown by both Christian pilgrims as well as the Turks,[6] who are sworn enemies of the name of Jesus Christ. We must not be too surprised at this, for in ancient times the Prophet Micah had foretold, "And you, Bethlehem, in the land of Judah, are not the least among the princes of Judah; for from you shall come a ruler who will govern my people Israel" (Mt 2:6).[7] And so it was, for where was He born, He who was to rule and govern Israel? In Bethlehem. And from which land did He come forth, He who was long-expected to be a light to the Gentiles? From which land? Bethlehem. Where is the stone that was cut out of the mountain without hands, that is, where is the Messiah and Saviour of the world, Jesus Christ, who was born of a pure Virgin without her knowing man? In Bethlehem. Today, Catholic Listeners, we have come to Bethlehem among innocent people, among shepherds who live in all simplicity and honesty, without deceit or guile.

Therefore, those people who are tainted with sin and wickedness, and who are given over to lustful pleasures and deceit, let them stay away from the stable. Likewise, let the hypocrites and insincere of heart and those who speak with honey on the tongue but have bitter gall in their hearts, let them not approach the crib. For neither God nor His angels take pleasure in duplicity. See how today the angels have not been sent to Jerusalem to visit that sly fox Herod, nor to those hypocritical Scribes and Pharisees, but to Bethlehem to visit the innocent, simple shepherds, for in them is the Most High

---

6 i.e., the Muslims.
7 Here Matthew is quoting Micah 5:2.

well-pleased, to them He gives counsel for the salvation of man-kind. The Wise Man says, "His communication is with the simple" (Prov 3:32). Sacred Scripture praises the Prophet Jacob's simplicity, who, when compared to the rough and hairy Esau, was said to have been an innocent man living in a tent (see Gn 25:27). The virtue of simplicity was also praised in the Prophet Job by God Himself, for Job had rejected the devil who had tormented him in vain. The patient Job had placed his trust in the virtue of purity, and so he could acclaim with confidence, "Let God weigh me in a just balance, and let Him know my simplicity" (Job 31:6). King David also noticed that this virtue was very pleasing to God, and so he placed all his trust in it. He therefore exclaimed after having honoured God with a worthy sacrifice, "I know, my God, that you search the heart and love simplicity, and take pleasure in uprightness; in the simplicity of my heart I have joyfully offered all these things" (1 Chron 29:17). We need not seek examples of this praiseworthy virtue only in the Old Covenant; Scripture tells us that the disciples of Christ and the early Christians attended the Temple together, and by breaking bread in their homes they received their food with gladness and simplicity of heart, "They ate their food with glad and generous hearts" (Acts 2:46). O blessed simplicity, which was so often praised in the Holy Spirit! Catholic Listeners, we must love simplicity, and loving it we must embrace it, and embracing it we must put it into practice, so that, walking straight and simply with the shepherds, we may become strengthened with a sure confidence. "He who walks simply, walks confidently" (Prov 10:9).[8] We must not approach the Child Jesus as hypocrites, duplicitous of heart like present-day politicians, for "woe to them that are of a double heart!" (Sir 2:14). Woe to those who have sweetness on their tongues but deceit in their hearts.

But let us return to that blessed Bethlehem. If someone wants to know when Jesus Christ was born, He was born in the sixth age.[9] The first age is reckoned from Adam to the Great Flood; the second

---

8 Here simplicity takes the meaning of sincerely or uprightly.
9 The Six Ages are a historical periodization based upon Christian religious events. Each age lasts around 1000 years. They were first written about in the fourth century by St Augustine.

age is reckoned from the Great Flood to Abraham; the third from Abraham to David; the fourth from David to the Babylonian captivity; the fifth from the Babylonian captivity to the birth of Christ. If you want to know the time of the year, the day and hour of His birth, well then, He was born during the winter on a Sunday at midnight. Why was He born in the sixth age? Because God's grace and mercy would flow in abundance upon all those who through the ages had shown the abundance of their sins and wickedness. Why was He born in the middle of winter? Because the beginning of His life would be fraught with difficulties and toil. Why on a Sunday? To bring to an end the Sabbath of the Jews. Why at midnight? To fulfil Sacred Scripture, for as the Wise Man said long ago, "While all things were in quiet silence, and the night was in the midst of her course, your almighty Word leapt down from Heaven from your royal throne" (Wis 18:14–15). It likewise seems mysterious that Christ's birth happened during the reign of the Emperor Augustus who is portrayed wearing a tabard and holding an olive branch in his hand. Similarly, Jesus is the King of Peace who not only urged peace, but actually left peace with His disciples and indeed to all people; His peace means peace with God, peace with the angels, peace with man, and peace between right reason and our senses and strengths. How wondrous, then, that when He was born a fountain of oil sprang up in the city of Rome, as these following verses testify. These can be read even today in the church of the Blessed Virgin in *Trans Tiberim:*[10]

> *Dum tenet emeritus miles, sum magna taberna,*
> *Sed dum Virgo tenet, nive maior nuncupor, et sum.*
> *Tunc oleum fluo, signans magnificam pietatem*
> *Christi nascentis; nunc trado petentibus ipsam.*

Which in our language reads,

> Of old I was a hospice for deserving soldiers, a resting place;
> But now the pure and holy Virgin finds her rest in me,
> Then the oil flowed out, a sign of hope and grace
> For Christ is born; ask, and I'll impart that grace to thee.[11]

---

10 This is the Roman church of Santa Maria in Trastevere.
11 The church of Santa Maria in Trastevere was built c. AD 342 on the site of the old *Taberna Meritoria,* a hospice for wounded soldiers. According to

Is it then so wondrous when in the East precious balsam came to be produced in the vineyards of Engaddi? (see Song 1:14). It is not so wondrous, but it is a sign that the new-born Prince of Peace would let the oil of mercy flow out over His works, and that He would spread the abundant balsam of His divine grace.

Before we close our discourse, let us see, as far as is possible, how the birth of Our Saviour took place. On this point, it is true what the Prophet Isaiah said long ago concerning either His eternal or His temporal generation, "Who can explain His generation?" (Is 53:8). St John the Evangelist tried to explain this great mystery in just four words, "The Word became flesh." In what way? In what manner did the Blessed Virgin Mary bear her only Son? Forgive me, O eternal Majesty, for even trying to explain this miracle, because, to tell the truth, this perplexes and astonishes me. Nevertheless, I will rely on what the Catholic Church has always stated on this matter. She bore Him in the way that stars shoot out their beams, or hills give off their fog, or the fire its heat, without pain or blemish. For just as this second Eve, this pure Virgin Mary, was freed from all sin, so she was also freed from any pain, because pain finds its origin in sin. And so pain cannot follow where there was no fault. The Son, who had come into the world to heal our ills and free us from sorrow, would not cause His own mother anguish. Therefore, the One whom she had conceived without human desires, she now bore without any pain. She bore Him without going into labour and had carried Him pure and spotless in her womb for nine months without being sick or vomiting. O wondrous exchange! O unfathomable mystery! Our natural intellect just cannot understand how it is that a Virgin can conceive without the help of a man, or how God could become human without diminishing His Majesty, or how a man could be born without deflowering virginity, or how a person could give birth without suffering pain and simultaneously be a Mother and a Virgin. So it is no wonder, then, that nature and natural intelligence must

---

tradition, on the day of Christ's birth, a mysterious fountain of oil sprang up in the middle of this hospice. The oil continued to flow for a whole day. Eusebius and others wrote about this event. This was later interpreted as signifying the coming of God's grace upon earth. The Latin verse is from a marble inscription still found near the main entrance to the church.

keep silent when the Creator of nature displays His almighty power. Therefore, we must adhere to what our Faith teaches us and not try to be too scholarly lest we are imprudent or indiscreet in our speech. Let us not be like those pompous men such as, for example, Marcion, Julianus, Eutyches, or Ebion[12] who originally, thanks to God's glory, had not fallen into very grave heresy, but because they later strayed from the path of the Catholic Faith, and the Catholic Church, they pronounced false lies and extreme errors. For you, O God, are the Most Holy among the holy, a hidden God who has revealed your mysteries not to the learned of the world, but to the small and humble, to shepherds and fishermen, to the simple and innocent. You, whose presence is everywhere, now lies wrapped in swaddling clothes in a stable. You, who are the Bread come down from Heaven, the fountain of life and eternal light, now suffer hunger and thirst in a dark and gloomy stable. "Truly you are a hidden God" (Is 45:15). Indeed, O Jesus! would not those who witnessed the marriage of Joseph and Mary have said that your conception had occurred in the usual way? And those who saw your sweet tears whilst you lay in the manger, would they not have said that your birth had taken place in the usual manner? Would not those who had seen the marks of your circumcision say that you had been made subject to the malediction of sin? Your frequent praying and calling upon your heavenly Father seemed to diminish your power and authority, and your having been nailed to a gibbet seemed to conceal your glory. I will not mention that you have hidden your teachings in words, your truth in parables and your grace in the holy Sacraments. "Truly you are a hidden God, the God and Saviour of Israel."

Even though He has hidden His Godhead, we must nonetheless acknowledge that He truly is God. Therefore, you who have not yet approached this new-born King, and you sinners who have become stuck in the mire of your sins, make haste to go and join the shepherds, and say with sincere devotion, "Let us go to Bethlehem." Let us

---

12 Marcion of Sinape (d. AD 160) preached errant theology. Emperor Julian the Apostate (d. AD 363) tried to re-establish paganism throughout the Roman Empire. Eutyches (d. AD 456), Greek archimandrite who was denounced at the Council of Chalcedon as a heretic. Ebion, a second century literary figure who gave rise to a school of thought which refuted Christ's divinity.

leave the centre of worldly delights and lusts and go to the Bread of Heaven and the Food of angels. See, the sweet Child Jesus is calling you, He invites you through the words of the Wise Man, "Come over to me, and be filled with my fruits" (Sir 24:26), both eternal and temporal. See, I do not call you by means of my Prophets or Patriarchs, but I call you personally, not as a strict or severe God, but as an innocent, gentle Child.

Let us then give ear to Him, Catholic Listeners, and embrace this sweet, blessed Child, saying with sincerity, O sweet Jesus! you took such delight in loving us, that you wanted to be born into the world as man. Give us strength to turn from hatred and intolerance to love you above all else. You, who desired to lower yourself by taking on the form of a servant, help us to turn from pride so that we might always be humble. You, who are the author of all purity, and in whom is found neither sin nor blemish, make us flee from sin as from a poisonous serpent. For you there was no room in the inn, but we present to you our souls and our strengths. You suffered cold and discomfort, we shall kindle within us the fire of fraternal love. O sweet Jesus! because of us you shed tears; we, too, shall weep, but for the sins and misdeeds by which we have angered you, who are all good. By promising to do this, may we become partakers of your divine grace, and thus secure our eternal glory. Who lives, etc.

On the Solemnity of Christmas—II

Peperit Filium suum primogenitum et pannis eum involvit et reclinavit eum in praesepio quia non erat eis locus in diversorio — "And she brought forth her first born son and wrapped him up in swaddling clothes and laid him in a manger: because there was no room for them in the inn" (Lk 2:7).

ATHOLIC LISTENERS, WHEN GOD'S Spirit compelled the Prophet Isaiah to prophesy to the world the wonderful tidings of the Incarnation of Our Saviour, Jesus Christ, about how He was to be born and the miracles that would be seen around His birth and even on the very day of His birth, he became speechless with wonderment and amazement and he cried out, "Who has believed what we have heard, and to whom is the arm of the Lord revealed? Who shall declare His generation?" (Is 53:1,8). Pope St Leo wrote in a sermon for today's feast, "The Prophet's words look not only to the divine, but also to the human birth of Jesus Christ, the Son of God. Faith believes that two natures were joined in one Person, but words cannot explain how."[1] And so I say, following the words and manner of speaking of this holy Prophet, "Who has believed what we have heard, and to whom is the humility of the Lord revealed? Who shall declare His birth?" Who can believe that God is a child, or that a child is God? Who can declare that a Virgin has become a mother while remaining intact, or that she has become

---

[1] *Quod in Christo Iesu Filio Dei, non solum ad divinam essentiam, sed etiam ad humanam spectat naturam. Utramque enim substantiam in unam convenisse personam, nisi fides credat, sermo non explicat.* Pope Leo the Great, On the Feast of the Nativity, Sermon 9.

the Mother of the Son who created her? Who can understand that God, who cannot be understood either in Heaven or on earth, had been enclosed for nine months within the blessed womb of Mary and has been born into the world? That is why, and not without good reason, the same Prophet added one more title to the list with which He honoured the Son of God, which is "Astonishing," for He truly is wonderful and astonishing. His conception, life and teachings were truly wondrous, so too were His death, Resurrection and Ascension. In relation to today's feast St Ambrose tells us, "Truly astonishing is His birth from a Virgin, who wrapped Him up in swaddling clothes and laid Him in a manger because there was no room for them in the inn."[2] What can be more astonishing, Catholic Listeners, than the Creator of Heaven and earth lying in a manger because there was no room for Him in the inn? What can be more astonishing than that the supreme Divine Majesty, in whose presence the pure spirits of Heaven rejoice, has taken up lodgings in a stable amongst dirty, earthly beasts? This is why on this day the angels sang, *Gloria in altissimis Deo*—"Glory to God in the highest Heaven," because from Heaven they could see the Lord lying submissive and humble below them on the earth. The birth of the Son of God into the world is therefore no less profitable or astonishing for us. On the one hand, we might freely question with amazement the wisdom of God in this matter; on the other hand, we must praise the endless benevolence of His works. As St Maximus tells us, "Today the Judge of Heaven and earth has appeared to us, He has ripped up the record of our offences and His mercy has wiped away our guilt. Today has been born the Lord who lifted off our shoulders the yoke of our ancient slavery; the world now rejoices with its new-found everlasting freedom. Today we see the gentle King who walked the earth with heavenly righteousness and crushed the proud tyranny of our enemy from hell. Today has been born for us the second Adam, the Lord of Paradise, who shall be neither deceived nor tempted by the beauty of the forbidden tree, nor by the perversion of the serpent nor the seduction of the woman. Today is seen a light in the darkness, a light in which the heavens rejoiced. The world has received this light, but

---

2   St Ambrose, Commentary on Luke 2:41–42.

it did not know it. 'He came unto His own, and His own did not receive Him.'"[3]

The Fathers of old witnessed many countless wonders and miracles. For example, "Man ate the bread of angels" (Ps 77:25), or, "He struck the rock, and made water flow from it, and the streams overflowed" (Ps 77:20). And also, "The sea fled at the sight, the Jordan turned back on its course" (Ps 113:3). So, too, "At the sound of the trumpet the walls collapsed" (Josh 6:20). We are also told that the sun stopped in the middle of the sky and delayed going down for about a full day. There is no doubt that our Old Testament Fathers had seen some strange signs and wondrous miracles. Even so, they did not witness the most wondrous event ever to be seen, namely, that the formless Word of the Father, the only-begotten Son of the Most High, before whom the heavenly powers thunder and quake, would be born into the world. He would become like men, and He would unite His divine nature to a human one, becoming one Person. This was such a remarkable event that no human tongue could merit to sing about it; that is why it was left to heavenly voices, and in particular those of angels, to sweetly announce the glory of God from Heaven on high. But seeing that our human condition leads men to think they can explain the secrets of God to one another, let us first beg the grace of the Holy Spirit through the intercession of Mary, who bore her first-born Son, wrapped Him in swaddling clothes and laid Him in a manger, by presenting to her the angelic salutation,

Ave Maria

WHEN THE FULLNESS OF TIME HAD COME AND THE MOST favourable hour had arrived, as St Paul the Apostle writes (Gal 4:4), Almighty God resolved to assume human nature so that He would pay the debt for people's sins; for, after He had given them all kinds of created things, He now decided to give Himself as well. He gave Himself through an inextricable bond that could never be undone, which was that God should become man, and man become God. And so in a great and incomprehensible mystery, He chose a Virgin whose name was Mary, from the tribe of Judah, and through the

---

3 St Maximus the Confessor, On the Nativity of the Lord VII, Sermon 13.

power of the Holy Spirit she would receive in her blessed womb the eternal Word, which she would bear while still remaining a virgin; she would become His true Mother, and He would be Her true Son. He chose a Virgin who was the most pure among all His creatures and the most blessed among women, endowing her with every virtue and privilege, as was only proper for the Mother of God. He wanted her to come from the tribe of Judah, which was also David's lineage, and she had to be a descendent of the Patriarch Abraham, because God had promised them that the Messiah and Saviour of the world would be born from their household. As God said of Abraham, "All the nations of the earth shall be blessed in him" (Gn 18:18), and to David He promised, "I will raise to your throne heirs of your own body" (Ps 131:11). It was God's will that this blessed woman would descend from the illustrious blood of the Patriarchs, Prophets, Kings, Princes, Judges, and Rulers of the people of Israel and that both the royal and the priestly bloodlines would unite in her; for she was to become the Mother of the Supreme High Priest and the King of Heaven and earth. God willed that when the time had arrived for her to conceive, she should be married to a holy man of the same tribe, whose name was Joseph, so that she would have someone to keep her company and also so that no one would make dishonourable assumptions about her virtue, since she had conceived without being married. Furthermore, it was also to avoid the Jews rejecting her Son by them claiming He had been conceived in sin, which would harm His Mother's honour more than it would His own dignity. "The Lord preferred that men would doubt His own origin rather than cast doubt on His Mother's purity," as St Ambrose writes.[4] Even though He was conceived by the Holy Spirit, He feared that His Mother's honour could be endangered, and so He agreed to be known as the son of Joseph. He had come to teach us humility and that we were not to set our hearts on the temporal things of this world, such as wealth and plenty, which are not found in Heaven, where poverty is held in great esteem. Therefore, He desired that His Mother and St Joseph, whose son the people thought He was, should be poor, and

---

4   *Maluit autem Dominus aliquos de suo ortu quam de matris pudore dubitare.* St Ambrose, Commentary on St. Luke's Gospel, Book 2, ch. 1.

that they would experience neither sadness nor sorrow in their poverty. To show that He came to save sinners and that we were not to place our trust in men of flesh and blood, He allowed some people in His lineage of ancestors to be sinful, wanton women.

To bring about this great act, the Divine Majesty first sent the Archangel Gabriel to the Blessed Virgin Mary to announce the mystery and to assure her that, even though the mystery would be fulfilled in her, the flower of her virginity would not in the least be defiled. Whereupon, at the very moment this purest Virgin gave her agreement to the angel, she conceived within her blessed womb the Son of God through the power of the Holy Spirit, who overshadowed her, so that she would be able to endure and sustain the rays of the Sun of Righteousness and the Divine Fire (which had come to kindle the world). For nine months she carried Him in her womb and during this time she visited her cousin Elizabeth; her greeting and presence brought blessings upon Elizabeth's still unborn son, John the Baptist. During those days the Emperor Augustus had issued a decree "that the whole world should be registered" (Lk 2:1). To make this onerous task easier, and to avoid inaccuracies and deception, Augustus ordered that everyone should be registered in their place of birth. Seeing that Joseph, Mary's husband, had been born in Bethlehem, he had to travel with his wife from Nazareth, where he was living, to Bethlehem so as to carry out the royal decree. And so it happened that the good Jesus, who had come into the world to raise man up after his fall through disobedience, already began to demonstrate His obedience whilst still in His Mother's womb, by desiring that His parents should also be obedient to the laws of a temporal prince.

It was no mere coincidence that the Sovereign of Heaven was born during the reign of the world's greatest monarch, and that the Prince of our salvation was subject to the most noble ruler of the Roman Empire. You see, Catholic Listeners, the time had come for the Prophets' predictions to be fulfilled, namely, that the Messiah and Saviour of the world would come before the Jewish governance had completely come to an end. As the Patriarch Jacob lay dying he called his sons to bless them and to predict what would happen in the days to come; and he told his son Judah, "The sceptre shall not depart from

Judah, nor the ruler's staff from between his feet, until tribute comes to him; and the obedience of the people is his" (Gn 49:10). Thus, the Emperor's decree of registration had been issued at the exact time when it had been predicted that the law of the Messiah would go out from Zion and the Word of the Lord from Jerusalem. His is not a strict law, but one that is gentle and mild; His law does not bother people, but it strengthens them by God's grace; it is not a law that extorts money through violence or war, but one that demands love and obedience to God and provides good maintenance of the soul. "The law of the Lord is unspotted, converting souls: the testimony of the Lord is faithful" (Ps 18:8). Augustus wanted the names of his subjects registered because he was proud and arrogant; Christ was born into the world to record the names of those who believe in Him so He could show them mercy and grace. Augustus conquered the princes of the world so there would be peace throughout the entire empire; Jesus came to conquer the prince of darkness, and through His Blood brought peace to those in Heaven and on earth. Those who aligned themselves with Augustus thereby acknowledged their slavery to him; those who aligned themselves to Jesus received the power to be called children of God. "He gave them power to become children of God" (Jn 1:12).

It was, therefore, no coincidence that Jesus Christ's birth occurred at the exact time when a general census had been proclaimed. He wanted to make known that in time He would reveal Himself in a human nature, He who has now registered His elect for all eternity. St Gregory asks, "What does it mean that the whole world was to be registered when Christ was born? Unless it means that the One who has registered His elect for all eternity has Himself appeared in the flesh?" How are they registered? He registers them by recording His elect in the Book of Life, in which His name comes first as the Head of everyone and everything. "In the head of the book it is written of me, that I should do your will" (Ps 39:8–9). He registers their names in His heavenly palace so that their names can never be erased or scratched out, "Rejoice that your names are written in Heaven" (Lk 10:20). He writes them in His blessed hands so that He will never forget them, "See, I have engraved you on the palms of my hands" (Is 49:16.) Here we have a reference to His death on the Cross. That is why St Augustine says, "O Lord, your hands have moulded me and fashioned me: your hands, that were nailed to the Cross have fashioned me; O Lord, do not despise the work of your hands. I look at your deep wounds, my name has been engraved on your hands! Read my name and deliver me!"[5]

But we are now speaking of a new-born Child, who holds the elect in His heart, thereby offering them only love and affection. His heart is the paper on which they are written; the crib is His writing desk; the ink, His bitter tears and His pen is the Spirit of the living God. Catholic Listeners, if we could look into the heart of this sweet, blessed Child, we would find our names engraved there with indelible letters of love. For Jesus knew from the very first day who belonged to Him; He knew who would reap the fruit of His birth. That is why He was born during this general census, for He had subjected all the nations of the world under His feet and had engraved their names in His heart. He, the Lord, who had been born in time, would recount their names in eternity. Furthermore, this census was a sign that peace and calm had come to the entire Roman Empire. The great temple of Janus, which was only open during times of war, had been closed shut,[6] and all the people were to be ruled under one emperor. And so, Jesus was born in Bethlehem to show that He had to bring another kind of peace. It was to be a spiritual, divine peace: peace between God and man, peace between man and his conscience, peace between right reason and sensuality. God wanted us to share in this peace. O Jesus, whom the Prophet Isaiah calls "Prince of peace," pour into our hearts this peace, which surpasses all understanding. Give us peace with your heavenly Father who has broken our sins; give us peace with our conscience, which our wickedness had disturbed; give us peace

---

5 *Manus tuae Domine fecerunt me, et plasmaverunt me: manus inquam illae que affixae clavis sunt pro me; opus manuum tuarum Domine ne despicias: vulnera manuum praecor ut aspicias. Ecce in manibus tuis Domine Deus descripsisti me: lege ipsam scripturam, et salva me.* St Augustine, Soliloquies, Book 1, ch. 2.
6 In ancient Rome, the main Temple of Janus stood in the Roman Forum. It had doors on both ends, and inside was a statue of Janus, the two-faced god of boundaries. The Temple doors were closed in times of peace and opened in times of war, which was very often.

with our neighbours who have dwindled away because of our wicked words, our immoderate passions, and harmful actions. The Emperor Augustus did not himself experience this spiritual peace and calmness of soul, nor could he give it to anyone else, but it was the God of love and peace who today declares this peace through the message of the angels who have come down from Heaven singing with gladness and rejoicing, "Glory to God in the highest, and on earth peace to men of good will" (Lk 2:14). Peace to those who are poor in Christ's name, and who spurn the wealth and splendour of the world; peace to those who, because of His humility, detest pride and the world's vanity; peace to those who, because of His gentleness, have forgotten any injury or injustice done towards them; peace to those who, because of His moderation and sobriety, have given up gluttony and drunkenness. But to those people who continue to pollute their conscience with sin, and those who argue and quarrel with their neighbours, who live in hatred and envy and spend all day in the tavern drinking away the feast days, all these people can expect to hear Almighty God's threatening voice which He speaks through the mouth of the Prophet Isaiah, "Woe to those who rise early in the morning to run after their drinks, who stay up late at night till they are inflamed with wine" (Is 5:11). Woe to those who do not notice the works of the Lord, works of love and humility, of grace and mercy, which He demonstrated by His birth for the salvation of the world. So then, we must flee from wickedness when Innocence appears in the world; we must cast away all traces of bitterness, hatred, envy and enmity when the Prince of peace makes His entrance into the world, when the sweet Child Jesus, the God of peace and love, is born on earth.

While everyone travelled to their own towns to be registered, according to Emperor Augustus' decree, so Joseph and Mary also set off on their journey, not just in obedience to the royal command, but principally because they had been directed to do so through divine prudence. Nevertheless, the expectant Virgin showed herself among the people, travelling through various lands and always assured of her dignity and purity. She did not think it scandalous to travel with a carpenter and to be considered his wife, even though she knew what kind of fruit it was that she carried in her womb, namely, the Son of the Most High, the Creator of all, the glory of the angels and the Lord of Heaven and earth. They came to the small, innocent town of Bethlehem, whose only claim to fame was that David had been born there and had built it up. Thus was God's great mystery revealed in the flesh, and what had been shown to the angels was preached to the heathen and believed throughout the world. "And she brought forth her first born son and wrapped him up in swaddling clothes and laid him in a manger: because there was no room for them in the inn." Catholic Listeners, Mary bore her first-born son in Bethlehem, not by mere coincidence, but so that not one iota or dot of God's plan would be changed, as the Prophet Micah prophesied and St Matthew so clearly recorded for us, "And you, Bethlehem, in the land of Judah, are by no means least among the leaders of Judah: because out of you will come a leader who will shepherd My people Israel" (Mt 2:6). Notice how the birth of the Messiah, who is the leader of God's people, is described according to the location in which the event took place. Despite being the Lord and Creator of the entire world, he was born in Bethlehem where He owned neither land nor field. He who came to dispel the night of sin and the darkness of wicked desires was born around midnight, when all things were still and the heavens seemed to drop down their dew like sweetest honey. He came to reconcile us to His heavenly Father, who is no God of quarrelling and disharmony; it was His wish to pour into us the dew of His grace and obtain for us the sweetness of Heaven. The Blessed Virgin Mary bore a Son to show that He truly was her Son, that He was truly man, thereby refuting the errors of Nestorius and Valentinus. She bore her first-born Son to show that she had born no others before Him, and that He, being the first-born, would accept all of us as His brothers in the Faith. In the *Life of St Gertrude the Great* it is written that one day as she was meditating she became puzzled by the title of 'first-born' in relation to the Son of God. Should He be called the first-born of His Mother, or the only-begotten? Our Lady herself appeared to St Gertrude and related these words, "They ought not to call my sweetest Jesus my only Son, but rather my first-born Son. I conceived Him first in my womb, but after Him, or rather, through Him, I conceived every one of you to be His brothers and to be my children, adopting you in the womb of my maternal charity."[7] That is why Mary is not only called the Mother of God but also the Mother of all the elect, that is, of all the children of God.

She bore her first-born Son without pain or injury, sadness or sorrow, "As a lily gives off its perfume, so the Blessed Virgin, without defilement, brought forth the Saviour and wrapped Him in swaddling clothes," says St Thomas of Villanova.[8] This is not without mystery, for Jesus had wanted be wrapped in swaddling clothes to teach us to reject worldly excesses and desires and to teach us deep humility. He allowed Himself to be bound in swaddling clothes in order to hide Himself from the glory of the world and the vanity of men, thereby giving us an example that we, too, should hide and distance ourselves from wealth and glory and look to the poverty and mockery that Our Lord had to endure. Furthermore, He allowed Himself to be bound in cloths as a sign that the wretched human race, which was wounded by Adam's sin, might become strong, as the Prophet Ezekiel tells us, "It has not been bound up for healing or wrapped with a bandage, so that it may become strong" (Ez 30:21). This human race had not become wounded, even though it had been injured through Adam, just for the purpose of again receiving His healing, nor was He wrapped in linen cloths so that this race might once more obtain His power, but He been wrapped in cloths in order to bring health and healing to wretched humanity. He was wrapped in swaddling clothes as a sign that He would avert from us the rags and tatters of misery and sorrow and clothe us with the robe of glory and immortality, as St Augustine commented, "Your rags He cast away, your impure robe He tore asunder. He pitied you that He might adorn you. He adorned you, that He might love you."[9] O blessed infancy of Jesus

---

7 *Nequaquam unigenitus, sed congruentissime primogenitus dulcissimus Iesus meus, quem primo clauso utero procreavi, et post ipsum, imo per ipsum, omnes ipsi in fratres, mihi in filios, maternae charitatis visceribus adoptando, generavi.* St Gertrude the Great, The Herald of Divine Love, Book 4, ch. 3.

8 *Sicut enim lilium spirat odorem, ita Virgo beata sine corruptione peperit Salvatorem, et pannis eum involvit.* St Thomas of Villanova, Sermons on the Nativity, Sermon 2.

9 *Abiecit pannos tuos, discidit cilicium tuum, misertus est ut ornaret; ornavit ut amaret.* St Augustine, Sermons on the New Testament, Sermon 12.

Christ in which we grow and mature, attaining to the whole measure of the fullness of Christ! O happy cloths, for the One who had lain in you has come to shoulder the sins of the world. O most-blessed birth! Through you man can see God on earth, humble and gentle, kind and merciful.

Listen! In days of old, man had four reasons to complain against Almighty God. The first reason was that He seemed inaccessible because no one could approach Him. As King David said in Psalm 41, "My tears have been my bread day and night, while people say to me continually, 'Where is your God?'" (Ps 41:4). David longed with all his heart that God would reveal Himself to the people. The second reason was that the people thought God's hand was too severe and strict. In the words of the Prophet Job, "Withdraw your hand far from me!" (Job 13:21). The third reason was that His words were harsh and cutting. Thus the children of Israel said to Moses, "You speak to us; let not the Lord speak to us, lest we die" (Ex 20:19). And the last reason was that the people were terrified of God, for He showed Himself as a great Judge, sitting on a high, majestic throne, "I saw the Lord sitting upon a throne high and elevated" (Is 6:1).

On this day, Catholic Listeners, all these complaints cease; today all things have changed; today the angels bring other tidings to the shepherds by wishing them peace and telling them, "You will find the infant wrapped in swaddling clothes and lying in a manger" (Lk 2:12). In other words, 'Well now shepherds, well now people, no longer do you have a reason to complain about your God, for He is no longer inaccessible, but you can see Him with your own eyes and feel Him with your hands; His hands are not severe and strict, but small and tender and bound in cloths; His words are not harsh and cutting, for He is a mute child, a child which cries and whimpers; nor is He seated on a majestic throne accompanied by the Cherubim and Seraphim, but instead He lies in a crib surrounded by animals, an ox and an ass. Come then, O people, to your God! Do not fear His majesty, do not be frightened of His glory. See how a tender Virgin swaddles Him in cloths and lays Him in a manger, under the warm breath of the animals. "And she wrapped Him in swaddling clothes and laid Him in a manger.'" This was all according to God's wisdom, for the first human, our father Adam, not understanding the honour he had been given, changed his grace and eternal happiness into eternal unhappiness by eating of the forbidden fruit, thereby becoming like the beasts, as King David says, "And man when he was in honour did not understand; he is compared to senseless beasts, and he becomes like them" (Ps 48:20). In order to restore man's misfortune, the Saviour, the second Adam, has come to make His debut into the world. He has taken up lodgings in a stable, which is a home to beasts; He has come naked into the world, in order to clothe us; He came poor to make us rich; He came humble so that we might be raised up; He came crying and blubbing like other children, so that His tears would earn for us heavenly joy.

Today, then, Catholic Listeners, let us use our intelligence; let us remove ourselves from the busy noise of the world, and with lively faith observe the condition of this stable. Let us accompany the humble shepherds and come down from the hills of pride to approach the crib. Without a doubt we will see wondrous things. Notice that in this stable we see neither carpets nor tapestries, but we see dung and spider-webs, even though the King of Kings is lodged here. In the stable we see neither furniture nor household items, and yet the Lord of the world has come here, with all that that involves. This small, freshly-born Child lying in the manger can barely open its eyes; it is agitated and cries bitterly. As a human being it already knows everything there is to know; full of wisdom, it is the Master of all scholars and Teacher of the angels. But as God, even though this Child lies in a manger, it rules the entire world, it adorns Heaven, it tames the winds and moves all things. This is surely a wondrous Child. Come, and look closer. See, these tiny, tender fingers once shaped Heaven and earth; this silent tongue once gave the Law to mankind; these small eyes, which can hardly bear daylight, see through Heaven and hell, they see everything that happens throughout the universe. Surely then, every Catholic Christian who observes with the eyes of his mind the miracles that occurred in that stable on the day of Our Lord's birth, must openly admit that today is the most wonderful day ever to have seen the sun's rays, for this day is full of the Lord's wondrous mysteries and loving miracles. What do you think? Is it not a wonder that the Son of God became the Son of man? That the eternal One was born in time? That the One who from all eternity sprouted from the heavenly Father's fertile mind is this night born from the womb of a Virgin? That the One whom the heavens themselves could not contain, is now lodging in a stable? These are doubtless strange things, but no wonder, for today all things have changed. Temporality is changed to eternity; slavery to freedom; death into immortality; humanity into divinity; disdain into honour and poverty into abundance. See, God has become man. He who was immortal has become mortal; He who was outside of time, has been born in time; He who was invulnerable has become vulnerable, and He who was immeasurable has become measured. Approaching this from the other direction, we can also say that man has (in a manner of speaking) become God; the created has become the Creator; the one who was subject to time has become eternal and the subject has become Lord and Master. O man! What will you give the Lord for all He has done for love of you? This birth did not take place for the redemption of devils, nor for the salvation of angels, but only for the benefit and advantage of man. What shall man therefore give in repayment for this remarkable deed and wondrous act of love and mercy, which was performed not for the angelic spirits, but for this creature, man? So then, Catholic Listeners, seeing that this birth happened for our sake, we should celebrate it with true love, with pure hearts and a good conscience, coming to the manger to worship Our Saviour Jesus with true humility. The poor may go join the shepherds; the righteous may join St Joseph, and the pure in heart may join the pure Virgin Mary. But what do we advise sinners who do not want to confess or better their lives or even acknowledge the Lord's good deeds on the occasion of this great solemnity? They may go join the beasts, the ox and the ass, thus hopefully coming to their senses. "The ox knows his owner, and the ass his master's crib" (Is 1:3).

So come, you sinners, with humility. Place yourselves in a blessed situation, and even if you cannot weep because of your sins, at least ask the Child Jesus to give you the strength of His bitter tears. For today He is born into the world precisely to draw sinners to Himself, so that He can lighten the burden of sinners' misdeeds. In the

Epistle for today's solemnity St Paul the Apostle speaks clearly when he says, "For the grace of God has appeared for the salvation of all men, training us to renounce irreligion and worldly passions, and to live sober, upright, and godly lives in this world, awaiting our blessed hope, the appearing of the glory of our great God" (Tit 2:11–13). We must live soberly, seeing that the new-born Child Jesus scorned useless, excessive things, and even things that were necessary. What do you think? Could He have lived more simply or used the things of this world more frugally seeing He had already chosen a stable over a palace, and a hard manger over a soft bed? His servants were an ox and an ass, and His carpets were spider-webs and animal dung. Furthermore, we need to live upright lives seeing that even Jesus, before His birth, travelled with His parents to pay the Emperor's census tax, and now after His birth He could not find room in the inn, but out of poverty had to make do with a stable. Finally, we are to live godly lives, seeing that the godliness He had towards His heavenly Father moved Him to be born and to die a bitter death. The silent Child Jesus teaches us these lessons, and more, on this special day.

Catholic Listeners, we must often be mindful of the great love God showed us. He was born into the world to become man, a poor man nonetheless, so that, following His example, we will not set our hearts on the passing things of this world, but rather, by leaving these temporal things we will live sober, upright and godly lives, looking for the blessed hope, future immortality and the coming of the glory of our great God and Saviour, in the joy of Heaven. Who lives, etc.

On the Feast of Saint Stephen, Martyr

Video caelos apertos, et Iesum stantem a dextris virtutis Dei—"Behold, I see the heavens opened, and the Son of man standing on the right hand of God" (Acts 7:56).

CATHOLIC LISTENERS, MARTYRDOM, by which one sheds his blood and gives up his very life for the true Catholic Faith, was considered to be of extremely great value by the Church Fathers. In fact, they openly testify that there is nothing more worthy or meritorious in our Catholic religion. St Thomas, the Angelic Doctor, is also of this opinion, for he elevates the Martyrs above the Confessors and Virgins.[1] St. Thomas's opinion is not unfounded, seeing that our blessed Saviour Himself says in St John's Gospel, "Greater love than this has no man, that a man lay down his life for his friends" (Jn 15:13). In other words, there is nothing more meritorious, there is no greater love possible than for us to make friends of our enemies through love, and to pour out our blood and pledge our life for their sakes. Every Martyr has done this, especially the first among the Martyrs, St Stephen, who, because of his fearlessness and courage and his steadfastness and perseverance, saw the heavens opening and Jesus standing at the right hand of God. "Behold, I see the heavens opened, and the Son of man standing on the right hand of God." St Paul the Apostle stored such great value in the title of *Martyr* and the qualities inherent in that name, that he placed it before all others. At one time he had called himself an Apostle of Jesus Christ, but seeing that this holy and blessed name caused him to be imprisoned, chained, handcuffed, tortured and beaten, he put

---

1 See St Thomas Aquinas, *Summa Theologiae*, II–II, Q 124, A 3.

aside the name and title of Apostle and started calling himself a poor prisoner, "Paul, a prisoner in Christ; I am a prisoner in the Lord" (Eph 3:1; 4:1), thereby placing the name of Martyr before that of Apostle. And not without reason, for when the great lords of this earth progress from being a lesser authority to one of greater honour, as when a count, baron or marquis advances to the greater honour of king or duke, they accept the new title as being of great worth and excellence. So, too, St Paul, who was called an Apostle, a chosen vessel, a trumpet of the holy Gospel and the teacher of the Gentiles, was raised to the honour of Martyr because he chose to be imprisoned and tortured in the name of Jesus; and so he kept only this title and renounced all others, no matter how honourable or excellent those titles were that the world had ascribed to him. St Stephen, whose feast we celebrate today, was the Prince of Martyrs. After the Ascension of the Lord he was the first man to confirm the holy Gospel with his blood, and as stones and rocks painfully rained upon his head, he raised his eyes and heart to Almighty God, to whom he delivered his soul, whilst saying the words, "Behold, I see the heavens opened, and the Son of man standing on the right hand of God." Before explaining these words in greater detail, let us first pray for the grace of the Holy Spirit through the intercession of the Blessed Virgin Mary, by presenting to her the angelic salutation,

Ave Maria

THE ACCOUNT OF ST STEPHEN'S BLOODY MARTYRDOM has its origin in the Acts of the Apostles. It relates that within the city of Jerusalem there were various synagogues or schools that operated like colleges, and many young students of Jewish extraction came from around the world to study there. In this city, which was the capital, there was the Temple of God where the liturgy of their religion flourished. They would learn the Law of Moses and the traditions by which Almighty God wished to be served. The five individual colleges were made up of freedmen and students from Cyrene, Alexandria, Cilicia, and Asia. Some students had come to debate with Stephen about religion. They quickly saw that he was so learned and zealous and filled with such grace and strength of preaching, that he soon stirred up the people and, assisted by many wondrous signs and miracles, he converted them to believe in Jesus Christ, whom they had considered the enemy and seducer of the people. They often debated with each other, but Stephen won them over every time. In the end, they realised they could not resist the force of his arguments nor the strength of his reasoning, nor his lively spirit, and so, ashamed and confused because they had been vanquished by someone they did not like, they reached the point *a verbis ad verbera*[2] of conspiring to take his life; and so they decided to strangle him on the pretext that he had blasphemed against God and Moses. Sacred Scripture is silent about the particular charges of blasphemy brought against him. Even so, the same still happens today among the Reformed Brethren, for when their errors are challenged by profound reasoning and true witness, they burst out with blasphemies and evil words against God and His Saints.

In order to strengthen their thick veneer of slander, the Jews brought in false witnesses, and being charged by the court, Stephen was sentenced to death, "And casting him out of the city, they stoned him" (Acts 7:57). This must surely be one of the cruellest torments that a man can do against another. The Patriarch Moses himself had such an abhorrence for this practice, that when faced by the people's rebellion, he began to invoke Almighty God, calling and shouting for His help and aid, that he might not be stoned by the people, as Sacred Scriptures tells us, "And Moses cried to the Lord, saying, What shall I do to this people? Yet a little more and they will stone me" (Ex 17:4). Today, Stephen, too, has been condemned to suffer these torments, which he endured with such courage that it was as if he had not suffered at all, "The stones of the brook were sweet to him."[3] The harder these cruel executioners cast their stones, the more he seemed to grow in courage; the greater their torments, the more comfort he received from Heaven. Therefore, that which King David said in his psalm may be appropriately applied to Stephen, "How wonderful is God in His Saints: He will give power and strength to His people" (Ps 67:36). He will give them strength to overcome all

---

2   Latin proverb, "from words to blows" or "one thing leading to another."
3   *Lapides torrentis, illi dulces fuerunt.* Roman Breviary, Feast of St Stephen, antiphon at Lauds.

torments, and steadfastness to resist all kinds of pain and grief; that Stephen also received this help is no wonder, for just as a vigilant general has an eye out for the bravest and strongest of those soldiers who stand in the front-line of a battle, thereby bearing the brunt of the enemy's attack, so too Almighty God, in order to confirm and support His Catholic Church in her true faith, has given the Martyrs the particular strengths and gifts of the Holy Spirit they need to fight all their enemies, for the protection of the faithful.

In a similar way, just as Noah's Ark, which saved the human race, was raised higher towards Heaven as the waters rose because of the heavy rain, and made little of the wind, storm, and thunder, so today St Stephen is floating on the sea of persecution whilst stones and rocks are being hurled at him; and even though he is overcome by cruel pains and torments, he raises himself up towards Heaven, calling, "Behold, I see the heavens opened, and the Son of man standing on the right hand of God." In times long ago, the Patriarch Jacob had a marvellous vision. He dreamed that he saw a ladder standing on the earth, with its top reaching up into heaven; a stairway for the angels of God to go up and come down, as Sacred Scripture tells us (see Gn 28:12). The Patriarch had seen in a dream a ladder which stood on the earth and reached to Heaven; angels moved up and down along this ladder. This imagery is still part of our subject, because yesterday we were shown the wondrous ladder of Jesus Christ, who through His birth touched Heaven with His divinity and earth with His humanity. The blessed Jesus, whom the Prophet Isaiah calls an "Angel of Mighty Counsel" (Is 9:6), descended from Heaven along this ladder together with a great company of angels, and today St Stephen climbed up that ladder like an angel, "and all that sat in the council, looking on him, saw his face as if it had been the face of an angel" (Acts 6:15). It was he who first ascended that ladder, showing the way to the Martyrs coming after him; it was he who was the first, after the Ascension of our Lord, to have crossed the dangerous sea, and who passed trouble-free through the valley of tears. For him it was without a doubt a glorious honour and an honourable glory.

St Paul the Apostle mentions his tribulations and persecution, and the pains and sufferings he endured for the true Faith and on behalf of true believers. In fact, St Paul the Apostle thought his sufferings so important that he even ventured to say that not only men were amazed and impressed by them, but even the angels. Hear now his words, "For we have become a spectacle to the world, to angels, and to men" (1 Cor 4:9). We suffer such great persecution that man on earth, the angels in Heaven and even the entire world, are astonished by it. Today, St Stephen tells us more, namely, that not only man on earth and the angels in Heaven were astonished and astounded by his torments and suffering, but even God Himself, who witnessed his meekness and patience, his steadfastness and courage, heard him say the words, "I see Jesus standing on the right hand of God." He is there to support me and give me courage. In other words, what he was saying was 'How lucky I am, what happiness to see what I can see! I see the heavens opening; I see the angels of God who regard my plight and who give me courage to suffer somewhat. I see my Saviour Jesus, who calls out to me, "Courage, Stephen! It is only by means of many tribulations that one can enter Heaven. Have courage, brave soldier; you endured the stones, I carried the Cross; you are being stoned, I was crucified; you see the heavens opening, I saw the sun darkening; you are dying outside the city of Jerusalem, I died on Mount Calvary; you are being martyred at the feet of the young Saul, and I was crucified between two murderers. Be brave, Stephen! and show courage as a true witness; be a witness to my greater honour and glory, and show them how I have opened the gates of Heaven by my Blood.'"

He was joyful, without a doubt; he was joyful because he had received the singular favour that no one else would ever receive. He easily surpassed all other apparitions and visions; for example, Noah had seen an Ark, Abraham saw the angels, Jacob had his ladder, Moses had the burning thorn-bush, and Aaron his flowering rod; nonetheless, no one else had ever seen the heavens open except the Martyr Stephen, "And raising his eyes to Heaven, he saw God's glory, and Jesus standing at God's right hand." There was a reason he cast his eyes up to Heaven, says St Luke in the previously mentioned Acts of the Apostles, because from there comes our help and support. Catholic Listeners, our solace and consolation can only come from

Heaven. King David also knew well where to find this place, when he was beset with trials and tribulations. That is why he wrote, "To you I lift up my eyes, to you who are enthroned in the heavens" (Ps 121:1). What he meant was, "O God, during all my tribulations and suffering I have found no greater solace than by raising my eyes up to you who live in the heavens; this has been my remedy and place of shelter, my hope and my trust." No wonder, for Christ Himself, when He was about to raise Lazarus from the dead, first raised His eyes to Heaven, as if imploring His heavenly Father for the help He needed to carry out that wondrous act. Raising one's eyes to Heaven, and being mindful of God's omnipotence, and contemplating the eternal glories of Heaven, all have the effect of giving courage to the fearful person, and to the anxious it gives a generosity of spirit in their tribulations and trials, and to the cowardly, strength and forbearance in their pains and sufferings. St Jerome says something similar in his letter to the Roman virgin Eustochia, when he told her that in the midst of the trials and tribulations of this present life, there was nothing greater or more powerful than to contemplate the company and glories of Heaven, "Emerge, I pray you, for a while from your prison-house, and paint before your eyes the reward of your present toil, a reward which 'eye has not seen, nor ear heard.'"[4] For, "Blessed are they that suffer persecution for justice' sake: theirs is the kingdom of Heaven" (Mt 5:10).

St Paul the Apostle, while still a member of the Jewish sect, went about cruelly persecuting the Christians and was converted when he saw a light coming down from the heavens accompanied by a voice, to which he answered, "Lord, what do you want me to do?" (Acts 9:6). So it is no wonder that St Stephen made light of the hail of stones raining down on him by lifting his eyes to Heaven, where he saw the heavens opening, revealing the glory of God. But, some might say, how is it possible for the heavens to open up? My answer to this is that the heavens did not part from each other in order to let Stephen see Christ, but that they opened, in a manner of speaking, because Stephen first had seen with his own eyes the blessed Son

---

4 *Egredere de carcere, et praesentis laboris, tibi ante oculos pinge mercedem quam nec oculus vidit, nec auris audivit.* St Jerome, Letter 22, *Ad Eustochium.*

of God, Jesus, who is in Heaven. How had he seen Him? How can someone on earth see Jesus, whose throne stands above the highest heavens, according to the Angelic Doctor, St. Thomas?[5] To this I answer, together with the learned Estius, that the Body of Christ, having been imbued with extraordinary light and brilliance, could naturally be seen from far away, just as we, standing on the earth, can see the sun and the stars, despite us being far removed from them by distance. So then, Christ could send out over extraordinary distances, in a supernatural and miraculous way, the clear and brilliant rays of His beauty. Either way, this generous Martyr Stephen, half dead after suffering the pains of stoning, raised his eyes and hands to Heaven, and whilst kneeling on the ground, began to pray for his enemies and in particular for those who had stoned him, saying, "Lord Jesus, accept my spirit, and do not hold this sin against them." That is, 'Take my soul into your protection and take pity on my enemies.' From whom had he learned this lesson? This lesson he had learned and memorised in the school of the heavenly Master, Jesus Christ, who, whilst hanging on the gibbet of the Cross, made the same request of His heavenly Father, saying, "Father, forgive them, for they know not what they do" (Lk 23:34). 'O merciful Father! I am asking you a favour, and I hope you will not refuse me. Forgive the sins of my enemies, and do not punish them, even if they deserve it, but instead, by your grace grant them mercy and forgiveness. I know their sin is great, and they act out of ignorance rather than malice, being unaware of what they are doing. They think they are hanging a thief on the gibbet; they think they are executing a false prophet and troublemaker; they are crucifying the Messiah, they murder the Son of God, the Saviour and Redeemer of the world.' This was the prayer of Jesus Christ our Redeemer, which Stephen, being a clever disciple, had remembered. However, between the two there is this difference, namely, that our Redeemer, hanging on the Cross, had first prayed for His enemies and then commended His spirit into the hands of His heavenly Father. Stephen, on the other hand, had first said, Lord Jesus, accept my spirit, and do not hold this sin against them. Why did Stephen first commend his soul into

5   See St Thomas Aquinas, *Summa Theologiae*, III, Q 57, A 4.

the hands of Jesus Christ, and then pray for the forgiveness of his enemies, while His Redeemer had done the contrary, namely, He had first prayed for His enemies, and then commended His soul to God's care? The reason is clear, for Christ could not deviate from the path of righteousness, and so, being assured of Himself, He first prayed for sinners, for whose salvation He had suffered a bitter death; but seeing that Stephen was still travelling along the path, and was not assured of his salvation, it was natural for him first to be concerned out of love for his own soul by seeking a happy union with Christ, after which he then prayed for the forgiveness of his enemies, "Lord Jesus, accept my spirit, and do not hold this sin against them."

Where are they now, those people who for days and years have cast anger and fury against their neighbours? Where are they who did not want to forgive those who trespassed against them, thereby increasing their enmity and jealousy, choosing instead acts of revenge and retaliation? They earnestly need to imprint in their minds the above examples of love and benevolence. See how Christ our Saviour has been a mirror of virtue for each one of us, so that we might follow His example. For as St Peter the Apostle says, "that you should follow in His footsteps" (1 Pet 2:21). See how He prayed for those who crucified Him. Stephen, the first of the Martyrs, like a true disciple, followed in the footsteps of his heavenly Master; he had forgotten the injuries he suffered at the hands of those who stoned him. Is there anyone who still wants to wreak revenge? Is there still anyone who wants to be obstinate and stubborn against love after seeing the deeds of his Saviour, the example of Stephen, and knowing the commands of Jesus Christ? Hear now the direct commandment He gives us in the Gospel of St Matthew, "But I say to you, love your enemies: do good to them that hate you" (Mt 5:44). If you do not do these things, you will not be called children of your Father who is in Heaven. As we know, some people complain about this commandment, and say it is impossible to keep, and that it should be enough just to avoid hating one's enemies, and that one should not be obliged to love them. St Jerome gives a clear answer to this, "They should know, that this which Christ commands is not impossible, albeit perfect. This is what David did in respect of Saul and Absalom; the Martyr Stephen also prayed for his enemies, even while they were stoning him."[6] When our Redeemer, during His bitter Passion, hung on the gibbet of the Cross to give up His spirit, He called out, "I thirst," and they gave Him gall and vinegar to drink. Why do you think they did this? It was not to heighten any mystery, but to teach us that He was concerned for our salvation, and He wanted to take with Him the gall and vinegar, that is, the injury and injustice, the offences and acts of revenge, the passions and hatred of this world; those Catholic people who have become infected have become nothing more than gall and vinegar. That is why the heavenly Bridegroom, whilst praising His beloved Bride and marvelling at her extraordinary beauty, said amongst other things, that "her eyes were like those of a dove" (Song 5:12). For just as a dove is a sweet creature and a gentle bird, having no gall or wrath, so the heavenly Bride sees a Christian soul as something that merits praise, and is worthy to take Jesus as her Bridegroom, provided she is pure in soul and sweet and gentle in body, having neither the gall of hatred and enmity, nor the vinegar of wrath. These are the type of souls which are loved in Heaven. St Stephen saw the heavens open as a sign that the gates of Heaven had been opened for him because he was kind and gentle towards his enemies, who without a second thought forgave the injustices and injuries they inflicted upon him.

There is a well-known story about the eloquent Cicero, who was at court successfully defending Quintus Ligarius before Julius Caesar. Cicero attributed to the latter this honourable and commendable quality, "You forget nothing except for wrongs." "Mighty Caesar" he said, "it is indeed true that your fortunate victories cause fear throughout the world, and your triumphs and victories have made your name legendary and have spread your renown throughout the world. Now you have the opportunity to show mercy; your natural disposition is to grant pardon to your enemies. These qualities make you great in the sight of the people, and, I have to admit, one of your great virtues is that you forget nothing but injuries."[7] These flattering words were

---

6 *Sciendum est, Christum non impossibilia praecipere, sed perfecta. Quem fecit David in Saul, et Absalon: Stephanus quoque martyr, pro inimicis lapidantibus deprecatus est.* St Jerome, Commentary on St Matthew's Gospel, Book 1, chs. 5 and 6.
7 Cicero, For Ligarius, Book 6, ch. 45.

likely spoken by this heathen to the Emperor Julius in order to flatter him, in the hope of advancing his goal. In all honesty, today we can also say the same about the Prince of Martyrs, Stephen, namely, "You forget nothing, O Stephen, except for wrongs." O worthy Martyr, full of love and kindness, you are admired by the people for your patience. Your courage makes you glorious to the angels, and your steadfastness makes you precious to the Divine Majesty. Above all, you were raised to the heights, when in your kindness and benevolence you forgave your enemies by praying for those who persecuted you and by pleading for the lives of those who condemned you to death, "Blessed the meek, for they shall inherit the earth." Not the earth of the world where there is continual conflict and discord, but the earth of the living, where the Blessed live forever in glorious peace and tranquillity.

We have heard how the ancient Greeks marvelled at the gentleness and sweet nature of the philosopher Aristides, because when he had been banished unjustly from the city of Athens he had fallen to his knees outside the gates, praying and calling upon the gods not to remember the injustice committed against him, and begging them to spare his Fatherland from the punishment of plagues. How much more, then, should we marvel at the praiseworthy life of the martyr Stephen? He had been sentenced, not to eternal banishment, but to a cruel death; when he was about to leave this world, he fell on his knees, and, raising his eyes to Heaven, he prayed to the one, true God for his enemies, and having no regard for the injustices and injuries committed against him, he called with a loud voice, "Lord Jesus, receive my spirit, and show mercy and forgiveness to those who stone me" (See Acts 7:59–60). With these words he clearly showed that he was a child of God, his heavenly Father.

As I mentioned previously, in chapter five of St Matthew's Gospel we read of the love and affection we should have towards our neighbour; we must love our enemies and do good to them that hate us, and pray for them that persecute and calumniate us" (see Mt 5:44). Why? For what reason? He tells us in a few words, "So that you might become children of your heavenly Father" (Mt 5:45). The Father lets His sun rise over both the bad and the good: He sends down the rain over both the unrighteous and the righteous. So then, the person who is a child of God shows love and affection towards his enemies, forgetting all occasions of injustice and hurt. On the contrary, we might also say that the person who is not a child of God is a child of darkness and the devil; his heart is filled with anger and wrath.

The onus is on us, Catholic Listeners, to learn from the holy Prince of Martyrs, St Stephen, the way to our heavenly Father. Some have reached Him along the path of pains and torments, others by gallows and crosses. He, however, reached his destination through stones and rocks. We, then, at least need to be patient in our trials and tribulations. Above all, we need to learn from this generous soul that we must love our enemies, and forgive and forget the injustices committed against us, without wanting to take revenge. In this way we hope to be forgiven our own trespasses, thus hoping to enjoy forever the eternal glory of Heaven. Who lives, etc.

On the Feast of Saint John the Evangelist

Conversus Petrus, vidit illum discipulum, quem
diligebat Iesus—"Peter turned around, and saw
the disciple whom Jesus loved" (Jn 21:20).

ATHOLIC LISTENERS, SOMETIMES
we discover hidden truths found in fables written
by the poets of old. For instance, we see that the
eagle in particular seems to have been appropriated
by the god Jupiter as his messenger and arms-
bearer; the bird appears to have carried the stuff with which to make
the god's thunderbolts. Today we see an eagle, not of the false Jupiter,
but of the true God. He does not arise from the poet's fables, but
from Sacred Scripture. For the eagle is counted among the four mysterious animals that pull the triumphal wagon of the Divine Majesty
and His glory, as described in the first chapter of the Prophet Ezekiel.
This eagle soars through the clouds and heavens "and makes his nest
on high," as the Prophet Job tells us (Job 39:27). He flew up to Mount
Lebanon where he took the pith of the cedar tree, that is, the mysteries of the Blessed Trinity; he has shown and made known to us
through his holy Gospel the knowledge of the eternal Word of the
only-begotten One, who, as it were, abides as divine pith in the bosom
of the heavenly Father. This eagle is the Apostle St John the Evangelist, whose feast we celebrate today.

St Augustine says, "St John the Apostle is not undeservedly compared to the eagle, for he has elevated his preaching higher and far
more sublimely than the other three evangelists; and thus have our
hearts likewise been lifted up."[1] The other evangelists, despite having

---

1 *Sanctus Ioannes Apostolus non immerito Aquilae comparatus, altius multoque*
sublimius aliis praedicationem suam erexit; sicque corda nostra etiam erigi voluit.

walked on this earth with the God-man, mention little about His divinity; but John, who seemed to abhor staying close to the earth, as he shows at the beginning of his Gospel, raised himself up, not just above the earth and the vault of the heavens, but also above all the hosts of angels, above all the choirs of invisible powers, finally reaching Him who shaped and created all things, as he said, "In the beginning was the Word, and the Word was with God, and the Word was God" (Jn 1:1).

Just as the eagle is the only bird that can gaze at the sun's rays with the naked eye, so John is the only Apostle who had foreseen the brilliant rays of the Godhead's mysteries and perfections; not only did he make these known to the world, but he also silenced the heretics with regard to the perfections of the Divine Being. St Basil confirms this in his fine commentary on this subject, "Just as birds suddenly cease their twittering as soon as they catch sight of an eagle flying overhead, so worthless chattering and lies fall silent in the presence of St John the Evangelist."[2]

It is indeed a weighty matter trying to worthily declare and make known the praises of John, in whom the Divine Majesty had infused every perfection, for he was a prudent Apostle, a learned Evangelist, a holy Prophet, and a courageous Martyr. Therefore, before speaking further in praise of him and for our own edification, we shall first pray for the grace of the Holy Spirit through the intercession of the Blessed Virgin Mary by presenting to her the angelic salutation,

Ave Maria

SEEING THAT CHRIST OUR SAVIOUR HAD COME INTO the world to be a doctor, a teacher, and a master to all men, "your eyes shall see your teacher" (Is 30:20), do you think it was merely a trifling honour for John to have been a pupil or a disciple of Jesus Christ? Not at all, because to John the title disciple meant something illustrious and praiseworthy. Alexander the Great took pride in

---

St Augustine, Tractate 36, On the Gospel of St John, ch. 1.

2   *Universum simul mendacium suppressum silentio est; quemadmodum Aquila aliunde advolante, ac desuper conspectam, futili garrulitati loquacium avium, quam occiissime silentium indicitur.* St Basil the Great, Commentary on the Prophet Isaiah., ch. 2.

his master Aristotle; Marcus Tullius extolled his poet Archias; and Plato esteemed Archytas, despite him having erred on many things. Our eagle has set his eyes on someone else. John received his divine education from a different Master, namely, from uncreated Wisdom, from the Truth Himself, from the Second Person of the Blessed Trinity whom God the heavenly Father has given to be a witness to all nations and a leader and teacher to the heathen. John, then, was a disciple of Jesus Christ, not in some pitiable school, not of the natural or written law, but in the law of grace. In this he was counted not among the least, but among the first and the most diligent, for he was "the disciple whom Jesus loved." It was for him indeed of great advantage to be loved by Love Itself, to be thought of highly by Jesus, to be on familiar terms with the Son of God; it was a great privilege for him to be the particular object of divine love.

Some people will ask, Our Saviour does not normally single out people, so what is the reason He showed such tender love towards John in particular? My answer to this is, "Likeness is a cause of love."[3] There was a great likeness between the purity of these two. We read in the Divine Office for this feast, "Jesus loved him, because his singular gift of purity made him more worthy of love."[4] Furthermore, Christ his Master was love personified, "God is love," and John the disciple, burning with ardent love, offered up the flower of his youth to his Saviour, "He chose him for a virgin unto Himself, and a virgin he remains forever."[5] Moreover, he shunned the pleasures and delights of the flesh, preferring instead to join his Master in remaining celibate rather than becoming separated from Him like married people. "But he who is married is anxious for the things of the world and how to please his wife; and he is divided" (1 Cor 7:33).

See the heights our eagle has reached; he has followed the footsteps of the Sun of Righteousness. God grant that we be of the same disposition and that we may be reckoned among those who are loved

---

3 *Similitudo est mater amoris.* St Thomas Aquinas, *Summa Theologica*, I–II, Q 27, A 3.
4 *Diligebat autem eum Iesus, quoniam specialis praerogativa castitatis, ampliori, dilectione fecerat dignum.* Divine Office, responsory at Matins for the Feast of St John the Evangelist.
5 *Virgo electus ab ipso, virgo in aevum permansit. Ibid.*

for doing good. God grant that we may bear some likeness to the One who loves us and that we may be free of bitterness, bile, or anger, or, to sum it up in a few words, that we may be disciples of Jesus Christ. But who could honestly dare to pride himself on being a disciple of Christ? For if a disciple is a student who has placed himself under the discipline, direction, or instruction of a master, then you need to take a good look at yourself, O man! and ask whether you are a disciple of Christ or of the world? Are you a disciple of the eternal One, or of one who is temporal and will pass away, together with his wants and desires? Of course, it is true that we can find many Christians who, unfortunately, are disciples of Christ in name only, seeing that they seem to care little for His commandments and teachings. They are stubborn and rebel against Him and are lazy, negligent, and slothful in the things that pertain to their eternal salvation. Not only have they deprived themselves of God's love, but they are filled with hatred and envy, ambition, and anger. To tell the truth, perhaps there will be some who say, I do not know if I love my Lord and God with a pure and upright love. O man! how is it you do not know? Stop and reflect upon the condition of the person who loves with an upright love. Behold, he will let nothing stand between him and the object of his love. "Nothing is difficult for a lover."[6] He takes every care to love the beloved; he speaks gladly of his beloved, he thinks day and night about that which he loves. But if you seek only to love people, can you still claim to be a servant of Jesus Christ? Do you claim to love Him for whom you cannot be bothered to perform the smallest deed, or about whom you hardly ever think, being instead more concerned about your physical comforts and placing no value in the Word of God and in His promptings, which you find distasteful and unpleasant? These are certainly not signs of love of God, but they are signs of love of self, which love leads to laziness in loving things that pertain to God and our salvation. A true sign of loving God is to rest with John in the bosom of Jesus Christ, to enjoy the peace that surpasses all understanding, to remain united with the eternal good, to consider all worldly things as mere vanity and to love God with all one's strength as far as is possible in this present life.

---

6 *Amanti nihil est difficile.* Cicero, Letter to Brutus.

But let us return to our topic. If God is love, and he who remains in love remains in God, and God in him, then it is certain that John remained in God, and God remained in him, seeing that he was solely enkindled by love, and that he prized this virtue above all others, impressing it upon his heart and recommending that others do the same, continually telling those under his direction, "My children, love one another."

St Jerome tells us[7] that when he became so old that he needed to be accompanied to church and was no longer able to hold lengthy discourses on the teachings and commandments of Christ, he would then in a few words sum up love as the principle among all the virtues. Yes, the blessed name of Jesus is a name full of sweetness and love. Jerome repeated this name so often in his writings that he is with good reason lauded in the words of Deuteronomy, "The most beloved of the Lord shall dwell in safety in Him" (Dt 33:12).

Moreover, not only was John the beloved of the Lord, but Christ was also John's beloved Lord. Do you wish to hear of some signs of Christ's love towards him? Then listen! John was present when the daughter of the synagogue official was restored to life. He was one of the three Apostles to have witnessed the glorious Transfiguration on Mount Tabor; he was sent to Jerusalem to make everything ready for the Last Supper, during which he rested on the Saviour's breast; he was present in the Garden of Olives where he beheld Christ's blessed face, not shining like the sun, but deathly pale and dripping with sweat and blood; and right at the end he stood beneath the gibbet of the Cross; it was here that to him was entrusted the greatest treasure of the world, namely, the holy and blessed Virgin Mother of God, Mary. Do you not think, Catholic Listeners, that these particular graces and privileges openly show Christ's love for him? But let us see this eagle fly even higher. John was not only an Apostle, that is, a messenger of God sent to announce the holy Gospel throughout the world; not only did he receive together with the other Apostles the power to perform miracles, to heal the sick, to forgive sins or to bind them; not only did he receive clear knowledge of the mysteries of God's Kingdom without the aid of parables or examples, but above all, he was

---

7 St Jerome, Commentary on Galatians. Book 3, ch. 6.

also an Evangelist, and a secretary to the Blessed Trinity. He is the Prince of the Evangelists, on the one hand because he finished writing the holy Gospel, and on the other hand, because he, as it were, beheld the Sun of Righteousness with the naked eye. The other Evangelists, when compared to John, do not seem to climb up but they remain here below on the earth. John seems to have flown up to Heaven to patronise it. St Augustine says, "But this Evangelist, as if he disdained to walk on earth, soared not only above the earth and above the whole compass of air and sky, but even above the whole army of angels."[8] The other Evangelists only spoke of Christ in His humanity. John spoke of the eternal Word and His divinity, when commencing his Gospel with these mysterious words, "In the beginning was the Word, and the Word was with God, and the Word was God." If you want to know about the eternity of the Word, he tells you clearly, "In the beginning was the Word." Do you want to know about the distinction of Persons? "And the Word was with God." Do you want to know about the same substance and being of the Persons? "And the Word was God." Do you want to know about the omnipotence of God, by which thousands of heretics were set to flight? "Through Him all things were made." I will not talk about his banishment to the island of Patmos under the cruel Emperor Domitian, where he wrote a book full of wonders and mysteries, which is called the Book of the Apocalypse, or Revelations, in which he clearly illustrates the Godhead and promises the longevity of the holy Catholic Church. He shows himself to be a wondrous Prophet by revealing so many profound secrets and mysteries about the Blessed Trinity. And not without reason, Catholic Listeners, for as St Augustine says, "What he had drank in, the same he gave forth; seeing that at supper he reclined on the Lord's bosom, in which were concealed all kinds of treasures and wisdom, it stands to reason that from that breast he secretly drank; but what he drank in secret he gave forth openly, that there may come to all nations not only the incarnation of the Son of God, and His bitter Passion and glorious Resurrection, but also what He was before His Incarnation, that is, the only Son of the Father,

---

8   *Iste autem quasi piguerit in terra ambulare, erexit se non solum super terram, sed super omnem etiam exercitum Angelorum.* St Augustine, op. cit.

the Word of the Father, coeternal with Him that begot, equal with Him by whom He was sent."[9]

Furthermore, not only had John been an Apostle, an Evangelist and a Prophet, but he was also a martyr, carrying like a special friend the livery of Christ our Saviour, the Bridegroom of the Catholic Church, and even though being "white and ruddy," (Song 5:10)[10] for his life did not actually end by martyrdom, he may still be called a martyr because of the thousands of travails he had to endure on the island of Patmos in order to propagate the Catholic Faith. Not only this, but in Rome the tyrant Domitian, who was called a second Nero because of his cruelty, had him cast into a cauldron of boiling oil before the Latin Gate. To this day one can see the chapel built on the site as an eternal memory of the event; on one side of the entrance one reads these words, *Ioannes Christi Apostolus, Evangelista, Propheta, et Martyr, e dolio ferventis olei vegetior exivit* — "John, an Apostle, Evangelist, Prophet and Martyr of Jesus Christ, emerged from the cauldron of boiling oil renewed in strength." Above the door we read these verses,

> *Martyrii calicem bibit hic athleta Ioannes,*
>   *Principii Verbum cernere qui meruit.*
> *Verberat hunc fuste Proconsul, forfice tondet,*
>   *Quem fervens oleum laedere non valuit.*
> *Conditur hic oleum, dolium, cruor, atque capilli*
>   *Quae consecrantur inclyta Roma tibi.*

Which in our language reads:

> The athlete John drank the cup of martyrdom,
>   who merited to understand the Word at the beginning.
> Here the proconsul beat him with a rod and cut him with pincers,
>   whom the boiling oil was unable to harm.
> Here are stored in a cask the oil, his blood and his hair,
>   which are consecrated to you, glorious Rome.

It is obvious from this that John was a Martyr who was not afraid of death; rather, death was afraid of him. The Apostle Peter knew well

---

9 St Augustine, op. cit.
10 A reference to red and white martyrdom. Red martyrdom occurs through an actual spilling of blood for the Faith; white martyrdom is "dying" to the world by totally offering one's life to God. (Trans.)

that the honour and glory of the Apostles lay in dying for the blessed name of Jesus; he understood from Christ, albeit obscurely, the kind of death he would undergo to glorify God, and so, according to his usual impetuous way, he hastily asked about John, "What shall this man do?" Lord, what have you planned for John, the one who was so pleasing to you, the one you loved? What glorious death shall he whom you especially loved undergo? If I am to be honoured by dying on a cross, what will happen to the beloved who rested upon your breast, who remained steadfast with you throughout your Passion, and whom you called your brother when you made him the son of your most loving Mother, "Woman, behold your son"?

Indeed, the highest honour martyrs could hope for was to suffer torments for love of the name of Jesus, and throughout the difficulties and persecutions they had to endure they would contemplate the tenderness of God's friendship towards them. For Almighty God will not abandon those who suffer and fight for His glory. The more they labour, the more they are strengthened. Truly, then, may King David say, "When the pains in my heart are many, your consolations cheer my soul" (Ps 93:19). In similar manner did God console the Apostle Paul within the walls of Jerusalem when he was attacked, stripped, tortured, beaten and thrown in prison (Acts 16). So, too, did God free the Apostle Peter from the dungeon by sending the help of an angel to loosen the two chains with which he had been fastened; in such manner did the Shepherd of the Catholic Church regain his freedom. Similarly, as St Stephen the proto-martyr was enduring death by stoning, God comforted and gladdened him by opening the heavens to show that He was personally present. No less happened to St John the Evangelist. In Rome, did he not taste of the divine assistance when he emerged safe and sound from the cauldron of boiling oil? And during his exile on Patmos, did the angel not reveal to him the state of the Catholic Church, the torments of the martyrs, the eternal suffering of the damned souls, and the glory of the chosen ones? On Mount Calvary, when he beheld with great sadness the blessed yet disfigured Body of his Lord and Master, bleeding and pierced through with nails, did he not take great comfort in receiving the blessed Mother of God into his care and protection?

Of course, it is true that many worldly and narrow-minded people let themselves be overcome by misfortune and difficulties, and they often let themselves be led into serious sin by grief or despondency. This does not happen because of any medical issues, but through their own spiritual imperfections and illnesses, when they use remedies to their own detriment; like mud, they become hardened in the fire of tribulation, whereas they should have become soft and pliable as wax, patient and meek, saying together with Job, that patient Prophet, "If we receive good things from the hand of God, should we not also receive evil?" (Job 2:10). The fire of tribulation manifested its power and operation in a very different way in St John, who was kindled into a divine, pure an upright love. There is little comparison between this love and the examples put forward by worldly people, who at best only put on a false appearance of holiness. There are various instances, as Valerius Maximus claims, of some heathens displaying images that represent love, for example, when Pylades was prepared to die for his cousin Orestes, or when Portia, hearing of the death of her husband Brutus, had wanted to kill herself, and many such similar kinds of examples; these are, however, not examples of virtuous love but only signs of natural affection or fondness by which a person wishes good on another person. True love is the virtue of a Christian person towards his neighbour, which virtue cannot be perfected without the love and knowledge of God. It is this neighbourly love rooted in the love of God that St John so frequently mentions in his letters and so often tries to inspire within us as being a kind of summary of all the virtues, "He that loves his neighbour has fulfilled the law" (Rom 13:8). Therefore, those who try to banish this virtue from the earth would do better by trying to steal the sun from the heavens. For love holds all the other virtues in its grip and sway; in this it is not unlike the heavens, which let rain and dew fall down upon the just and the unjust alike, and on both the fertile fields and the dry heath. Love therefore includes all people, strangers and acquaintances, friend and foe alike. St Basil so often laments about the duplicity found among the Catholics and Christians of his day, but alas! this is still to be found in our times. Where can one find a person completely on fire with a pure and upright love? Where can one find a person who has compassion on a neighbour who suffers misfortune, or who is overjoyed when a neighbour has good fortune?

> A rival's eye is close by, a potter emulates a potter;
> one smith envies another;
> a beggar loathes a beggar,
> but he is faithful.[11]

Where can one find a person who lives according to the teachings of St Paul the Apostle, who weeps with those who weep and rejoices with those who rejoice, who weeps for the wickedness of his neighbour, and rejoices in his virtues and godliness? These are the signs of true love, and those who carry these signs "do not love in word or speech, but in deed and in truth" (1 Jn 3:18). There are people who delight in uncovering their neighbour's sins; there are those who work at goading their neighbour to do wicked deeds, and those who aggravate their neighbour to cause scandal. Can we say that these people are imbued with the virtue of charity? "Love is not jealous or boastful; it is not arrogant or rude. Love does not insist on its own way, it seeks not her own, it is not resentful; it does not rejoice at wrong, but rejoices in the right" (1 Cor 13:4–6).

I will conclude this discourse with the other virtues and perfections of this holy Evangelist. He always upheld the admonition of St Paul, "As for a man who is heretical, after admonishing him once or twice, have nothing more to do with him" (Tit 3:10). As one flees from the plague, so he fled from the conversations of all heretics, especially ones like Ebion and Cerinthus, knowing well that they were heretical, as St Paul said, and wicked in preaching errors, thereby sentencing themselves to damnation. I shall say nothing about him being the bishop of Ephesus and archbishop of Asia, and the first Patriarch of all the churches in that area. After the death of the holy Apostles Peter and Paul, he assumed care of all the faithful throughout that region, thus with good reason could he say, "Who is weak, and I do not feel weak? Who is led into sin, and I do not inwardly burn?" (2 Cor 11:29). These truths appear clearly in his writings and works.

---

11 *Aemulus est vicini oculus, figuloque perosus est figulus, fabroque faber, nec egenus egeno, est fidus.* Hesiod, Works and Days, 1.

Cardinal Baronius, in his entry for the Year of Our Lord 98, writes that both Eusebius and Clement of Alexandria claimed that after his exile on Patmos, John went to Asia Minor to examine the state of the churches, where he met a young man, strong and fair of complexion, with a pleasing aspect, but crude of mind. He gave the youth into the care of a certain Asian bishop to be trained in the Catholic Faith, thereby receiving all the virtues. The bishop instructed and baptised the youth, but he was too soft-handed and permissive with him, and since our corrupt nature is more inclined towards evil than good, the young man was lured towards the company of sinful wretches and, quickly forgetting the precepts of religion, had become a villain and a robber. He took flight to the mountains where he joined a company like himself and practised wickedness with impunity. But when the opportunity presented itself, John went to speak to the bishop, asking him to restore to him what he had entrusted to his care. The bishop thought John was asking him for a trust of money, the likes of which he had not seen, but John had to explain that he meant the young man and the soul of his brother which he had left in his custody. The bishop, with sighs and tears, said the young man was dead, at least in his soul, and he had given himself over to wickedness and had withdrawn from the sheepfold of the holy Catholic Church. He had become a robber and ran off to the mountains. John, always aflame with zeal for souls which had been ransomed by the Precious Blood of Jesus Christ, reprimanded the bishop for not having taken better care of the lost sheep, so he went into the mountains to search for that sheep, which, having been found, was returned to the sheepfold. He embraced the young man, and with kind words moved him to turn from sin to a virtuous life. The murderer and brigand repented with a flood of tears and was saved. St John could then honestly say, "Rejoice with me, for I have found the sheep that was lost" (Lk 15:6).

These have been some of the privileges, virtues, and perfections of the holy Apostle, St John the Evangelist, Catholic Listeners, which might serve us as a mirror by which to reach Christian perfection. John had been a disciple of Jesus Christ; we too must work at being His disciples, not the kind that pay lip-service to God and then spurn any good works; nor should we be like those children of the world who take great care with their temporal profits but are blind at working out their salvation. We must not be disciples of that wisdom, which St James calls earthy and unspiritual, but we must be disciples of Christ in the wisdom that comes from above, which is peaceable, full of mercy and good fruits (cf. Jas 3). John loved purity of body and soul, and this we must also embrace, not only by suppressing inordinate lusts of the flesh, but by abstaining from illicit desires out of love for perfection. He offered the best part of his life to his Saviour; we, too, must learn from our earliest days to carry the sweet yoke of the Lord. For the glory of God he suffered untold hardship and persecution, exile and the dungeon, and so we should not give up the merits of patience for the slightest offence committed against us. Finally, John loved the most Blessed Virgin and Mother of God, Mary, and showed her great respect and honour, and so we, too, should devoutly love, serve, and invoke her, so that through her intercession we may share in divine grace, thereby meriting to enjoy heavenly glory in the life to come. Who lives, etc.

On the Feast of the Holy Innocents

Herodus, videns quoniam illusus esset a Magis, iratus est valde, et mittens, occidit omnes pueros, qui erant in Bethlehem, et in omnibus finibus eius — "Then Herod, when he saw that he had been tricked by the wise men, was in a furious rage, and he sent and killed all the male children in Bethlehem and in all that region" (Mt 2:16).

ATHOLIC LISTENERS, AMONG THE disordered desires that might be found in a rich and powerful person, there is none stronger and more powerful than the desire to dominate. Once an ambitious soul becomes possessed with this vice, she forgets God and right reason, she rejects all decency and orthodoxy, she tramples underfoot the laws of God and the world and refuses any other. In order to bolster and strengthen her frenzy to dominate, she uses hatred and anger as instruments to bring forth heinous revenge and unheard-of cruelty. In addition, one could also say that those who are ambitious are also often cruel; and those inclined to dominate others are inclined to murder. How often do we see tyrants being afraid of everything, even their own shadow? They become suspicious and will judge and murder anyone they do not trust. They use evil suspicions and false accusations to justify murder and cruel deeds, showing respect for neither friend nor foe, age nor innocence. By means of strange maxims, which they call state laws, they are not ashamed to perform or set into motion things forbidden by other laws, and whatever is illicit in nature to them becomes reasonable and licit, not because of any rational proof, but merely because of their evil wills. According to the testimony of

Valerius Maximus,[1] when Lucius Sulla assumed sovereign dominion over the Republic of Rome, his extraordinary ambition spurred him on to such cruelty that, going against his own promise, he had four regiments of soldiers massacred, along with four thousand inhabitants of the city of Praeneste, and another four thousand seven hundred citizens of Rome who opposed his proposals. All these people tasted his bloody sword because of his anger and vindictiveness, and to confirm his lust and tyrannical dominion.

In Sacred Scripture we read that Abimelech, the bastard son of Gideon, murdered each and every one of Gideon's seventy licit children so that he could rule over the citizens of Shechem (see Judg 9). Even so, these atrocities, which arose from an ambitious passion to rule over others, so to speak, can hardly be compared to the atrocities committed by Herod as recorded in today's Gospel, which arose from an unfounded distrust; he thereupon unleashed the full fury of his anger and wrath, not over men who could defend themselves and whose strength would have frightened him, but over innocent little children whose fragility and innocence would offer him no resistance. He performed this barbaric cruelty and misdeed without any hint of excuse, and it shows us the extremes to which a tyrant's blind passion can push him. "Then Herod, when he saw that he had been tricked by the wise men, was in a furious rage, and he sent and killed all the male children in Bethlehem and in all that region who were two years old or under." In order to express this in broader terms, let us first pray for the grace of the Holy Spirit through the intercession of the Blessed Virgin Mary by presenting to her the angelic salutation,

Ave Maria

THOSE PEOPLE WHO POSSESS A KINGDOM, NOT LAWFULLY but unlawfully, and not justly but unjustly, often display the characteristic of mistrusting others because they are frightened of losing what they had appropriated. One of these people was Herod, king of the Jewish nation, who had been placed in charge of that kingdom by the hands of the dishonest Romans. He had become infected with an inordinate ambition to rule, and it made him suspicious, fearful,

---

1 Valerius Maximus, Memorable doings and sayings, Book 9, ch.2.

and distrustful of people. He was in the thirty-second year of his reign when Jesus was born in Bethlehem, and during this time he strengthened his authority, not through kindness and gentleness, but through violence and cruelty, by instilling in his subjects fear rather than love. He was, therefore, always in a bad mood, because he knew well that rulers who only cause fear among their subjects will consequently be hated by them, and hatred will seek any possible means to liberate itself from oppression and subservience. Furthermore, he was concerned about a common belief held among the Jews that a king would be born of their race and ancestry who would free them from slavery under the Romans, and who would establish a kingdom as of old, in splendour and freedom. In this way would the words of the Prophets be understood, that a Messiah would be promised them. This Messiah would reign like a great king, establishing righteousness upon the earth and liberating Judah from slavery and oppression. "Behold, a king shall come, and he shall execute justice and righteousness in the land; in his days Judah will be saved" (cf. Jer 23:5-6). The Jewish people understood these and similar passages literally, for they promised a king who would oust the Romans and set them free with strength and weapons. Even the scholars of the Law, being no more spiritual than their disciples, did not realise that such prophecies should be understood in the sense of a king who was coming to rule them spiritually, and who would free them from slavery of the devil. They therefore did nothing to correct the erroneous beliefs of the people, for they themselves were blind. The Jewish people had for years nourished the hope that one day they would be liberated by a king, and this cry reached the ears of Herod, partly through his minions, and partly through his scribes, and he became pensive. And so when the Three Kings came to Jerusalem after having followed the star, they asked, "Where is He that is born King of the Jews?" (Mt 2:2). When Herod heard this, "he was troubled," the Evangelist tells us. He became worried and frightened, for he feared that the old prophecies of a promised Messiah, which heretofore he had always regarded as mere fables, may have in fact come true. "He quickly called together all the chief priests and scribes of the people, and inquired of them where the Messiah was to be born" (Mt 2:4). He most probably asked this question not to hinder that king, but more likely because he was curious, or perhaps because he had wanted to give instructions to the kings who had come from far to find and worship that king.

Once Herod's scribes had told him that Bethlehem would be the birthplace of this king who was coming to rule the people of Israel, he "privately called the Wise Men" (Mt 2:7) to come to his palace, thereby showing his guile and duplicity, for he did not trust the Jews. Having called the Three Kings, he questioned them thoroughly as to the exact time, day, and moment when the star had appeared. In this way, once having found out from the chief priests where the King of the Jews was to be born, he would come to know the time of birth, based on the information the kings would tell him about the star, and so, informed as to the place and time of the Child's birth, he would be able to find the Child in order to kill it. He disguised his wicked intention and hypocrisy before the Kings, whom he had seen devoutly seeking the very child he was planning to murder in order to defend his dominion, and so he said to them, "Go and search diligently for the Child; and when you have found Him, bring me word so that I may also go and pay Him homage" (Mt 2:8). But Almighty God, who could see through Herod's two-faced, deceitful heart, sent the Kings back to their countries by another road after they had found the new-born King and had worshipped Him and given Him gifts.

Even though the Evangelist attributes Herod's anger to the Kings not having kept their word, we may nonetheless assume that he became bitterly enraged and perplexed because he (who imagined himself to be far elevated above other people in duplicity and falsity) had been so gullible to believe foreigners and strangers. For there is nothing that upsets a crooked man or swindler more than when he realises that he himself has been duped, and that his deception has come to naught. Some months after the departure of the Kings, Herod became increasingly suspicious, not of them finding the Child, but of them perhaps not having been able to find it and then quietly hurrying off so as not to reveal their embarrassment at having so easily believed in a star that could well have been due to a natural occurrence, such as mist or moisture in the heavens. This opinion of

Herod is attributed to St Augustine,[2] and is not without foundation. What other reason could there be for Herod not to have examined this matter closely, seeing that maintaining his reign and status was at stake? He was of the opinion that the Kings had not found the one they sought, and, acknowledging the foolishness that they had let themselves be deceived by the vision of a star, they had been ashamed to return to him and had gone home by another route. There are indeed many godless people who are attached to the world and its fortunes and who give no thought to Heaven or heavenly signs. That is why Herod considered this celestial, shining star that the Kings claimed to have seen in the east to be a phantasm or a natural phenomenon, thinking that the Kings had wanted to cover their shame without the city of Jerusalem or indeed the entire world knowing about it. He therefore made no further attempt to investigate the Child that had evoked such fear in him. St Epiphanius and other scholars claim there were two years between the birth of Our Saviour and the scandalous murder of the Holy Innocents.[3] What is the reason, someone might ask, that Herod's fear and anger were rekindled to the extent that he furiously shed innocent blood? The answer to this we find in St Augustine's aforementioned work, where he tells us that when Our Saviour had been publicly presented in the Temple of Jerusalem, many people had witnessed the marvellous words spoken over Him by the righteous Simeon and the Prophetess Anna, and this news quickly spread through the land of Judah, eventually coming to the ears of Herod. He began to realise that the stories and experiences of the Three Kings had not been illusions, but that this Child about whom so much was being told could indeed one day usurp his crown and sceptre when He came of age; he was well aware of the immense hatred the Jews had towards him, and their fervent hope in the coming of the Messiah.

A new fear, doubled in intensity, gripped Herod, and he gave free reign to his enraged fury and wrath, partly because he felt cheated by the Kings, partly because he had deceived himself by trusting their words, and also because he feared losing his crown. He gathered all

2 St Augustine, On the Harmony of the Gospels, Book 2, ch. 11.
3 See St Epiphanius of Salamis, Against Heresies, 30, 31.

these reasons together, and in his anger resolved to put to death all the children of Bethlehem and the surrounding regions, up to two years old. Sacred Scripture does not tell us how he put his plan into action, that is, whether he sent his servants and executioners to each house of Bethlehem and the surrounding countryside, or whether he gathered all the mothers with their children to a certain place, using the pretext of wanting to grant them some favour or benefice, which was a common practice among tyrants, who never show a more heinous face that when they need to do something out of the ordinary. It is the opinion of St Antoninus that Herod enticed all mothers and wet-nurses who had children two years old and younger to a certain place under the pretext of promising them some kind gesture, and once in place he unleashed his cruelty. Others are of the opinion that he waited for some solemn feast-day on which mothers would normally take their children to the Temple; in this way, he could attack them without being seen, and so accomplish the murders he had sworn himself to do. In any case, who can even try to describe the strength and violence with which the cruel executioners had ripped those tender, innocent children from their mothers' arms to slay them before their very eyes? We see a tug-of-war between the barbaric servants pulling the children on one side, and the mothers defending them on the other. It is a struggle between strength and love; strength pulls, love resists. But even though love is strong in the hearts of mothers, it weakened in the hands of the women, who, having no other weapons than the tears in their eyes, could no longer offer resistance in the face of such brute violence. They used every strength they possessed to save the fruits of their wombs, but seeing that their tears had no effect to move such cruel men, they used everything a mother could procure to overcome such tragedy; but what could naked arms do against armed soldiers, apart from becoming wounded and bloodied with the innocent blood of their children? For if they tried to free their children, they would be placing themselves in danger of death; their fragility in trying to ward off a blow of the sword would in fact cause two blows, one on themselves and one on the child. They were therefore struck twice with one blow, once on their arms and once in their heart.

Just imagine what a cruel spectacle that would have been, Catholic Listeners, to see a child violently ripped from its mother's arms and massacred before her very eyes. O cruel tyrant! said one despondent mother: With one blow you strike down two; with one blow you commit two murders; you pierce the heart of the mother with the same sword you used to open the breast of her son. O merciless executioner! cried another. For which crime do you perform this execution? For the crime of the son or of the mother? My son is too young to have thoughts in his head, so it must be the crime of the mother; aim your cruelty at her and spare the innocent ones. Another mother, seeing the sword unsheathed against her beloved child, placed herself between the two to spare his life, but it was her own that she lost. As he raised the sword she cried out, O you pitiless man! do not hurt me twice by sparing my life and taking the fruit of my womb. The mercy you show me is much more cruel than the death of my child alone. Therefore, if you want to show any mercy at all, then either kill the two of us, or spare us both. Yet another mother tried to flatter the soldier who was about to rip apart her child. My friend, she said, see how sweetly this innocent child looks at you, not knowing the evil you want to do to it; see how lovingly he smiles at you and how he places his tiny fingers on your sword, almost as if he thinks you to be his nurse or father. Would you really have the courage to kill it? Would you exchange its caresses for injury, its smiles for wounds, its childish innocence for five or six stabs of the sword? If my tears cannot move you, then at least be moved by its affectionate innocence. Another mother thought the fear of God's justice might have some effect to allay those cruel men, and so she put on a performance, calling out that any spilt innocent blood would call down Heaven's vengeance, and that God is superior to any king; He is more mighty than the mighty and He shall severely punish those who are unjust and who forcefully oppress the innocent. What is more, anyone found to have taken part, through their own will or consent, in this cruel tyranny, even if they be kings and princes, shall be subject to severe judgement. Others tried to ransom the fruit of their wombs with money or goods, thereby demonstrating that blood can make no one rich, but that friendliness, gentleness and kindness are praised in every kind of person.

Summing up then, these wretched, oppressed mothers used a variety of methods to try to save the lives of their innocent children. But seeing that the fury and anger of these blood-thirsty tyrants was increased even more by the bloodletting, just as fire becomes more ardently stoked by using drier and better quality fuel, so nothing could soften their hearts, neither tears, nor prayers, nor promises of money or goods; yet despite the children's screams, the mothers' wailing, the clamour of the onlookers and bystanders, they performed their barbarous task with precision. Catholic Listeners, what advice could we give these sad mothers, whose tears were in vain and whose strength was lacking? I do not doubt they took refuge in the comforts of Heaven and the assistance of the omnipotent God, seeing they could find no hope among the people. When they heard that this cruel event occurred because of just one Child, which the Prophets claimed had been promised as God's Messiah, they called out, 'O Almighty God, protect your inheritance! It was because of your Messiah that our children were taken from us; we beg your assistance and pray that you will offer your protection; avenge this misfortune that happened according to your will. Make these tyrants understand that even if they oppress the people, they will never be able to withstand your divine strength. You, O promised Messiah! You yourself are being sought and followed by the tyrants; do not allow the sacrifice of our innocent children to be in vain. "Come, come, O Saviour, how long must we wait for you? You are Almighty, come and save our children. Come, for you are mighty enough to protect yourself and to free us. Come, commence the liberation of Israel by sparing our innocent children."[4] In these words did the poor mothers beseech the Lord, and Almighty God seemed not to hear their cry. But He did hear their cry, because the very first fruits of the Redemption wrought by the Messiah were applied to those children, not in the manner hoped for by their mothers, who wanted nothing more than to be spared the fury of persecution, but in a vastly better and more profitable manner, for when they were slaughtered by the sword they assumed the crown, the reward, and

---

4   *Veni iam, veni Salvator mundi: quamdiu quaereris? Nullum times: videat te miles, et nostros non occidat infantes.* St Augustine, *Sermons on the Holy Innocents*, Sermon 1.

other privileges of the glorious Martyrs. That is why St Augustine says, "Behold, the profane enemy could never have benefitted the little ones by kindness as much as he did by hatred."[5] For by befriending them he would only be able to offer them temporal honours, passing goods, and deceptive pleasures. But instead, in his hatred and anger he honoured them with the crown of eternal glory, the likes of which no worldly pleasures, delights, honour, or glory could equal. Of course, by persecuting them he did not intend to benefit them, nonetheless, they can attribute their salvation to his merciless sword, seeing that without this they would not have received from God this precious crown, from which the drops of their innocent blood drips down like so many pearls, gems, and diamonds.

Furthermore, the benefits these innocent children received from Herod's cruelty have been described by St John the Evangelist in the Book of Revelation and taken up by the holy Catholic Church, which sings on today's feast, "These were purchased from among men, the first fruits to God and to the Lamb" (Rev 14:4).[6] By applying these words to those blessed children, the holy Catholic Church wanted to make known that they had been selected to be the first fruits of the Redemption, as an offering to Almighty God and to Jesus the Lamb immediately after His birth. This was no doubt an extraordinary grace and a particular privilege. Catholic Listeners, you all know how pleasing first fruits can be. Apart from the goodness they contain in themselves, the eye finds a certain pleasure and value in their newness, and so they are handled and stored with care. These innocent children are like the first fruits of the law of grace that flourished during the first days of the nascent Catholic Church, when the Sun of Righteousness was rising to visit the earth, warming her and making her fertile. They received the first rays of the light of grace that Jesus brought into the world, and the first application of Our Saviour's Precious Blood, which He had come to pour out in order to water the aridity of our corrupt nature. Thus they were the first among the human race to be ransomed and offered to Almighty God, who, under the Old

---

5 *Ecce, profanis hostis, nunquam beatis parvulis tantum prodesse potuisset obsequio, quantum profuit odio.* St Augustine, op. cit., Sermon 3.
6 Antiphonarium Praemonstratense, Versicle at Vespers for the Feast.

Law having commanded that all first fruits be offered to Him, now expected these, too, as truth follows image. The Lamb of God who had come into the world to offer Himself as a pure sacrifice to God had sent these souls ahead of Him as heralds of the great Sacrifice that would follow, not by Herod's sword, but on the gibbet of the Cross through the hatred of the Jews. The first fruit He presented to His heavenly Father was the blood of the Innocents as a sign that innocence itself would follow the reconciliation of the entire world.

Finally, these tender children have the honour of being called the Flowers of the Martyrs, because they flowered in the spring of the Catholic Church. Their abundant harvest was an indication of the ripe fruits and holy persons who would follow in high summer through the searing heat of persecution. They received this honour, I say, through Herod's cruelty, which coloured the white lilies of their innocence a deep rose-red through martyrdom. Before persecution they had merely the white of innocence, which undoubtedly they would have lost soon enough as they got older; but Herod's sword, painting them with their own innocent blood, made a gracious mixture of white with red, preserving their innocence while turning them into glorious Martyrs. I could tell you about many more privileges with which these souls had been honoured, such as their continual presence before the divine throne, and their being untainted by any impure acts, whether of desire or thought. Furthermore, they accompany the Lamb of God wherever He goes as honorary pages, adorned in His livery of red and white. But I shall pass these over, concluding my discourse with what the Catholic Church attributes to them in particular, namely, that they confessed the praise of God and His Holy Name, not by speech but by dying, not with their tongues but with their blood. "Not by speaking but by dying did they bear witness."[7] That is why in the Collect of today's feast the holy Catholic Church asks Almighty God to grant to the faithful the grace to declare their faith, not only by what their tongues confess but also by their godly lives and actions. Those people who are satisfied to confess God with their mouths whilst in the meantime denying

---

7 *Non loquendo, sed moriendo confessi sunt*, Divine Office, Collect for the Feast of the Holy Innocents.

Him by performing works contrary to the Faith, have moved far away from glorifying and honouring God's Holy Name. Their actions give occasion to heretics and infidels to blaspheme and slander the Almighty, "God's name is blasphemed among the Gentiles because of you" (Rom 2:24). Their confession does not honour God but dishonours Him; instead of salvation they cause themselves grief and damnation. Indeed, how could one simultaneously acclaim God and anger Him? How could one confess Him with the mouth and despise Him with actions? This tendency can also be found among Catholic people who try to unite confessing God and embittering Him, paying no notice to what King David says, "They would lie to Him with their tongues; their hearts were not loyal to Him, they were not faithful to His covenant" (Ps 77:36–37). Therefore, what use will it be to you, O man! to remain obstinate in your sin, and for people to consider you a Catholic, while God counts you among the godless? How will it benefit you to be considered a believer when before God, who knows the state of your soul, you will be deemed an infidel? "They were not faithful to His covenant." God shall not judge you according to man's opinion of you, but according to His own knowledge; the severity of the sentence you receive shall not be based on the tongue with which you profess faith in Him, but on your wicked, sinful lives with which you angered Him. "For He will render to a man his work" (Job 34:11).

Therefore, Catholic Listeners, let us be mindful of the prayer the holy Catholic Church places before us on this feast-day and of the way in which the Holy Innocents praised and professed God, not by their mouths but by their deaths. May we profess faith in His Holy Name through virtuous and godly lives, so that by having a lively faith and practising good works we may attain the crown of eternal glory in the life to come. Who lives, etc.

On the Sunday nearest Christmas (within the Octave)

Ecce, positus est hic in ruinam, et in resurrectionem multorum, et in signum cui contra-dicetur — "Behold, this child is destined to bring about the fall and rise of many, and to be a sign which men will refuse to acknowledge" (Lk 2:34).

ATHOLIC LISTENERS, IN OLD TEStament times there could be found within the Ark of the Covenant both a hard substance and a sweet substance, namely, the rod of Aaron and manna from Heaven. During these days we see the Blessed Virgin Mary, whom the holy Fathers often compared to the Ark of the Lord, experiencing both great joy and extreme sadness. She was filled with joy and gladness because she had borne without pain the Saviour of the world who had been worshipped by the angels, served by the shepherds, honoured by the Three Kings, and praised by Anna, the God-fearing widow. Even so, she also heard the words of the holy priest and Prophet Simeon, "And your own soul a sword shall pierce" (Lk 2:35). No doubt she felt great pain and anxiety at these words, and the ones that followed, "Behold, this child is destined to bring about the fall and rise of many, and to be a sign which men will refuse to acknowledge." The Wise Man in the days of old summed this up well, "Even in laughter the heart may ache, and rejoicing may end in grief" (Prov 14:13). It is indeed so, for Almighty God has a custom of not giving joy without sadness, or comfort without discomfort, even to His devout friends on earth. We see an example of this with the Patriarch Abraham, who after many years of longing was finally granted a son by his barren wife Sarah. He named his son Isaac. Yet even during this period of joy, he was commanded by Almighty God to offer his son as a sacrifice to Him. What do you think of this? Would this not have been an occasion of extreme sadness for Abraham and Sarah to have to sacrifice the son upon whom their entire dynasty depended? In similar manner did the Blessed Virgin Mary bear her only Son Jesus, who would be the Saviour of the world and "a light to enlighten the Gentiles." Today she hears the words, "Behold, this Child is destined to bring about a fall, and to be a sign which men will refuse to acknowledge." This was no doubt an occasion for much sadness, and that is why the Evangelist hastened to add that Joseph and Mary marvelled at what was said about Him. Before examining some points of today's Gospel for our edification, let us first pray for the grace of the Holy Spirit through the intercession of the same Mother of God, Mary, by presenting to her the angelic greeting,

Ave Maria

VARIOUS HOLY FATHERS, SUCH AS ST AMBROSE, ST FUL-gentius, St Bernard and the Angelic Doctor St Thomas, have expressed their surprise at St Luke's words in today's Gospel when he says, "Joseph and Mary, the Mother of Jesus, were astonished at what was being said about Him" (Lk 2:33). It is said that "astonishment is the daughter of ignorance," because a person only becomes astonished when he is told something he did not know before. Therefore, would someone dare to suggest that the Blessed Virgin Mary and the righteous Joseph did not know what was to happen to their blessed Son Jesus? I am not saying that someone would try to veil their holiness with this ignorance. Perhaps we should say that the Blessed Virgin Mary's astonishment is akin to the astonishment expressed by her Son, Christ Our Saviour, when He became astonished at the centurion's faith, as St Mark recounts in chapter eight of his Gospel, "When Jesus heard him, He was astonished" (Lk 2:33). The Angelic Doctor, St Thomas, when explaining these words, said that there are two kinds of astonishment. The first arises from ignorance, which is not the kind that involved Christ or the Blessed Virgin Mary. The other kind arises from the excellence or perfection of the matter placed before us. For example, we might be astonished at the enormity of the world, the breadth of the earth, the height of the heavens, the depth of the sea and the beauty of the sun and moon, even though we have a good knowledge of these things.

Today the Blessed Virgin Mary and the righteous Joseph's astonishment did not arise from ignorance, but from the rarity of what they heard. For these two holy and blessed souls, Joseph and Mary, were completely certain that this Child was the Son of God and the Saviour of the world. This certainty was given them through what the Holy Spirit had revealed to them through the angel's greeting, the arrival of the Three Kings, the adoration of the shepherds, the prophecies of the Prophets, and everything else that happened around the birth of Our Saviour Jesus Christ. Even so, these two people were astonished when they attentively listened to everything the priest Simeon and the prophetess Anna were telling them about this Child. No wonder, Catholic Listeners, because the more the divine benevolences are known, the greater the astonishment they cause in the souls of men, and the more they are reflected upon, the greater clarity they give us of God's mercy and kindness. That is why King David said, "Your testimonies are wonderful; therefore my soul has sought them" (Ps 118:29). In other words, 'Seeing, O God, that your testimonies, your mysteries, and your gifts are excellent and perfect, my soul has been zealous in reflecting upon them.' Ignorance, ungratefulness and tepidity are some of the problems that beset many Catholics these days; they arise because people do not follow the example of the Blessed Virgin Mary and the righteous Joseph in reflecting and meditating upon the gifts and works of God, especially His humble birth, for it is certain that nothing in the world moves the heart of man more than the thought of God's gifts to us. King David experienced this for himself, for he wrote, "My heart grew hot within me, and in my meditation a fire shall flame out" (Ps 38:4).

Precious spices or ointments do not give off any perfume while they remain sealed in jars or boxes, but once they are brought out into the open or cast on the fire they give off their scent; similarly, expensive rugs and carpets cannot display their beautiful patterns and colours while they are folded and packed on top of each other. So, too, do the divine mysteries and gifts seem of little value if they remain packed up and hidden away. But if they are attentively observed and opened up in devout meditation, then their full value shall be realised; one shall taste their sweet honey and observe their majesty and excellence.

The events that happened to the Blessed Virgin Mary and the righteous Joseph caused them to reflect with astonishment on the Incarnation of Jesus Christ, and especially His humble birth and all the other extraordinary circumstances that surrounded that birth. Let it be an example to us, so that we should know how to occupy our thoughts during these holy days; we would do well to reflect attentively upon the divine gifts and be thankful for them, especially the birth of the Son of God, which gift was so noble and excellent that it not only astonished common people but also holy Prophets. This is illustrated clearly by the words of the Prophet Habakkuk, "O Lord, I have heard of your renown, and I stand in awe" (Hab 3:2). So, too, the Prophet Isaiah said, "Lord, who has believed what we have heard? To whom has the arm of the Lord been revealed?" (Is 53:1). Lord, who would have believed that you should be born in a stable and laid in a manger? Surely the Blessed Virgin Mary and the righteous Joseph would have known more about this great mystery than all the Prophets together? Today they hear the Prophet Simeon and the widow Anna speak of these things, and they were greatly astonished at the greatness of God's benevolence. The example of these holy persons should therefore inspire us to seriously observe this mystery of God's love, which is so sublime and excellent that God's Wisdom could give us nothing better than the joining of our human nature with the divine nature in one Person. These words are not mine, but they come from St John Damascene, who said, "There is nothing greater than that God was made man."[1] In other words, what he is saying is that the Incarnation was such a sublime, divine and supernatural work that God never repeated it. For by assuming a human nature, Almighty God elevated and ennobled man's nature

---

1 *Nihil maius, quam quod Deus factus sit homo.* St John Damascene, An Exact Exposition of the Orthodox Faith, Book 3, ch. 1.

by uniting it to the divine nature of Our Saviour, thereby elevating man to a height that surpasses even the choirs of angels in the glory of Heaven. Pope St Leo explained this truth well to the people in his sermon on the birth of Jesus Christ, "O Christian, acknowledge your dignity, and becoming a partner in the divine nature, refuse to return to the old baseness by degenerate conduct."[2] But dear Pope St Leo! You will find very few people these days who think about the dignity and honour they received through the Incarnation of Jesus Christ. We should rather say together with King David, "When man was in honour he did not understand: he has been compared to senseless beasts, and made like to them" (Ps 48:21).

The reason why today the Blessed Virgin Mary and the righteous Joseph were astonished is because of the humility of the Son of God, who humbled Himself to descend from Heaven to earth; the omnipotent Creator has become a weak creature, the Lord has become a servant, the Immortal One has become mortal. "He emptied Himself, taking the form of a servant" (Phil 2:7). We can understand that God, who is great, can do many unusual things, but the fact that He becomes small, submissive, and rejected is something that does not cease to astonish the human mind. Furthermore, these two righteous people were amazed at the merits, perfections and qualities of this small Child, who, while being tender, nonetheless possesses all strength and power. Even though it cries and blubs, it is imbued with all the wisdom and prudence, grace and gifts of the Holy Spirit. St Augustine sums it up well, "Just as the head contains all the senses, so in Christ are contained all graces."[3] The Prophet Isaiah adds to this, "There shall come forth a shoot from the stump of Jesse, and a branch shall grow out of his roots; and the Spirit of the Lord shall rest upon him: the spirit of wisdom and understanding, the spirit of counsel and might, the spirit of knowledge and fear of the Lord. And his delight shall be in the fear of the Lord" (Is 11:1–2). With these words the Prophet wants to make known that Jesus, while

---

2 *Agnosce o Christiane dignitatem tuam, et divinae consors factus naturae, noli in veterem vilitatem degeneri conversatione redire.* Pope St Leo the Great, Sermon I On the Nativity, ch. 3.

3 *Ut in capite omnes sunt sensus; ita et in Christo fuerunt omnes gratiae.* St Augustine, Letter to Dardanus, Sermon 187, ch. 12.

still a small child, was endowed and honoured with all the gifts and graces of the Holy Spirit.

Finally, the Queen of Sheba, who had come from distant lands, had been greatly amazed when she heard with her own ears and saw with her own eyes the wisdom and prudence with which King Solomon ruled over his house and family. So, too, was the Queen of Angels, the Blessed Virgin Mary, filled with wonderment when she heard all that the angels, shepherds, kings, the Prophet Simeon, and the Prophetess Anna were saying about the wisdom and holiness of her Son, especially when the old pious Simeon took the Child into his arms, and, weeping with joy, pronounced to the Blessed Virgin those prophetic words which we have taken as the theme of our discourse, "Behold, this Child is destined to bring about a fall, and to be a sign which men will refuse to acknowledge." For those who do not know God's endless love, the mystery of the Incarnation will indeed be an aggravating stumbling block and a source of contradiction. For, in the first place, when Almighty God created the angels in the fair heavens, He made known to them that through the mystery of the Incarnation, the Second Person of the Divine Godhead would take on a human nature, and if they wanted to remain steadfast in glory, that they were to honour and worship Him, as St Paul made known to us, "When He brings His first-begotten into the world, He said, Let all the angels of God worship Him" (Heb 1:6). All the good angels who kept themselves in grace by following this commandment reverently bowed down low to worship and honour this Person, but Lucifer and his companions were puffed up with pride and were deceived by the perfection they had received from God Himself; they remained obstinate, and he who was the most sublime among the angels thought it unworthy to have to worship and honour a mere human. In this way had Jesus led to contradiction and downfall in Heaven, whilst He was expected on earth through the eternal decree of Almighty God, "He is destined to be a sign which men will refuse to acknowledge." We can add to this that Lucifer and his disobedient followers were the first unbelievers, the first infidels, the first enemies of Jesus Christ. In short, he was the author and father of all those who later followed him in the wickedness of this contradiction.

Secondly, Almighty God Himself revealed this same mystery long ago in the earthly Paradise through the sin of our first father Adam, adding to this that they would have to suffer the resistance and the struggle of the godless, as Sacred Scripture shows us in Genesis where God proclaims to the devil, who had taken the form of a serpent, that there would be enmity between him and the woman, between his offspring and hers (Gn 3:15). The holy Fathers, when explaining this passage, considered the woman to be the Blessed Virgin Mary and her offspring the Son of God, Christ Our Saviour. So, too, they understood the devil's offspring to be all wicked and evil people, "You are from your father the devil" (Jn 8:44). They are the ones who, because of their wicked deeds and obstinate wicked wills, are called children of the devil. This war was already announced by Almighty God, for Cain murdered his brother Abel, Jacob was persecuted by Esau, as was Joseph by his brothers, David by Saul, the people of God by the Philistines, and the Maccabees by the tyrants. Thus had all the righteous people of the Old Testament been persecuted by the godless; they had experienced the continual warfare the children of the devil had sworn against the children of God — they were a type of the contradiction that Christ had to suffer from hell and the world. He Himself was then born into the world, and the devil, who had resisted and opposed all those who prefigured Him, immediately assembled his artillery against that sacred Person. Observe, no sooner had He been born into the world, than the righteous Simeon had begun explaining to His Blessed Mother the contradictions and persecutions that had been prepared for Him, "He is destined to be a sign which men will refuse to acknowledge." Herod begins to fulfil the prophecy by using every means to find and kill Him, thereby forcing Him to flee to Egypt. Once He had reached maturity, John the Baptist acknowledged Him, "Behold the Lamb of God, behold Him who takes away the sin of the world," but no sooner had he done so than the devil tried to tempt Him in the desert, but without success. Nonetheless, the devil stood perplexed before His divine teachings, His miracles and wondrous deeds; he was confused by His holiness and jealous of His glory. And so, the devil roused the Scribes and Pharisees and practically the entire Jewish race, which spouted forth all kinds of vile objections and contradictions against Our Saviour. He could thus truly say what the Prophet Jeremiah had said about him in days of old, "He has set me as a mark for His arrows" (Lam 3:12).

The heavenly Father had sent Him into the world as a sign, or as a target for arrows to shoot at, for from the very beginning man had attacked His innocence and tested His patience with their sins and wickedness. Alas! He had brought from Heaven nothing more than the bow of mercy and the arrows of goodness with which to wound the people with gentleness and love, yet He found them armed with bows of contradiction and arrows of persecution with which to pierce and kill Him. He came from Heaven to be a target of endless goodness, yet we used Him as a target upon which to shoot our innumerable misdeeds. Indeed, the Jewish Scribes, Pharisees, and priests had contradicted and opposed Him and sentenced Him without motive to death on the gibbet of the Cross. Indeed, subsequent Emperors and tyrants persecuted and tortured His followers and poured out an abundance of innocent blood of the righteous and glorious martyrs. Indeed, even today the unbelievers and heretics still contradict His divine teachings. But alas! We too must admit and confess, and not without sorrow, that He was destined to bring about the fall of many, being a sign that many will refuse to accept, including many Catholic Christians when they disregard the benefits wrought by the birth of Jesus Christ, through which the very foundation was laid by which we might be freed from the slavery of sin. These Catholics transgress and contradict the commandments of God and His holy Catholic Church; this contradiction is much worse than that of the Jews, the heretics, the heathens, or infidels. Perhaps I am speaking broadly, but I think St Bernard sums it up when he says, "Bitter indeed was the Church at first in the slaying of the martyrs, more bitter in later times in the struggle with the heretics, but now most bitter of all in the corrupt morals of the members of the household."[4] This will not seem so shocking when one considers that the persecutions under the godless tyrants, since they were strangers outside the Church of

4 *Amara prius persecutio Ecclesiae in fece martyrum, amator post in conflictu haereticorum, amarissima nunc in moribus domesticorum.* St Bernard, Sermon 33 On the Song of Songs, ch. 7, 16.

God, were somewhat bearable; the persecution of the heretics was less dangerous because they were an obvious and clearly defined enemy; but worst of all is persecution by one's own children, through the sins, wicked ways, and godless lives of the very Catholics themselves: this is persecution by hidden, furtive enemies. For the godless tyrants only persecuted the Church with pains and torments, by which she displayed her invincible steadfastness. The heretics opposed her with contradictory doctrines, which only served to strengthen her pure truth. But wicked Catholics persecute her by doing wicked and evil deeds, which are unbecoming of a Christian person and provide an opportunity for heretics and infidels to defame and dishonour the Church through blasphemy and slander.

We therefore need to test our lives according to Jesus the touchstone.⁵ Are we true gold or fool's gold? Are we children of God or children of the world? For as the righteous Simeon said, Christ was not only destined to bring about the fall of many, but also the rise of many. But how can we know this? Listen! Simeon surely was not referring to the resurrection of the body on the Last Day, but the resurrection of the soul from a state of sin to a state of grace, which occurs through Christ's grace in the holy Sacraments. Hear the words of St Paul the Apostle, "Since, then, you have been raised with Christ, set your hearts on things above, not on earthly things" (Col 3:1). St John the Evangelist records Our Lord's words on this, "I am the resurrection and the life" (Jn 11:25). With this He is saying, 'I am the resurrection and the raising up of sinners (for no one can rise up from a state of sin without God's grace) and the life of dead souls.' If you have prepared for this solemnity by having confessed your sins with sincere contrition and a firm purpose of amendment, and if you have received the Most Holy Sacrament of the Altar with devotion and piety, and if you have resolved to observe in the future all God's commandments and those of the holy Catholic Church, then you may be confident that Jesus will not bring about your fall and ruin, but your resurrection to new life. The Prophet Isaiah tells

---

5 Touchstone: 1. a black stone related to flint and formerly used to test the purity of gold and silver by the streak left on the stone when rubbed by the metal. 2. a test or criterion for determining the quality or genuineness of a thing.

us that Christ will be sent into the world for our sanctification, our righteousness, and our salvation, "He shall be a sanctification to you" (Is 8:14). But if we remain in sin, if we choose not to obey either God or the Holy Church, in short, if we disregard the salvation of our souls, then what shall I say? I shall tell the truth — it is a sure sign that we do not value the great benefit Jesus Christ's birth has brought us; it is a sign we will stay trapped in the rut into which we have fallen, thereby undermining our own salvation.

So then, Catholic Listeners, let us not be foolish and hard-headed, but rather let us abide in the grace of God, so that having distanced ourselves from sin and using the means He left us for our salvation, we may enjoy heavenly glory in the life to come. Who lives, etc.

On New Year's Day

Postquam consummati sunt dies octo, ut circumcideretur Puer, vocatum est nomen eius Iesus — "When eight days had passed, the Child was circumcised and given His name, which was Jesus" (Lk 2:21).

ATHOLIC LISTENERS, THE WRITers of old held the opinion that there was no better way of glorifying Almighty God than by keeping silent, because such sovereign Majesty could better be praised through intense contemplation than by undignified speech, for not even the heavenly tongues are fully capable of singing the praises of the Divine Majesty. The celestial Seraphim are so called because they are inflamed with the fire of love, yet they cover their mouths with their wings as a sign that the sovereignty of the Divine Majesty cannot be explained by any creature. No matter how high we aim our praise, we end up never getting off the ground, because the Lord, who made Heaven and earth and all they contain, can never be completely understood by anyone apart from Himself. St Gregory Nazianzen expressed this well when he said that God is an eye of Himself and He has the nature of an ineffable Being. He is light and is able to see into all things. No one can ever behold Him, and no one can ever fully explain His name.

Of course, all this is indeed true. You might therefore easily think that I am terribly arrogant, so to speak, by today climbing into the 'seat of truth'[1] to announce to you the power and dignity of the

---

1 i.e. the pulpit. Perhaps a reference to the "Seat of Moses" in Mt 23:2. In the synagogue, only those who sat in the Seat of Moses could have the authority to interpret the Mosaic Law. In the Catholic Church, it is the place from which God's Truth, and so that of the Catholic Faith, was preached (Translator's note).

sweet, blessed, and holy Name of Jesus. Nevertheless, I hope I might merit to be excused for my arrogance, seeing that the same great God invites us to examine various passages of Sacred Scripture, so that we will laud and praise Him, especially through the mouth of King David, "Praise the Lord, you children; praise the Name of the Lord" (Ps 112:1). I wish I were an innocent child, clean of all stain of sin. I wish one of the celestial beings would come to purify, rule, and direct my lips. I wish Divine Love would come to inflame you, and me, so that we might announce the power and strength of the blessed Name of Jesus and be able to explain why the One who was given this Name had been willing to endure the shame and physical pain of His circumcision. For as the Evangelist says in today's Gospel, "When eight days had passed, the Child was circumcised and given His name, which was Jesus." To explain this further, let us first pray for the grace of the Holy Spirit through the intercession of the Blessed Virgin Mary by presenting to her the angelic salutation,

Ave Maria

THE ANCIENT JEWS WROTE THE NAME OF GOD, *JEHOVAH*, with four letters. So great was their reverence for the Holy Name that they did not even dare pronounce it. The High Priest wore on his forehead a golden headband on which was engraved the Holy Name. Only he was allowed to utter the Name, and then only at certain times and hours of the day. If this was so for the ancients, then what great reverence and honour should we Christians bestow on the Holy Name of Jesus? St Paul the Apostle says that at the name of Jesus every knee should bow, in Heaven and on earth and under the earth. Your name, O Jesus! is both holy and terrifying; it stirs up in our hearts both love and fear. It is a Name full of honour and reverence. It is a Name invented by the Blessed Trinity, announced by an angel, and given to Joseph and Mary. It is a Name of salvation and grace. There is no Name higher than this blessed Name by which man can obtain salvation. In your Name, O Jesus! did the wondrous exchange occur between humanity and divinity, by which we were saved. In your Name, O Jesus! are contained wisdom and power, goodness, love, and all the other divine properties. Your Holy Name flows with oil and is like a precious ointment. When oil is pressed from sweet-smelling spices and herbs, the air becomes filled with a pleasant odour; so, too, most sweet Jesus, does your Name give off the fragrance of love and reverence, which makes Heaven and earth rejoice. This blessed oil was first tapped in the land of the Jews, and from there it flowed throughout the world. Thus we, too, have shared in its fullness and our lamps have not been extinguished by the dark night of sin. The Name of Jesus is a light, food, and medicine, says the mellifluous St Bernard.[2] It is the manna from Heaven, which contains in itself every delight to make the soul rejoice and give strength to the body. Well might we say, together with King David, "How majestic is your name, O Lord, in all the earth!" (Ps 8:2). So, too, the heavenly Bride says in the Book of Songs, "Draw me; we will run after you to the odour of your ointments" (Song 1:3).

And yet, notwithstanding the sweetness of this holy, blessed Name, the Reformed Brothers, like birds of prey circling dead, stinking corpses, cannot abide the sweetness of the Name of Jesus, for they find pleasure in the stench of error and the filth of sin. Woe to these pathetic people who say evil is good, and good, evil! How they labour to cure their ailing bodies! They are not in the least concerned for their immortal souls, even though a powerful and effective medicine can easily be found. For as the same St Bernard tells us, calling to mind the Name of Jesus softens the impetuosity of anger, it quenches the fire of lust and concupiscence, it conquers pride and overcomes the thirst of avarice.[3] This should come as no great surprise, Catholic Listeners, for what springs to mind when we hear the Name of Jesus mentioned? And do not say what you have read in books, for that would be a gross stupidity. So what image comes to mind? We should imagine a man who is powerful, prudent, gentle, God-fearing, moderate, and pure, merciful and humble of heart. I say 'man' but He is also God; He can heal us because He is Almighty, and He wants to help us because He is goodness itself. Damned, then, are those people who constantly have the name of the devil on their lips by cursing and speaking evil and blaspheming the Name of God. Likewise, there

2 St Bernard, On the Song of Songs, Sermon 15.
3 See St Bernard, Sermon on the Holy Name of Jesus.

are people who, every time something goes wrong or falls flat, misuse the Name of God because they are not careful enough to put a seal on their lips — they are to be despised.

Let us by-pass these people and look to those who seek to obtain their salvation with godly fear. Who would not forsake all vanity? Who does not inwardly rejoice? Who is not strengthened upon hearing the blessed Name? There is no doubt that in this Name miracles have been wrought and many devils have been cast out and driven away. "They will cast out devils in My Name" (Mk 16:17). It was in this Name that Saul was changed into Paul, a bloodthirsty wolf became a meek lamb. In this Name St Peter made the lame walk and Stephen prayed for those who stoned him. And the holy martyr St Ignatius was so gladdened by this Name, that after his death, according to some, they found this Name written in gold letters on his breast. Therefore, we are not surprised that it is not permitted for anyone else to be honoured by bearing this Holy Name, no matter how perfect he might be in holiness. Of course, in history there were occasions when people bore the same name. For instance, we think of Jesus ben Sirach who wrote the Book of Wisdom.[4] Then there was Jesus Josedech[5] and Jesus the son of Nave.[6] The former brought the people of Israel into the Promised Land, and the latter led them out of the Babylonian captivity; both were a type of the Saviour of the world. Yet neither could actually bring salvation to the people, or save them from their sins. This power and privilege could only be wrought by the Name of God, as the Wise Man tells us in the Book of Proverbs, "the name of the Lord is a strong tower" (Prov 18:10). It is a parapet, an unconquerable shield, and an arsenal of various weapons. Look at how the young David, when armed with these weapons, went into battle against the giant Goliath; the haughty giant scorned him with pompous audacity, and cursed the army of the God of Israel, whereupon David said to the giant, "You come to me with sword and spear and javelin; but I come to you in the name of the Lord of hosts" (1 Sam 17:45). What shall I say about Moses who carried in his hands

4   The Book of the Wisdom of Sirach, also known as the Book of Ecclesiasticus.
5   See Zech 3:1.
6   See Sir 46:1.

the staff of God? According to Alfonso Tostado, the staff of God is so called because on it were engraved the four letters that make up the Divine Name,[7] through whose power Moses performed so many wonders, miracles and deeds in the presence of Pharaoh. Finally, if Joshua, who was also called Jesus, could make the sun stand still in the heavens, and if the Creator of the heavens out of reverence for the Name of Jesus was obedient to the voice of a man, and if the same Joshua could conquer the Amelechites, who represent the devils, and if the figure and image of Joshua's name can conquer enemies and set them to flight, then imagine what power is contained in the blessed Name of Jesus Himself.

Therefore, Catholic Listeners, if you tempt the devil or given in to demonic temptation, if some wicked passion has overcome you, if you suffer injustice or injury or if you experience some difficulty, if the waters of tribulation seem to have risen right up to the keel of your soul so that you are about to fall into desperation and despair, then call upon the Name of the Lord, invoke the power of the sweet Name of Jesus, and you will be protected and find rest for your soul. "For whosoever shall call upon the name of the Lord shall be saved" (Rom 10:13). The Son of God taught us to pray in the name of His heavenly Father, with the promise of being heard, "Whatever you ask of the Father in my name, He will give it to you" (Jn 16:23). And St Paul the Apostle exhorts us, "Whatever you do, whether in word or deed, do in the Name of the Lord Jesus" (Col 3:17). It is the Holy Name that the holy Catholic Church petitions for the forgiveness of sins, "Forgive us our sins, O Lord, for your name's sake" (Ps 78:9). Finally, those who leave behind the world for the sake of the Holy Name, will receive back a hundredfold and shall obtain eternal life. Seeing, then, that our prayers will be answered in the name of Jesus, and our works will become meritorious, and our sins shall be forgiven so that we may enjoy the blessed life of eternal glory, what better can I give you, Catholic Listeners, for this new year than the sweet, blessed Name of Jesus? Of course, when in olden times people

---

7 The four letters, or tretragrammaton, that make up the Hebrew Holy Name are YHWH. The most widely accepted pronunciation among Hebrew scholars is "Yahweh" (Translator's note).

honoured each other by giving sweetmeats on New Year's Day as a wish that throughout the year they would enjoy sweet happiness and happy sweetness, then what could be sweeter, more loving, and more lovely than the Holy Name of Jesus? It is sweeter than milk and honey and more precious than gold or gems. In Him are hidden every treasure of wisdom and knowledge. In Him the fullness of the Godhead is physically present, not only in being, presence, and power, but also through justifying grace and the personal union of divinity with humanity in one Person. So then, take this invaluable gift, this hidden treasure, this pearl of great price; take and receive for this new year the wisdom of our heavenly Fathers, and say together with the wise Solomon, "I esteemed her more than sceptres and thrones; compared with her, I held riches as nothing" (Wis 7:8). Therefore, nor would I want to compare her to precious gems, when even gold and silver are like mud in her presence.

O Jesus, King of glory! Your majesty is great, and your name is worthy to be praised. You are the lawgiver of all the laws, the image of the Divine Being; no guile is found in your mouth, nor the least trace of sin in your soul. Why then on this day did you subject yourself, like a servant or a slave or even a sinner, to the law of circumcision, which was given as a remedy for original sin? Did you not in truth say, "Which of you convicts me of sin?" (Jn 8:46). Catholic Listeners, He did indeed remain pure and untainted by any sin, although how this happened will always remain a mystery to us. Even so, the One who stood above the law of circumcision allowed His Body to be subjected to it, as an example of humility and obedience. And even though He was not obligated by the Law, He nevertheless upheld it, so that we might abide by His laws that bind us. He subjected Himself to the Law in order to free those bound by that same Law. "God sent His Son to redeem those who were under the law" (Gal 4:4–5). He became subject to the law of sinners because He had come in the likeness of those who had sinned, for circumcision is a mark of sin. It is a truly remarkable sign of love that God wanted to be born in a poor town in a dirty stable in the cold winter, and to be circumcised on the eighth day, with tears and sadness, to uphold the Law, which He Himself had given, not for the righteous but for the unrighteous, not for holy ones but for sinners. Therefore, today we might say that the Light has become obscured, the Almighty has been governed, and Wisdom received instruction. Yes, joy becomes sorrow, strength becomes weak, and life becomes death. Is there anyone who will not marvel when observing the judgements of the Divine Majesty when He sees His Divine Son, at the age of only eight days, shedding His Blood for love of mankind by being circumcised? Is there anyone who, with all his heart, with all his soul, with all his strength, and with all his mind, will not love Him who first loved us by pouring out His Blood for us at such a tender age?

Christian Listeners, the circumcision of the Old Law came to an end after Christ's circumcision, and the old figure was replaced by a new truth, that is, a spiritual, internal circumcision. Allow me, then, to comment on this, seeing that circumcision was not only useful and necessary under the Old Law, but also now has its place under the law of grace. The Prophet Jeremiah spoke of this when he addressed the people of Israel, saying, "Be circumcised to the Lord" (Jer 4:4). Now He did not want those who had reached a ripe old age and who were already circumcised in their bodies to have to undergo circumcision again, but seeing that they were uncircumcised in their hearts and ears, He made known to them their need for a spiritual circumcision of the heart, as St Paul the Apostle says, without which a bodily circumcision has no benefit. We still need this circumcision of the heart even today, namely, we need to cut ourselves off from any wicked desires and lustfulness that may harm the soul. The human heart harbours lustfulness, which is the origin of all evil passions and immoral inclinations such as avarice, gluttony, wantonness, and other such evils. Our Saviour Himself tells us in St Matthew's Gospel, "For from the heart comes forth evil thoughts, adulteries, fornications, thefts" (Mt 15:19), by which He tells us that sin finds its origin in the heart. Therefore, we need to take an axe to the roots of this deadly tree, so that, once chopped off, it will wither and be exterminated. So, too, should its wicked branches be pruned and lopped off. This is what the Patriarch Moses commanded the people of Israel to do in ancient times, "Circumcise then the foreskin of your heart, and stiffen your neck no more" (Dt 10:16). In other words, take the sword of godliness and lop off the shoots of sin which originate in the heart and sprout forth from it as if from a fountain. King David was well acquainted with the purity of heart that comes from this kind of circumcision when he prayed, "Create a clean heart in me, O God, and renew a right spirit within my bowels" (Ps 50:12). That is, create in me a spirit of righteousness, modesty and holiness, that I may do what pleases you and that I may bring to completion what you have commanded me to do. When this was granted him through God's grace, he called out with great joy, "My heart and my flesh have rejoiced in the living God" (Ps 83:3). They have rejoiced in God, who is not only life itself, but who brought me to life through the forgiveness of my sins and by His divine friendship.

Furthermore, since man's nature is entirely infected by original sin, it is not only the heart that needs to undergo spiritual circumcision, but also the other members of the body. In his Sermon on the Feast of the Circumcision, St Bernard tells us, "We must be circumcised not just in one part only, but in the whole body."[8] What shall I then say about the eyes or our sight? These too must be circumcised with great care, so that no one will later be able to join the Prophet Jeremiah in saying, "My eye has wasted my soul." If your eye tends to wander, or if you find pleasure in improper images, vulgar people or any other kind of disagreeable frivolity, then you must pray together with King David, "Turn away my eyes that they may not behold vanity" (Ps 118:37). Lord, turn away my eyes, so that in the end you might joyfully say together with the patient Prophet Job, "I made a covenant with my eyes, that I would not so much as think upon a virgin" (Job 31:1).

In secular history Scipio Africanus is rightly praised, for when he was in Spain his men captured a noble and fair maiden, yet he did not even want to behold her, instead issuing an order that she be delivered unharmed to her intended fiancé. So we see that even pagans knew that curious or flighty glances can lead to immoderate love and affection. But who are these people who have uncircumcised eyes? They are those of whom the Apostle Peter says, "They have

8 *Circumcidi necesse est, non in uno membro, sed in toto corpore simul.* St Bernard, First Sermon for the Feast of the Circumcision.

eyes full of adultery" (2 Pet 2:14). They are those who, as soon as they see a woman, straight away give in to wicked desires, immodest longings, and impure thoughts. In chapter nine of his book, the Prophet Jeremiah bewailed the fact that many people's eyes were defiled, "For death is come up through our windows," that is, through the eyes, which are the windows of our body, and it entered into our dwelling, which is our soul. We must then circumcise and close these windows and these eyes, so that the death of sin cannot enter into our souls and minds.

Moreover, a Christian must also circumcise his ears so as not to let enter wicked desires and delights by listening to gossip and backbiting, or to dishonest words and songs, or to the counsel of wicked people who often use empty promises to undermine our happiness. Here we must take heed of the Wise Man's warning, "Hedge in your ears with thorns, hear not a wicked tongue" (Sir 28:28). Therefore, if we hear someone trying to destroy another's good name and character with gossip or slander, we must walk away as if we are deaf; we must not add anything to this wickedness otherwise we will become accomplices in that same sin. Here it would do us well to follow the practices of Ulysses who, according to the historical witness of Homer, while bound to the mast of a ship, heard the beguiling song of the mermaids; he realised how deceptive and dangerous they were, and by spurning them he managed to sail past the rocks and cliffs without any harm. In a similar way, we, too, should be deaf to the flattering tongues of scandalmongers and not encourage them by giving ear to their gossiping or by delighting in their dishonest proposals. We must avoid the rocks of sin by keeping our souls pure and by circumcising our ears for our salvation.

But we should also mind our tongue, for even though it is only a small member, it has the potential to do much damage. It is not for nothing that nature has enclosed the tongue behind two rows of fortifications, namely, the teeth and the lips, almost as a warning to us not to flap the tongue indiscreetly. For as the Wise Man says, both death and life depend on the tongue. "Death and life are in the power of the tongue" (Prov 18:21). St James the Apostle confirms this when he says with great clarity, "So also the tongue is a small member, yet it boasts of great exploits. How great a forest is set ablaze by a small fire! And the tongue is a fire placed among our members as a world of iniquity. It stains the whole body, sets on fire the wheel of birth, and is itself set on fire by hell" (Jas 3:5–6). This wheel of birth he calls our mortal bodies, with which we were endowed at birth. Like a wheel it continually turns to carry us from birth to death, through sickness and health, changes, instability, and inconstancy. This wheel, or body, can become ignited by the allurements of hell and the temptations of the devil. It gives itself over to lies and deception, to cursing and swearing, to impurity and wantonness, to gluttony and drunkenness and a thousand other outrages. It is only right, then, that we circumcise this member, and let us use it to pray with King David, "Set a watch, O Lord, before my mouth, and a door round about my lips" (Ps 140:3). This will happen easily provided we seek to reforge our slippery tongues in the burning furnace of the blessed wounds of Jesus Christ. The anvil must be our Saviour's blessed back, striped and bloodied by His bitter Passion, about which King David remarks, "The wicked have ploughed my back" (Ps 128:3). Not only did they work and hammer when He received so many thousands of lashes on their behalf, but the wicked ploughed and cut furrows by means of their calumnies, blasphemies, and evil words.

Finally, the hands and feet are also in need of spiritual circumcision because humanity has received them for the purpose of performing works of love and mercy. And so the hands must not be used to hurt and injure people, nor for dishonest or unjust purposes, but they must be kept free of any impurity or contamination, whether bodily or spiritual. The feet, too, can be used as instruments for taking us to do evil things such as deceiving our neighbours or oppressing the innocent, or spilling blood, or they might lead us to taverns where we will find unsavoury company. Therefore, the feet must also be circumcised in order to ward off any scandals or aggression, according to the teaching of the Gospel. To sum up, all of our bodily members must be circumcised, for, seeing that today is the first day of the new year, each of us must be renewed. We must strip off the old, stinking Adam and put on a new man who is made righteous and holy in God's image.

Therefore, Catholic Listeners, remember the power and dignity of the blessed, sweet, and holy Name of Jesus, and ponder the words this tender little Child is saying to you today, "I have set you an example, that you should do as I have done for you" (Jn 13:15). I was circumcised with sorrow and tears whilst still a tender infant; you, too, must be circumcised, not in body but in spirit, even if it means suffering pain and discomfort, that is, you must live in this world as sober, upright, and God-fearing people, being righteous and holy before God all the days of your lives. In yourself you must be holy, with your neighbour you must be righteous, and before God you must be innocent, not just for one day but for all the days of your life, because "the backbone of a good work is endurance."9 Thus may you persevere in good works to the end, so that you may enjoy the eternal glory of the life to come. Who lives, etc.

---

9 *Virtus boni operis perseverantia est.* St Gregory the Great, Homilies On the Gospels. Homily 25.

On the Feast of the Three Kings (Epiphany)

Ecce, Magi ab Oriente venerunt Ierosolymam, dicentes: Ubi est qui natus est Rex Iudaeorum? Vidimus enim Stellam eius in Oriente, et venimus adorare eum — "Behold, Magi from the east came to Jerusalem and asked, 'Where is the One who has been born king of the Jews? We saw His star when it rose and have come to worship Him'" (Mt 2:1–2).

CATHOLIC LISTENERS, AMONG THE Scholastics there is a proverb which states that goodness does not want to be contained by borders, rather, it wants to share itself with others and is always seeking to spread and expand, "All good is self-diffusing and self-communicating."[1] Today we clearly see the truth of this saying, not in a created goodness, but in God Himself, who is the Author of all good things, created and uncreated. A few days ago the Word of the Father, the second Person of the Blessed Trinity, the Saviour of the world, was born in Bethlehem. His birth was announced by the angels to shepherds, "Listen, I bring you news of great joy, for this day has been born to you a Saviour" (Lk 2:10–11). The shepherds brought the news to the Jewish people. By means of a miraculous star, God Himself made the news known to Wise Men in the East, that is, to philosophers, kings, and priests living near the frontier with Persia, so that through them the birth of Christ would become known and celebrated among the Gentiles. It was therefore fitting that Christ would merge two walls together into one true

---

1 *Omne bonum est diffusivum et communicativum sui.* St Thomas Aquinas, *Summa Theologiae*, I, Q 73, A 3.

cornerstone; Jew and Gentile He would make into one Church. As St Paul the Apostle says, "For He Himself is our peace, who has made both one" (Eph 2:14). His purpose was to create one new humanity from two different religions through the covenant of His divine love. Likewise, King David gave testimony in Psalm 18 that "the heavens tell of God's glory," but today the heavens do not tell us of God's majesty or glory, nor of His power and greatness, but about something that astonishes us even more, which is the humility and abjection displayed by God when He demeaned Himself for man's salvation by taking on the appearance of a servant: "He emptied Himself, taking the form of a servant" (Phil 2:7). Behold a new star, a wondrous, brilliant star has revealed itself in the heavens as a message to mankind that God has become man for them, not in Heaven on high but in a stable, not on His heavenly throne but in a manger, not among the angels but among the nasty creatures of the earth, not in His usual majesty but in our self-abasement: "Fairer than the sun at morning was the star that told His birth; to the lands their God announcing, hid beneath a form of earth."[2] The holy Catholic Church tells us that a star whose light was fairer than the sun was sent to tell us about a miraculous occurrence—God has become a Child and is lying in a manger. That is why the Evangelist says in today's Gospel, "Behold, Magi from the east came to Jerusalem and asked, 'Where is the one who has been born king of the Jews? We saw his star when it rose and have come to worship him.'" Let us then go with the Three Kings to adore this Child, taking note of their piety and generosity by the light and the stars of God's grace. We shall ask for this grace through the intercession of the Blessed Virgin and Mother of God, Mary, by presenting to her the angelic salutation,

Ave Maria

THE SON OF GOD HAD FORESEEN FROM HIS ETERNAL throne that the entire human race would forever be lost, and so He assumed a human nature to redress the damage caused by sin. He

---

2 *Haec stella, quae solis rotam, vincit decore ac lumine, venisse terris nuntiat, cum carne terrestri Deum.* Epiphany Lauds hymn from the Divine Office.

fought a victorious battle against the attacks of the common enemy, the devil, and by His death He destroyed death's domain. It was out of pure, everlasting love for the human race that the Son of God took on this service, which was accepted and approved by His heavenly Father, who granted every honour to His only-begotten Son, as was only fitting, and He expressly ordered that the entire heavenly court, that is, all the angels, should honour and worship His Son who was made man. Yes, by being born of the Blessed Virgin Mary in the stable at Bethlehem, He laid the foundation stone of the great work which finds its completion in the redemption of the world. The heavenly Father, therefore, once again ordered all rational creatures to wish His Son well, and that men and angels should together humbly worship their Creator. And so the entire heavenly court rushed out, so to speak, to worship this wondrous work of the Blessed Trinity, that is, the tender Child Jesus who lay in the crib between an ox and a donkey. They worshipped the birth of their King with heavenly songs of praise. St Paul says it well, "And again, when He brings the firstborn into the world, He says, 'Let all God's angels worship Him'" (Heb 1:6). And yet, the heavenly Father was still not content with the affection shown towards His only-begotten Son, and so He sent His messengers from Heaven to Bethlehem to give a sign to the shepherds encamped there that Christ the Saviour had been born in the city of David. He commanded His angels to tell the shepherds because they were to witness to the Jewish people that Christ had been born principally for them. Nonetheless, these joyous tidings had been revealed not just to the Jewish shepherds, but, in order that the Son of God's glory might increase, as I said at the beginning, the heavens themselves had begun to speak of God's glory by bringing forth an incredibly beautiful and brilliant birth-star of the new King. As the holy martyr Ignatius wrote in his letter to the Ephesians, "A star shone forth in Heaven above all the other stars, the light of which was inexpressible, while its novelty struck men with astonishment."[3] This account witnesses to the Wise Men,

---

3 *Stella fulsit splendore exuperans omnes quotquot ante fuerant; lux enim eius inenarrabilis erat, et stuporem incussit omnibus videntibus eam, rei novitas.* St Ignatius of Antioch, Epistle to the Ephesians, ch.19.

or Gentile kings, who were experts in reading the heavens and stellar constellations, and who had come with gifts to bear witness that Jesus was the King of all kings, and that from now on all honour, reverence and glory should be granted Him.

We have all heard about Pharaoh, king of Egypt, who dragged the chaste Joseph out of his dungeon and named him Saviour of the world, and honoured him with a fine ring and expensive garments, and placed him upon a triumphal chariot and ordered the entire people to honour him, all because Joseph had explained Pharaoh's dream to him. And then we read of King Ahasuerus who saved the innocent Mordecai from the gallows and placed him on the royal throne and adorned him with costly robes and the royal crown, all because he had done him some service; and King Balthasar had wanted to honour the exile Daniel with a golden chain and purple robes because he had read and interpreted words written on a wall, even though these words were to the king's detriment. If all these important people acted as they did, then how much more will Almighty God, who is the Father of mercy and the God of all consolation, do for His only-begotten Son, knowing well that He was the only One who could completely settle the guilt caused by our first parents. God knew that His Son would redeem the human race with His Precious Blood, and that He alone was worthy to open the book and to untie the seven seals, and that He would glorify and honour His heavenly Father in all His works, even if it meant being obedient unto death on the Cross. It is therefore with good reason, Catholic Listeners, that Almighty God had desired from all eternity that His Son should be honoured this day with a new kind of honour. He rightly desired that His Son be honoured and known by the Gentiles, seeing that He had, as it were, divorced Himself from the Jews because of their ungratefulness. The Son of God had come into His own, as St John the Evangelist writes, "And they received Him not." His own people, the Jews, His kinsmen, received Him not. There is no doubt that they had cried long and hard, "Rain down, you heavens, from above and let the skies pour down righteousness. Tear the heavens and come down. O Lord, send a lamb to be ruler of the earth!" (Is 45:8; 16:1; 64:1). When the fullness of time had come, God sent His Son into the world. But the Jews shouted with fury and rage, "Where does He come from, we do not know Him" (Jn 9:29). The Lord and Ruler of the world came down to earth, and they said, "We have no king but Caesar." The heavens rained down the Righteous One and the godless defamed Him. And they told Him, "Are we not right in saying that you are a Samaritan and have a demon?" (Jn 8:48). Therefore, Almighty God left the obstinate Jews, and from the depths of His mercy He turned to the Gentiles to be worshipped and honoured by them; and so, by the light of a star He led the Three Kings to Bethlehem to find there a new-born King.

That is why, Catholic Listeners, we should celebrate today's feast with godly zeal, seeing that at various times God deigned to perform for our benefit three wondrous miracles, as the Catholic Church sings, "We observe this holy day, ornamented with three miracles: Today a star led the Magi to the manger. Today wine was made from water at the wedding. Today in the Jordan Christ desired to be baptised by John, so that He might save us."[4] The adoration of the Kings taught us about His Divine Majesty; by changing water into wine at the wedding feast at Cana we came to know His omnipotence and through the baptism of Jesus Christ in the Jordan we observed His deep humility. We can see, then, that the foundation of our salvation lies in our knowledge of the Blessed Trinity, that is, one God in three Persons. This mystery has been clearly revealed to us today when the heavenly Father revealed Himself as a voice heard coming down from Heaven, "This is My beloved Son in whom I am well pleased" (Mt 17:5). The Son came in His human nature and the Holy Spirit came in the form of a dove.

This day, then, is characterised by a number of personalities. Principal among these is the wise and prudent Queen of Sheba who came from distant lands with a great retinue and entered Jerusalem in order to hear the wise words of King Solomon, for he was renowned to be the wisest among all the rulers of the world. She honoured him with gifts of gold and jewels and costly spices. This pagan Queen of Sheba

---

4 *Tribus miraculis ornatum sanctum diem colimus; hodie stells Magos duxit ad praesepium; hodie vium ex aqua factum est ad nuptias; hodie in Iordane a Ioanne Christus baptizari voluit, ut salvaret nos.* Magnificat antiphon at Second Vespers for the Feast of the Epiphany.

is a type of the Church of the Gentiles, which today has sent her gifts and presents to Christ, the true Solomon, "Behold, something greater than Solomon is here" (Mt 12:42). No one has ever been more serene in being the mediator between God and man than He, "the mediator between God and men, the man Christ Jesus" (1 Tim 2:5). No one has been worthier to be called king than He, who is Creator of the whole world. There has been no one wiser nor more intelligent than He, for He can see into our minds and hearts.

Coming back to our Kings, some of you might be wondering how it was possible that they were able to undertake such a great journey, even with the most ardent diligence, in just thirteen days, according to learned opinion. Well, this is not so remarkable given that they had the Holy Spirit to guide their voyage. He kindled their spirits and gave light to their path, and also made their bodies, which normally weigh down the soul, light in weight, just as a feather sails on the breeze. The Holy Spirit can also make wagons fly, and wheels, people, and animals, as the Prophet Ezekiel testifies, "They came and went, vivid as lightning-flashes" (Ez 1:14). Do you not think these holy men would have been overjoyed at beholding that star, as the Evangelist tells us, "And when they saw the star they rejoiced with exceeding great joy" (Mt 2:10), if it were not for the fact that shining through this star was the Holy Spirit? St Augustine writes about this in his work 'On the miraculous things in Sacred Scripture.'[5] Indeed, like God's grace, the Holy Spirit is also varied and diverse according to the circumstances of the situation. We see Him taking on the appearance of a dove to illustrate innocence and purity; and again He comes in the form of fiery tongues to kindle the Apostles and grant them eloquence, and as a pillar of cloud He provided refreshment and shade. Therefore, today it would not be so unbelievable for Him to assume the appearance of a star, in order to guide and illuminate. We might also assume, following this opinion, that the Kings left their houses and palaces and set off without fear on their journey, not shying from the difficulties and hardships they encountered along their journey; they crossed the border with Persia and in a few short days arrived

---

5   i.e., Pseudo-Augustinus Hibernicus, *On the miraculous things in Sacred Scripture*, Book 3, ch. 4, 4.

in a strange country to seek Jesus, and once having found Him, they adored Him, for they had been kindled and enlightened, within and without, by the rays and light of God the Holy Spirit. Here the words of St Ambrose ring true, "The grace of the Holy Spirit does not move at a slow pace."[6]

But better that I should keep quiet to let the truth speak for itself. The New Testament had to fulfil what was foretold in the Old Testament. Hear what Balaam had once said, "I see a star that rises out of Jacob" (Num 24:17), and St Matthew said, "Behold, the star which they had seen in the east went before them." (Mt 2:9). Furthermore, the Prophet David said, "before Him the Ethiopians shall fall down" (Ps 71:9), and the Evangelist says, "and falling down they adored Him" (Mt 2:11). The Prophet said, "The kings of the Arabians and of Sheba shall bring gifts" (Ps 71:10), and the Evangelist says, "They offered Him gifts: gold, frankincense and myrrh" (Mt 2:11).

Now tell us, you worthy representatives of the Gentiles, what stirrings went on in your souls, what gladness and joy of heart did you feel as you approached to adore, with great humility and reverence, that small Child dandled on the knee of His Virgin Mother? How was it to behold this Child in His Mother's arms, the fairest Child among all the children of men; what was it like to behold His divine countenance, which so many kings and prophets had longed to see, and beneath which another face lay hidden, one that the angels yearned to behold, and which you now enjoy gazing upon in the glory of Heaven? It is a face for which the heavenly Bride pines, saying to her Bridegroom, "Show me your face, let your voice sound in my ears" (Song 2:14). Your godliness has been truly remarkable, you Princes of the Gentiles, seeing that you were not in the least offended by the lowliness of His birthplace, nor by the humble simplicity of His Mother, nor by the plainness of their furnishings. I think that if one of those pretentious Jews or pompous Pharisees had seen with what reverence these newcomers to the Faith had paid their respects to the Child Jesus, I do not doubt he would have said with disdain, 'For whom do these strangers bend their knees? Who is this they

---

6   *Nescit tarda nolimina Spiritus Sancti gratia.* St Bernard, Sermons on the Annunciation, Sermon I.

are worshipping as their King, and who is it they recognise for them to present Him such magnificent gifts? Could this Child be the king of the Jewish nation? Where are His servants and advisers, where is His palace and crown and sceptre and royal magnificence? I surely do not see here any signs of royalty. In fact, I see quite the opposite. For a royal crown He has some poor rags, His sceptre is just straw and hay, His throne is simply a rough manger, His palace is a stable and His servants are an ox and an ass. I see here no rugs or tapestries but filth, stench, and cobwebs; no grandiosity but only wretchedness, no riches but utter poverty.' Nonetheless, these minor details did not at all deter the Kings, who fell to the ground on their knees, not so much adoring the Child's infancy, which had as yet no mental capacity, but rather adoring His divinity, which contains all things. And to the delight of the Blessed Virgin Mary, not only did they adore the One "who was desired by all the Gentiles," but they also offered Him their gifts, gold, frankincense, and myrrh, not as uncircumcised men, but as true Israelites, not circumcised literally but according to the spirit, not in the flesh but in the heart.

Seeing then, Catholic Listeners, that God our heavenly Father desires us to follow the example of the Three Kings in honouring His only Son, the blessed Jesus, who will open the door of His love to receive everyone that comes to visit Him, let us then also hasten to the stable at Bethlehem to honour Him with gifts, seeing that no one, according to the Law of the Old Covenant, should come before Him with empty hands, "None shall appear before me empty" (Ex 23:15). No one should complain that he is poor when he knows how easy it is to fill the hand of a child. But what am I saying, to the stable at Bethlehem? It is not necessary for us to undertake the journey to the distant land of Palestine, for even though we have neither the stable nor the manger, which the Kings honoured, nor the Child Himself, whom they adored, nor the swaddling clothes that bound Him or the star that guided them, behold, we do have Jesus who is truly present in the Most Blessed Sacrament of the Altar. The swaddling clothes are the appearance of bread that hides Him from our eyes, the star is the Faith that guides us to find and adore Him. The altar, says St Chrysostom, is to the Catholic Christian what the manger was to the Kings — they found Jesus wrapped in swaddling clothes, and they adored Him; we find and adore Him under the sacramental species. The Kings only had licence to adore Him, whereas we have consent, permission, and even the command to receive and consume Him. Therefore, we should bring Him gold. Not the gold that is imported with much toil and danger from the far Indies, but that which is forged in our innermost hearts, that is, pure love, which enriches, gives merit to, and gilds all our deeds. Indeed, if we lack pure love, we should turn to God, the divine goldsmith, who urges us, according to St John the Evangelist, to purchase from Him gold that is proved and tested by fire, and which ultimately comes from His own generosity. Furthermore, no incense is as sweet or powerful as a fervent prayer, for, as King David tells us, prayer rises up to God like a pleasing incense offering. Finally, Our Lord has no need for myrrh to preserve His Body from corruption, for death shall have no hold over Him, but do you know what kind of myrrh is most pleasing to Him? The myrrh of blessed mortification. Indeed, our members and our wicked passions and inclinations must be mortified and reined in with the harness of right reason. Therefore, we must do not only what is most agreeable, pleasant, and delightful to our corrupt human nature, but that which we are commanded to do by God, the holy Catholic Church, and our temporal and spiritual superiors. In this way, no one particular type of person shall be singled out to present their gifts to our Saviour. From children He expects innocence of life, from youths He expects purity of heart, from the bachelor He wants moderation and sobriety, and in those approaching mature age He wants to see the fullness of Christian perfection.

On this day, the Child Jesus awaits special gratefulness and thanksgiving from us for revealing His Divine Majesty in a human nature. Like the Kings, He expects precious gifts from all kinds of people. But alas! He seems to be honoured everywhere with nothing but indifference, outrage, sin, and wickedness. He expects of us the gold of pure love, which we owe Him and our neighbour. Instead, we use our material gold to make a god for ourselves, or we squander it on things that make us vain and proud, on lavish banquets and meals, on excesses and gluttony, thereby showing we care little for His great benevolence towards us by being born into the world. He expects from us the sweet incense-offering of fervent prayer; instead, we give Him the foul stench of impurity and lust, our licentiousness, and unfettered lives through which His holy and blessed Name is blasphemed and defamed. He expects from us the myrrh of blessed mortification, but instead we give Him the exact opposite by being neither obedient to His holy law, nor by tempering the members of our bodies; we prefer to hand over the reins to excesses and debauchery, to drunkenness and gluttony, as if there were no Lord to fear, nor a Judge to whom we must be accountable. Tell me then, O man! "Where is He who was born king of the Jews?" Where is the King of the Jews who was recently spiritually born into your hearts and minds on Christmas Day? Where is that kind Guest, the Son of the Blessed Virgin Mary whom you so fervently received in the Most Holy Sacrament of the Altar, after having made a sincere confession and having done penance and made amends? Alas! He has fled to Egypt, He has left your soul and mind, but you were the cause when you sought to murder Him, like Herod of old, when you sought to do away with Him, so to speak, by your sins and misdeeds.

"Be still, and know that I am God" (Ps 45:11). I am God who will be raised up among the Gentiles and glorified on earth. With this He is telling us to detest the world, flee from sin, especially greed and adultery which darken and obscure the light of the intellect. Instead, believe and open the eyes of your hearts so that you may see me in this Child, so that you might love and worship me in my willing humbleness. See, the angels have left their heavenly home, the shepherds have left the sheep, the Kings have left their countries and kingdoms in order to honour and adore me. So, too, should you be prepared to empty yourselves to find me, and having found me, to honour, adore, and love me, for I am your true God.

Thus may it be, O Jesus! You lie in the manger yet you thunder in Heaven; you cannot speak yet you are the Wisdom of the heavenly Father, you cry with your eyes yet you fathom the entire world; you are wrapped in swaddling clothes, yet you are omnipotent; you depend on the breasts of the spotless Virgin, yet you feed all creatures in due season; you are a Child just thirteen days old, yet you belong to eternity. You are God indeed from whom flows all virtue, grace, and benevolence and whether you lie in a manger, or in the straw, or sit on your blessed Mother's lap, you are worthy to be worshipped, praised and honoured by all the Gentiles, nations, and kings of this earth. Therefore, give us grace that we might join the Three Kings in presenting to your Divine Majesty our gifts: the gold of pure love, the frankincense of fervent prayer, and the myrrh of blessed mortification, so that we may enjoy the vision of your countenance in the glory of Heaven. Who lives, etc.

On the First Sunday after Epiphany

Cum factus esset Iesus annorum duodecim, ascenden-
tibus illis Ierosolymam, secundum consuetudinem diei
Festi, remansit puer Iesus in Ierusalem — "When He
was twelve years old, they went up to Jerusalem,
according to the custom of the feast; the child Jesus
stayed behind in Jerusalem" (Lk 2:42–43).

ATHOLIC LISTENERS, IMAGINE THE
great anxiety and sorrow experienced by the Patriarch Tobit and his wife Anna after their young son
Tobias had left them and they had received no news
about his well-being or state of health or happiness. They had sent him to the town of Rages in the land of Media
to collect a sum of money the father has deposited there, and to
conduct some other affairs. But Tobias stayed away much longer than
anticipated, and the parents started to worry, becoming distressed
and anxious and fearing that some misadventure may have happened
to him along the way, or some other danger may have befallen him.
Since the mother's heart was tender, and therefore more easily moved
than the father's, she did not hesitate, as Sacred Scripture tells us, to
run to the hills and byways, scouring the horizon for any sign of her
son's return, and when there was no sign of him she began to mourn
for him, weeping copious tears and lamenting with deep sighs, "Woe,
woe is me my son! Why did we send you to go to a strange country,
the light of our eyes, the staff of our old age, the comfort of our life,
the hope of our posterity?" (Tob 10:4).

Today, no less was the sorrow and anxiety of the Blessed Virgin
Mary and the righteous Joseph upon the loss of their sweet Child,
that is, the blessed Jesus, who remained in Jerusalem without His

parents' knowledge after they had gone to that city to celebrate a certain feast, according to today's Gospel, "When He was twelve years old, they went up to Jerusalem, according to the custom of the feast; the child Jesus stayed behind in Jerusalem." But the sorrow of the Blessed Mother of God, Mary, was great beyond measure because the love she bore her beloved Son was great beyond measure. If the parents of the young Tobias had felt great comfort when they finally saw him returning after his journey, well-nourished and healthy, well-married and financially successful, then imagine the unspeakable joy of the Blessed Virgin Mary and Joseph when after three days they found their Son in the Temple among the rabbis and scholars, who were amazed at the learning and answers of a twelve-year old Child. Before we explain today's Gospel in further detail, let us first pray for the grace of the Holy Spirit through the intercession of the Blessed Virgin Mary by presenting to her the angelic salutation,

Ave Maria

THE ANGELS SANG A MESSAGE OF GREAT JOY AT THE birth of Our Saviour: "Glory to God in Heaven and peace to people on earth." On the eighth day He was circumcised; through His immaculate circumcision our flesh was circumcised according to the spirit. He received the name of Jesus and was honoured by the angels, worshipped by man and feared by the devils. On the thirteenth day He used a star to guide towards Him the Three Kings, who offered Him gold, frankincense, and myrrh. Today we see Him as a twelve-year-old boy who, being eternal of nature, presents Himself as a master of all knowledge and a font of all wisdom. He sits among the scholars, like the sun sits in the middle of our world, and with mature earnestness questions and examines the learned doctors and scholars of the Jewish land. These in turn are amazed and astonished. "And all that heard Him were astonished at His wisdom and His answers" (Lk 2:47). Christ Our Saviour grew in years like every other person, and now having reached the age of twelve years, He daily showed and revealed sure signs of the divine power and supernatural grace hidden within Him. In order to make mankind firmly believe He had indeed assumed our human nature, from His very infancy He subjected Himself to the same wants and needs of the people around Him. The shepherds found Him wrapped in swaddling clothes, the Kings found Him cradled in His mother's lap, and the priest Simeon knew Him as an infant in the Temple; therefore, in no way did He differ from any of the other children. Moreover, it is necessary for our salvation to believe firmly that not only was He made man, but that He is also truly God, whose human and divine natures had been united in one single Person. As St Hilary says, "Let us ever remember to hold fast this truth of our profession, namely, that the Son of God is the Son of Man also. Were He one and not the other, then were He no Saviour for us."[1] He therefore moderated the signs of His divine wisdom and omnipotence, so that as He increased in age the characteristics of His divinity likewise increased and came to be revealed to the world. Furthermore, in order to demonstrate that in His youth He had acquired none of the sins of our human nature, nor the effects of sin, namely ignorance, this Sun of Righteousness today lets shine a few rays of His divinity by acting in a way far superior to anyone of His natural age; thus was He found in the Temple amongst the doctors and scholars, listening to them and asking them questions with such wisdom and respect that they were all amazed and astonished by His modesty and humility, both in the way He questioned them as in the way He listened and answered them.

St Luke the Evangelist gives us the reason Our Saviour today had travelled from Nazareth to Jerusalem, for he wrote, "And His parents went every year to Jerusalem, at the solemn day of the Pasch" (Lk 2:41). They did this to fulfil Almighty God's commandment given in the Book of Exodus, "Three times a year all your men are to appear before the Sovereign Lord, the God of Israel" (Ex 34:23). Since the Pasch was counted among these three feasts, the parents of this sweet Child Jesus took Him to Jerusalem for the occasion. However, it is clear from the afore-mentioned words that the women were not required to attend the feasts, but only the men. God, the prudent Lawgiver, followed the practise of an expert physician when

---

1 *Haec enim confessionis tenenda est ratio, ut sicut Dei Filium, ita et filium hominis meminerimus: quia alterum sine altero nihil spei tribuit ad salutem.* St Hilary of Poitiers, Commentary on Matthew, ch. 16.

he applies medication to a sore member in such a way that the healthy members are not harmed or affected; He well knows the tenderness of the women-folk, so He took care that those things pertaining to the propagation of religion should not harm their purity in any way. Therefore, it would seem more reasonable for the women to stay home together, rather than having to walk the streets and roads, thereby avoiding the public domain. Even though the Blessed Virgin Mary was not obligated by this commandment, she nevertheless chose to accompany her Son, for she could not bear to be parted a single moment from her sweet Jesus. Not only did she go out of devotion to her Son, but she also felt drawn, so to speak, by her Son's geniality. She was not bound by the written Law but the law of love obliged her to go. Of course, she could not suffer any danger to her purity, which was greater than the angels', for she was in the company of Purity Itself. But let us not dwell on the Virgin Mary's love, rather let us observe, Catholic Listeners, the greater love with which Our Saviour was kindled to advance the salvation of mankind. Observe how the Blessed Jesus, while still in His tender youth, wearied Himself by undertaking a difficult journey with His parents to celebrate this feast, on the one hand, in order to honour His heavenly Father, and on the other hand to humbly fulfil the Law He Himself had given. His actions were indeed praiseworthy, seeing that He had come into the world to be a mirror of perfection, humility, and submissiveness, "My food is to do the will of my Father" (Jn 4:34). In this way He gave us a reminder to follow in His footsteps, meaning that we, too, should always be humble and that we should take care to celebrate the obligatory feast days, and to fulfil the will of our heavenly Father by observing His divine commandments.

When the feast day had come to an end, "the child Jesus stayed behind in Jerusalem." Not to conduct affairs, not through the negligence or forgetfulness of His parents, but because of His devotion and desire to show the world, even from His youth, His concern and care for mankind, and His desire to promote true religion and an increase in honour towards His heavenly Father. In this He wanted to give us an example of how we might, from our part, (depending on whether our strength, our daily worries, and neighbourly love permits us) continually use our time in virtuous deeds and prayers, and in salvific and sanctifying practices. However, He did not notify His parents of His intentions, knowing well that they would have been too concerned and worried at the thought of leaving Him alone in the city of Jerusalem. They thought He was in the company of their friends and relatives, and when in the evening they did not find Him among that company, they quickly turned back after a day's travel, seeking Him among anyone they encountered along the way. But they did not find Him, and so, worried and anxious, they entered Jerusalem. But, some may say, this was negligence on the parents' part, for how could a twelve year old child go missing so easily? Listen to the opinion of Cardinal Baronius: His parents were ready to leave Jerusalem, together with the company of friends. They had been somewhat unexpectedly detained, though doubtless not without divine permission, and so they let the Child go on ahead with His friends. He did indeed go on ahead, but, unbeknownst to His parents, He did not leave the city, and, as so many children might, He left the travelling party and wandered off, going a different way. That night, when His parents had entered an inn, they could not find the Child in the company of friends, and they realised they had been misled. No tongue can describe the anxiety and fear Mary's tender heart must have felt. How many sighs and tears must she have shed! This is not surprising, Catholic Listeners, for even King David had grieved the death of his son Absalom, who was immoral and a murderer, and was even willing to die for him, "O Absalom, my son, my son Absalom, would that I had died for you!" (2 Sam 18:33). And if the Patriarch Jacob, who was surrounded by many children, lamented bitterly over the death of Joseph, whom he thought dead, then how anxious, alarmed, and sorrowful must the Blessed Virgin Mary have been when she realised she had lost her only Son, and what a Son at that! She was sad, partly because she was deprived of the sweet, loving face of her Most Beloved; and partly because of her meekness, for she considered herself to be unworthy to be the custodian of such a valuable treasure, from which she had now, in her humble and reverent opinion, been deprived. We can well imagine her raising her eyes to Heaven, beseeching our Heavenly Father, 'O merciful God! If I have in any way angered the eyes of your eternal, Divine Majesty, if I have in any way sinned or offended you, then see, I am ready to receive the punishments of your divine justice. You, O gentle, kind Father! had let a shining star rise in the east, with which to guide the Three Kings from distant countries to the crib, so that they might come to know your only-begotten Son. Send me a ray of your divine light, that it might lead me directly to the arms of your Son, so that I might know His whereabouts. O Angel of the Lord! who announced to me the glad tidings that I would conceive and bear a Son, if what you said to me was true, "the Lord is with you," how can He now have filled me with this sadness by departing from me, and depriving me of His sweet presence? And you, my sweet Son Jesus, what did you see in me that made you depart so suddenly? I pray you, do not hide any longer from me your countenance, but let my ears again hear your voice, let me embrace your sweet cheeks, let me kiss your blessed mouth.' Such were the sighs and laments of the Blessed Virgin Mary. We can also imagine what the righteous Joseph did, for he was wounded with a double sadness, both for loss of the Child, as well as the compassion he felt for his beloved wife. He did not let his feet rest, his eyes saw no sleep, and as he passed the night in the company of the sorrowing Mother of God, he fasted on the bread of affliction and the water of tears. This sorrowful Mother, having sought her Son and not having found Him, now experienced greater pain than when she bore Him, for when bearing Him she experienced no pain at all. And so she could have named Him a child of sorrow, rather than a child of joy, just as Rachel, who, having experienced the excessive pain of a difficult labour after bearing her second son, and feeling that she was close to death, called her son Ben Oni, which means 'son of my mourning,' but his father Jacob called him Benjamin, which means 'son of my right hand.'

O Catholic Listeners, if there is any love at all within your hearts for the Blessed Jesus, then learn from the Blessed Virgin how to search and find that Beloved One, not for her benefit, but for yours and your salvation. In a spiritual sense, Jesus was never separated from His Blessed Mother, but alas! we have unfortunately been separated from Him so many times, every time we commit a mortal sin. Therefore, if we want to be able to find Him again, we need to seek Him with tears, sorrow, and contrition, just as His Mother sought Him. We must beseech that same Blessed Mother to assist us with her prayers and merits, so that we might easily find Him. Think how this Blessed Virgin is like a pure dove that can both soar through the heavens and hide in the niches of a cliff; she both contemplates the divine mystery and deals with the angels. See how she now races through the streets and alleyways, spurred on by great love, sighing and asking everyone she meets, "Have you seen him, whom my soul loves? I adjure you, O daughters of Jerusalem, if you find my beloved, that you tell him I am sick with love. But what is your beloved like, O fairest of all women? My beloved is all radiant and ruddy" (Song 3:3; 5:8; 5:10). He is white as man and ruddy as God; white because of His Incarnation, and red-hued because of His divinity; white in mercy and red in righteousness. This is the manner in which a Catholic Christian should find Jesus after having lost Him through sin, namely, he must with true meekness, perfect contrition and sincere sorrow search the streets of his life and the alleys of his soul and conscience in order to purify himself through the holy Sacrament of Confession, thereby once more being able to enjoy the presence of Jesus through His friendship and by His divine grace. For when Reuben, the Patriarch Jacob's first son, did not find his younger brother Joseph in the cistern where he had advised his brothers to put him, rather than kill him, he tore his clothes in grief and could not be comforted, filling the surrounding countryside with his cries, "The lad is gone, and I, where shall I go?" (Gn 37:30). How fortunate should we be if our hearts displayed only a small portion of similar sorrow upon losing our sweet brother Jesus through our sins. Even so, if we have lost Him we should not tear our garments, but our hearts, saying, after the example of the Blessed Mary, "Have you not seen him, whom my soul loves?" O Jesus! By my sins I have spurned your friendship and grace. Where have you gone? How will I be able to find you again? You are the way, the truth and the life. Without the right way, where shall I go, except on crooked paths and into dead ends? Without the truth, where shall I go, except to fall into error and heresy? Without life, where shall I go, except to death and damnation? Show me, then, your face, O Jesus! and I shall be saved, for the right way and sound truth have no other end than eternal life.

But let us return to the holy Gospel. While the Blessed Virgin Mary was anxiously going about trying to find her Son, who had meanwhile taken care of His physical needs? Who was it that gave Him food and drink? It is unlikely He would not have eaten; nor is it conceivable that He miraculously produced meals for Himself, seeing that He Himself had not yet performed any miracles. We must therefore assume that He spent these three days asking for food and begging His bread from door to door. This was the opinion of St Bonaventure in his *Apologia pauperum*. St Bernard thought the same, as did several other holy Fathers who based their opinion on the words of King David, which were spoken in the Person of Our Saviour, "But I am a beggar, and poor" (Ps 39:18). Whatever the case may be, I do not doubt there would be anyone present here today who, if this innocent Child were to come to his door, would not straight away cheerfully invite Him in and generously treat Him to a hearty meal. Even so, Catholic Listeners, while we may not have seen Him personally standing in front of our door, begging our help and support, we can nonetheless earn the same indulgence and reward, for He tells us, "Come, you that are blessed by my Father, inherit the kingdom prepared for you from the foundation of the world" (Mt 25:34). But for what reason should we experience this good fortune? He adds to this, "For I was hungry and you gave me food, I was thirsty and you gave me something to drink" (Mt 25:35). But the righteous will say, we have not performed these charitable deeds to you personally, and that is why He answers in the same passage of Scripture, "Truly I tell you, just as you did it to one of the least of these my brothers, you did it to me" (Mt 25:40). With this He is saying that on the Day of Judgement we shall receive a great reward for the charity we have shown towards the poor and needy, for we would have done it to Him.

It therefore seems likely that by going from door to door begging His bread, Our Saviour wants to set an example, to rich people, on the one hand, by spurring them on to works of charity and mercy, and on the other hand to the poor by giving them comfort and urging them to bear their poverty with patience. He also wants to assure all those who, out of love for Him, have forsaken everything, thereby sharing in His exile and poverty; they will receive an abundance of heavenly gifts and enjoy His sweet presence among the angels in the glory of Heaven, just as the Blessed Virgin Mary rejoiced upon finding Him in the Temple among the doctors and scholars. See how this blessed Child sits among the scholars as the focal point from which flows wisdom, just as many lines converge on one central point. "All wisdom is from Him, and has always been with Him, and is before all time" (Sir 1:1). He sat among the scholars, explaining the correct meaning of the Scriptures, "listening to them and asking them questions" (Lk 2:46), and impressing upon them all the more deeply, by means of wise and prudent answers, the heavenly and divine mysteries of His Incarnation and divinity.

Oh, if only one could be found worthy enough to have been able to be present at that learned meeting! Oh, to have heard the discourses of the Eternal Wisdom, who fills the angels with knowledge, and makes children's tongues fluent and eloquent. Oh, how sweet it must have been to have seen His gracious, loving countenance. How pleasant to have heard the sweet, flowing, powerful words issuing forth from that blessed mouth! I do not doubt that the angels themselves would have been amazed at the humility of their Creator, seeing that the uncreated Wisdom that had descended from Heaven to be a divine teacher had now placed Himself amongst the rabbis and common doctors as a pupil and student.

O Blessed Virgin Mary, who can express the joy and gladness you must have felt when you found your blessed Son, whom you anxiously sought for three days, not among unsavoury companions, nor in illicit places where parents these days often seek their children, and find them, but you found Him in the Temple concerned with divine teachings, eager to promote and increase the honour and glory of His heavenly Father. There is no doubt that this brilliant sun, Christ Our Saviour, had illumined her soul and banished from her heart the dark clouds of sorrow and anxiety previously found there. She must surely have invited her friends, the angels, to rejoice with her, perhaps using these words found in the Evangelist St Luke's Gospel, "Rejoice with me, for I have found the coin that I lost" (Lk 15:9). I have found my lost coin, my Son, my Jesus, whom I had lost. But what causes the most astonishment is that which the Evangelist Luke writes further on in today's Gospel, namely, "He was obedient to them." For when the blessed Jesus saw His beloved Mother He immediately stood up and left the company of doctors to go to her. This is an example to all young men, daughters, and children, that they, too, need to be obedient and submissive towards their parents. For when parents want to prevent them from going to the inn, or when they are punished for committing some wickedness, or are scolded for their rough behaviour, children should not murmur and complain, nor should they be obstinate and rebellious. Instead, let them remember Almighty God's Fourth Commandment, "Honour your father and your mother, that you may live long on the earth" (Dt 5:16). Let children, I say, remember the words of today's Gospel, "He was obedient to them." The blessed Jesus, who was not only human but also truly God, was also obedient to His parents. Therefore, if God wanted to be submissive to His parents, how much more should children show every honour and obedience to their parents, from whom they received life, from whom they received instruction and education, and from whom they may expect so many good things and happiness. Even so, when the blessed Jesus approached His Mother, she said to Him, "Child, why have you treated us like this? Look, your father and I have been searching for you in great anxiety" (Lk 2:48). But He answered them, "How is it that you sought me? Did you not know that I must be about my Father's business?" (Lk 2:49). In other words, He said to them 'did you not know that I first of all have to be concerned with promoting and increasing the glory of my heavenly Father?' Even though this is the answer of a twelve-year-old boy, it nonetheless comes forth from the mouth of Truth; therefore, the daughters, young men, servants, and children would do well to imprint these words deep in the memory of their hearts. So then, if their parents or teachers refuse to give them time to attend the Holy Sacrifice of the Mass on Sundays and holydays, or if on those same days they are ordered to do menial work, or if they are forced to do something that is improper or illicit, they may freely answer: "Did you not know that I must be about my Father's business?" Father, mother, teacher, or mistress, do you not know that on Sundays and holydays I must hear the Holy Sacrifice of the Mass, that I may not do any menial work, or anything that is illicit, but rather that I must tend to my soul and my salvation, thereby helping to increase the glory of my heavenly Father? In case you do not know, I shall teach you. For we must avoid sin and work at our salvation. "God has more right to be obeyed than men" (Acts 5:29). We should obey God and our spiritual leaders more than anyone else, including our natural parents.

So then, Catholic Listeners, we must pray to Jesus, who chose to be sought for three days by His beloved Mother. May He similarly inspire within us the desire to zealously seek Him with great affection after we have lost Him through our carelessness, so that once again having found Him, we may partake of His grace here on earth and enjoy His countenance in the heavenly glory of the life to come. Who lives, etc.

On the Second Sunday after Epiphany

Nuptiae factae sunt in Cana Galileae, et erat Mater Iesu ibi: vocatus est autem et Iesus, et discipuli eius nuptias — "There was a wedding in Cana of Galilee: and the mother of Jesus was there. And Jesus and His disciples were also invited to the wedding" (Jn 2:1–2).

CATHOLIC LISTENERS, CHRIST OUR Saviour used various ways and means to reveal His glory and divinity to people. He demonstrated this, for instance, on the day of His birth by sending angels and celestial spirits from Heaven to the shepherds to announce to them, "Behold, I bring you good news that will cause great joy for all the people. Today in the town of David a Saviour has been born to you; he is Christ, the Lord" (Lk 2:10). On the day of His circumcision, He also revealed His glory and divinity, and He received the name of Jesus, which was the name the angel had given Him before He was conceived. "And they called Him Jesus." His identity was revealed by a star which He had placed in the heavens in order to bring the Three Kings to Bethlehem, who then recognised in Him a glorious, divine king. The righteous Simeon foretold that He would raise up many in Israel, and the devout widow Anna had given a good testimony of Him to all those who awaited the redemption of Israel. But today Christ Himself, who is truly God and truly man, begins to display the first fruits of His divinity to His beloved Bride, the holy Catholic Church, by performing His first miracle at the wedding feast in Cana of Galilee, by changing water into wine. As St John the Evangelist tells us in today's Gospel, "Jesus did this, the first of his signs, in Cana of Galilee" (Jn 2:11a). Of course, there are those who will try to conclude from this that Our Saviour performed no miracles during His youth, otherwise the Evangelist would not have written that this was the beginning of His miracles, but this conclusion is without basis, for St John the Evangelist is here speaking about the miracles Christ performed in public in order to reveal the glory of His power to the world, as revealed by these words, "He revealed His glory, and His disciples believed in Him" (Jn 2:11). Of these public signs, says St John the Evangelist, the first was the miracle recorded in today's Gospel, namely, when Christ turned water into wine. Nonetheless, it can certainly be possible that in His younger days He performed many miracles of which His parents, and not many other people, were aware. The Prophet Habakkuk long ago foretold that Our Saviour would reveal His glory through miracles, for when he mentioned the coming of the Son of God into the world, he added that, "His brightness shall be as the light" (Hab 3:4). When explaining this passage, the learned Rupert wrote that Our Saviour used His wondrous works and miracles to reveal His divinity to the world, not only through deeds, but also using a particular, evident clarity, just as the clarity of the day is a sure sign of the sun's presence. Seeing that the intercession of the Blessed Virgin Mary was the cause of today's sublime miracle where water was turned into wine, for she said to her Son, "they have no wine", then let us, too, pray through her for the grace of the Holy Spirit to say something wise and instructive, by presenting to her the angelic greeting,

Ave Maria

THE WORKS THAT ARE DAILY WROUGHT IN THE WORLD by Almighty God are so wondrous, and the creatures He daily creates for our needs and comfort are so extraordinary that not only should they lead us to a closer knowledge of the Divine Majesty, but also to a more generous love and affection for Him. St Augustine gives evidence of this when he is moved by the wonderful works of God to write in his *Confessions*, "And also the heavens, and earth, and all that is therein, behold, on every side they say that I should love Thee."[1]

---

1 *Et caelum, et terra, et omnia quae in eis sunt, ecce undique mihi dicunt, ut te amem.* St Augustine, Confessions, Book 10, ch. 6.

No wonder, for all creatures are like tongues whose sound constantly reminds us to praise the omnipotent Creator, even though, as the same Augustine testifies, the divine works and miracles with which He governs the entire world and administers the entire creation, are, by their familiar constancy, held in low esteem.[2] What is more, man's intellect is often clouded by the fog of wickedness, and this prevents him from clearly recognising Almighty God in His creation. For instance, if someone places on his nose an eyeglass made of red or green glass, then everything will appear to be red or green. Similarly, if someone is infected with a particular tendency to wickedness, he will try to turn everything to his own profit or advantage, giving himself matter to sin. And so the avaricious will try to amass money or possessions; the impure will seek to lust after the flesh, and the gluttonous will seek the comforts of the body. Therefore, these people pay no consideration to God's daily works of creation and the wondrous composition or diversity of creatures He has made; consequently, they do not lift up their hearts in order to obtain a clearer knowledge and greater love for Almighty God.

It was therefore necessary, so to speak, for Almighty God to perform certain works outside of the normal course of nature, so that by witnessing these works we would not only come to know His omnipotence and Godhead, but we would also love the same. For a son does not have much regard for his father's daily upkeep, and thinks only about his inheritance, yet if he were to put some money in his father's wallet, he would be moved to see how happy that would make him, and he would resolve to love his father even more. So even if we humans were able to fill the entire world with food and drink, we still could not change water into wine. We humans, I say, are quickly moved by this extraordinary event to want to know God better and to love Him more fervently. Catholic Listeners, God's mercy and goodness are unfathomable, for He has devised so many different ways to draw us closer to Himself. St Augustine commented on this, and he cried out from the depths of his heart, "O Lord, who am I, or what can I give you, you who have led me to your love by so many different ways and means?" Man would, without a doubt,

---

2   St Augustine, see Tractate 24, On the Gospel of John, 1.

be ashamed when he thinks about how many signs of love God has given him, and daily continues to give him; and he would be more ashamed when he considers his own apathy and carelessness to return that love to his Creator and Saviour. Our Saviour demonstrated one of these extraordinary signs of love in today's Gospel, where He was invited to a wedding together with His Blessed Mother. "There was a wedding in Cana of Galilee: and the mother of Jesus was there," and as we know, it was there that He changed water into wine.

Now, some of you might be wondering how it is that Our Saviour, together with His Blessed Mother and His disciples, had wanted to be present at this wedding feast of worldly people, from which the clergy normally excuse themselves, so that they would not be seen to be partaking of, or condoning, the disorderliness and impropriety and the excesses and gluttony normally found at such events. This might seem a mystery to us, but, as St Cyril tells us, Christ, along with His mother and disciples, wanted to be present there to show that marriage was an honourable matter of which He approved and which He instituted by His very presence.[3] St Augustine is of the same opinion when he says that Our Saviour did this to show that marriage was a worthy and sacred affair and His own institution,[4] for He well knew that there would later be heretics, hypocritical liars and other unsound people, as St Paul tells us, who would assert that marriage was an evil, and so would forbid people to marry. Among those was a certain Saturninus, of whom St Irenaeus wrote, and also a Marcion, whom St Jerome mentions, and St Epiphanius writes about a certain Tatianus, and there are some others; yet all of them with one voice denounced marriage as an evil matter, saying thereby that it was only introduced because of Adam's sin, opining that there would have been no marriage in the original state of innocence. But they were all wrong. Our Saviour quashed and overcame these heresies and errors by gracing this wedding feast with His presence and endorsing marriage as a praiseworthy act by performing a sublime miracle. Similarly, just as Our Saviour had chosen to be baptised in the river Jordan by John the Baptist, thereby sanctifying the waters

---

3   See St Cyril of Alexandria, On the Gospel According to John, Book 2, ch. 1.
4   See Augustine, Tractate 9, On the Gospel of John, 2.

by touching them, so to speak, with His blessed humanity in the ceremony of baptism, so He had chosen to be present at this marriage, so that by the witness of His presence He would endorse the value and sacredness of marriage, of which God was the Author. For Almighty God had united our first parents in the earthly Paradise, where He infused in Adam the first strong sparks of love towards His wife, and Adam said, "This is now bone of my bones and flesh of my flesh" (Gn 2:23).

Married people, then, can easily understand the love and unity there must be amongst themselves; they must always be honest and reasonable. For even though children must with singular love obey their parents according to Almighty God's commandment, "Honour your father and your mother, so that your days may be long in the land" (Ex 20:12), so much more must a man love his wife with his whole heart. For in Sacred Scripture in the Book of Genesis we read, "That is why a man leaves his father and mother and is united to his wife" (Gn 2:24). If someone wants to know in which manner a man should love his wife, then know that he must love her as Christ the Son of God loves His holy Catholic Church, for whose grace and favour He died a bitter death. St Paul the Apostle especially exhorts husbands to love in this way, when he writes, "Husbands, love your wives." Tell us, St Paul, in which way? Certainly not with the kind of hypocritical love with which Prince Shechem loved Dinah, nor with the kind of flattering love with which the strong Sampson loved Delilah, nor with the egoistic love of Adonijah towards Abishag, so that he could obtain much wealth and property, nor with the kind of dishonest, impure, and unchaste love with which Sarah loved her seven husbands. Then how should husbands love their wives? With affectionate, pure love, "just as Christ loved the Church" (Eph 5:25).

Christ Our Saviour so loved the Church that He married her, so that she would bring forth spiritual children for God's honour and for their own salvation. For example, the holy Apostles, Martyrs, Confessors, and Virgins are all born, not of perishable but of imperishable seed. "Through the word of the living God," says St Peter the Apostle. Christ did not marry the Church because He felt enticed or moved by her beauty, her abundance, her comfort, or sweetness. Not at all! The only thing that moved Him was God's glory and the salvation of the human race. In a similar way should marriage be entered into, not just in order to beget children to populate the earth, and even less in order to satisfy the desires of the flesh, but principally to raise up children in order to lead them to salvation, thereby filling Heaven with the elect. Almighty God expressed this same motive when He spoke the blessing over Adam and Eve, "Be fruitful and increase in number; fill the earth and subdue it" (Gn 1:28). St Chrysostom, when commenting on this passage from Genesis, chapter one, astutely observed that this first blessing of being fruitful, multiplying and filling the earth was the same one pronounced over the animals in verse 22, but the last section, "and subdue it," was only spoken to man, for only the righteous and chosen ones will possess the heavenly earth of the living, and shall subdue the world, spurning everything that is temporal and fleeting. Marriage was therefore instituted to fill the world with God-fearing, devout people, and Heaven with Saints and the elect. Those people err greatly who only see marriage as an occasion of inheriting great wealth, or as a means of satisfying the desires of the flesh, or from some other human or worldly aspect. Is it any wonder that we find in such marriages great bitterness and difficulties, poverty and need? No, it is no wonder, seeing that the first and main reason for poverty and difficulty found daily among the people is this, namely, because they set their hearts on worldly, temporal things. They rely too much on their own wisdom and ingenuity and not enough on God's Providence.

Therefore, if married people desire a marriage that is free from burdens and hardship, they need only focus on the content of today's Gospel, that is, they need to invite Jesus and Mary to their wedding. Jesus needs to be there so that He can supply any temporal deficiency from His Divine Providence and lighten any burden. Mary needs to be present so she can be like a mirror of virtue for any bride or housewife, and to be, I say, their Patroness and Advocate. Observe, Catholic Listeners, how Jesus, who had been invited to this wedding at Cana of Galilee, at once used His Divine Providence to remedy the lack of wine, and how Mary obtained this miracle of her Son through her intercession. It is lamentable that many people do not receive

179

Jesus into their homes because they do not run the affairs of their households, their commerce and businesses, according to the rules of Christian justice. True, they might worship Him in church, but they drive Him away from their tables and families. They outwardly profess Him as their God, but in their homes, their lives, their work, there often reigns another god, namely, the devil, whom St Paul the Apostle calls "the god of this age" (2 Cor 4:4). These people do not rely on God's Providence but on their own unjust business, on lies and deception, on pleasures and deceit. That is why Almighty God often confounds everything they do; He changes, as it were, their wine into water, their wisdom into folly, and all their work into a vain cloud of smoke, thereby setting into action what He once spoke through the mouth of the Prophet Haggai, "When you brought it home, I blew it away" (Hag 1:9). In other words, what He is saying to those people who are concerned day and night about things, 'You thought you had great riches that would never run out, but I have taken them away, I have blown them away as the wind blows away the sand.'

The miracle Jesus performed in today's Gospel was intended to show His kindness and generosity towards the newly-wed couple who were suffering a lack of wine. More than that, it was also designed to assure us that He shall not leave us in any kind of want, provided we invite Him to our wedding, provided we receive Him into our homes, provided we adopt His divine law with which to rule our families and affairs, and provided that we first of all seek the Kingdom of God and His righteousness. Regarding that subject, we might well say together with King David, "I have not seen the just man forsaken, nor his offspring eating bread" (Ps 36:25). Moreover, seeing that the miracle in today's Gospel occurred through the intervention of the Blessed Virgin Mary, when she said to her Son, "They have no wine," we detect in this her concern on the one hand, and the power of her prayer on the other. She showed her concern by wanting the newly-wed couple to avoid embarrassment because the wine had run out. The power of her prayers was shown when her Son, Christ Our Saviour, was moved by her compassionate words to order the servants to fill the jars with water, which He then changed into an excellent, delicate wine. This was His first public miracle.

There would simply not be enough time for me to preach about the concern, the mercy, and the compassion the Blessed Virgin shows towards mankind, and the prestige she has to obtain for us all graces and favours. Let me just say just a few words to help spur us on to serving her. Seeing that she was so eager to lend temporal assistance to those who had invited her to the wedding feast, as we read in today's Gospel, there can be no doubt that she would be even more concerned about the spiritual welfare of the souls of those who honour and devoutly serve her. For if her Son's respect for her here on earth were such that she could encourage Him to perform His first public miracle, then it is certain that the prestige she enjoyed in Heaven would certainly not be altered in any way, nor would there be a decline in the love she bears for mankind, or a decrease in her benevolence. Instead, there would be a heightening of her love for those who serve her and for those who are just and godly. For among the Saints and blessed ones, the very act of possessing the glory of Heaven has the effect of removing whatever is imperfect or incompatible with the state of holiness. Similarly then, it was through her favour that the very first miracle occurred, the effects of which shall continually flow through that same channel of grace to all those who honour Mary in this world and who faithfully serve her. Through her did we obtain the Saviour of the world, and so through her we will need to pick the fruits that lead to our salvation; through her we obtained the true vineyard laden with the wine of divine grace, "I am the true vine"; is it then any wonder that we must receive through her the fruits, that is, the wine of God's love and divine friendship?

I know very well that the Reformed Brethren oppose us on this point, and that they would completely refuse to admit that either the Blessed Virgin Mary or any of the Saints may be invoked by us, and even less that these Saints might pray for us in Heaven. All this despite the above being confirmed by Sacred Scripture, for as King David says, "I lift up my eyes to the mountains, from whence shall come my help" (Ps 120:1). St Augustine interprets this as 'I lifted up my eyes to the mountains, that is, towards the Saints, from whence shall come my help.' This has been approved and accepted by the learned and holy Church Fathers for more than a thousand years.

St Jerome, too, in his *Liber contra Vigilantium* refuted the heretic Vigilantius by writing, "Stephen, the first Christian martyr, entreats pardon for his persecutors; and when once he has entered on his life of glory with Christ, shall he have less power than before?"[5] And St Chrysostom says, "For if Paul, when he was here, loved men so much, that when he had the choice of departing and being with Christ, he chose to be here, much more will he there display a warmer affection."[6] With good reason, therefore, may we say the same of the Blessed Virgin Mary. For if she showed concern by asking her Son to address the lack of wine at the wedding feast of Cana in Galilee, how much more shall she in Heaven address our prayers and supplications by interceding on our behalf to supply the means and graces that are lacking towards our salvation? Therefore, there can be no doubt that, even from Heaven, she will assist those Catholic persons who invite her to their wedding feast, who call to her with all their heart and who seek to please her by their godly lives. Therefore, despite the raging of the Reformed Brethren, we should, and indeed must, say together with St Augustine, "Holy Mary, be a help to the helpless, strength to the fearful, comfort to the sorrowful, pray for the people, plead for the clergy, intercede for all holy women consecrated to God; may all who keep your sacred commemoration feel the might of your assistance."[7]

Perhaps someone will say, how can you commend us to seek the Blessed Virgin Mary's help and assistance when her plea might be refused or she may receive a stern response, as happened in today's Gospel when Our Saviour said to her, "Woman, what is that to do

---

5 *Stephanus primus martyr in Christo, pro persecutoribus veniam deprecatus est, et postquam cum Christo esse caeperit, minus valebit?* St Jerome, Against Vigilantius, Book 1, ch. 6.

6 *Si Paulus cum adhuc hic esset, usque adeo dilexit homines, ut cum dissolvi et cum Christo esse cuperet, elegerit hic esse, multo magis illic serventiorem amorem ostendit.* St Chrysostom, On the Epistle to the Romans, Homily 32.

7 *Sancta Maria succurre miseris, iuva pusillanimes, refove flebiles, ora pro populo, interveni pro clero, intercede pro devoto femineo sexu, sentiant omnes tuum iuvamen, quicumque celebrant tuam sanctam commemorationem.* The author follows a long-held convention that attributed this prayer to St Augustine. However, it is now known that the author is probably Bishop Fulbert of Chartres (c. 951–1029). The prayer appears in his *Sermo IX, De Annuntiatione Dominica.*

with you or me?" (Jn 2:4). It is true that this is the opinion of the Reformed Brethren, but we need not believe them, Catholic Listeners, seeing they are no devotees of Mary. For just as bees extract their sweet honey from the same flowers from which spiders suck their venom, so do the heretics extract erroneous poison from the same words of Sacred Scripture from which Catholics source the sweet honey of truth. We see an example of this in today's Gospel in the words, "Woman, what is that to do with you or me?" We Catholics, who are illumined by the light of faith, detect in these words nothing but praise for the Blessed Virgin, whereas the heretics in their erroneous ways use them to blaspheme against her. St Augustine wrote that the Manicheans and followers of Valentinian drew from these words the conclusion that Mary could not truly have been the Mother of Jesus Christ, because when He addressed her with the words, "Woman, what is that to do with you or me?" it was as if He had said, they claim, 'Woman, I have nothing in common with you,' or, 'Woman, I know you not as my mother.' But this slander has clearly been refuted by St John, also in today's Gospel, when the Evangelist twice calls the Virgin Mary the Mother of Jesus Christ. The first time was at the wedding feast, "and the Mother of Jesus was there," and again later, "the Mother of Jesus said to Him." St Jerome writes that yet others try to prove that the title "woman" is evidence, that after she had given birth Mary had lost her virginity. Those people who hold this opinion are wrong, because in Sacred Scripture the title "woman" is given to both virgins as well as married women. St Augustine demonstrates this when he takes an example from a passage in the Book of Genesis, chapter three, where Eve is called "woman" before she had known her husband Adam, "And the woman saw that the tree was good to eat." And further on, "and the serpent said to the woman," and again, "the woman, who you gave to me."

So then, when it comes to understanding the answer Our Saviour gave His Mother in today's Gospel, "Woman, what is that to do with you or me?", we must give credence to the explanations of the Catholic Apologists, such as Sts Justin, Euthymius, Epiphanius, and many others, who interpret for us the words "what is that to do with you or me?" These words, of course, refer to the lack of wine, and

Our Lord is saying, 'this is not our concern but that of the hosts who invited us.' Listen to the words of St Justin. When he was questioned whether it was lawful or not to disdain one's parents, he answered, No! And yet, said his detractors, it seems that Christ did disdain them when He said, "what is that to do with you or me?" But the Saint answered that there was no disrespect in Christ's answer, for the meaning of it was, as I myself said before, "If the wine runs out, then it is not my concern, nor yours. If, however, because of your great charity you are still concerned that the wine will run out, then tell the servants to do what I tell them. The Lord's words do not reprove His Mother but rather pay respect to her." Thus speaks St Justin, along with Sts Epiphanius and Euthymius. Both St Augustine and St Gregory who quotes him, say that when Our Saviour said, "Woman, what is that to do with you or me?" He was actually saying that she should not concern herself with what had been commanded Him by His heavenly Father by performing miracles and wonders. This is how Catholic scholars generally understand these words, which clearly show that Our Saviour did not refuse His Mother anything, for He immediately fulfilled her wish and desire. But there is more He wanted to teach and instruct us by these words, namely, that when dealing with spiritual things, that is, in important things that pertain to our salvation, we should not concern ourselves with what the flesh desires, but rather with what right reason and God's will demands of us. Furthermore, Our Saviour desires that we should learn from His holy and beloved Mother a truly firm and perfect meekness; we should be grateful, we should not despair or become narrow-minded or grumble if He were to refuse us something or if we did not immediately receive what we asked for, because God, from whom all good things come, knows what is best for us. Observe the example of Tobias, who longed to depart this world because of the many trials and tribulations that assailed him. Almighty God sent even more sorrow his way through the long absence of his son. So, too, St Peter, when trying to rebuke Our Saviour to protect Him from the terrible torments and bitter death He was to suffer for the redemption of mankind, heard the frightening words, "Get behind me, Satan! You do not have in mind the concerns of God, but merely human concerns" (Mk 8:33). Nonetheless, these holy and perfect men had been patient through their deep sense of humility, which is the root, the foundation, and the mother of all the other virtues. In a similar way, the words found in today's Gospel did not affect Mary, the Blessed Mother of God, but she was strengthened in hope, seeing that she said to those serving at table, "Do whatever He tells you."

So then, Catholic Listeners, if any one of you should desire a prosperous marriage, a marriage without bitterness or troubles, poverty or scarcity, then you should invite Jesus and Mary to your wedding. It is in Jesus that the bridegroom must place his trust, and not in his own resourcefulness, or the world's. It is in Mary that the bride must see a mirror of all the virtues, and she should follow her in all meekness and humility. If they do this, the newlyweds will enjoy divine graces here on earth, and the glory of Heaven in the life to come. Who lives, etc.

On the Third Sunday after Epiphany

Accessit ad Iesum centurio, rogans eum, et dicens,
Domine, puer meus iacet in domo paralyticus — "A
centurion came to Jesus, asking for help. 'Lord,' he
said, 'my servant lies at home paralyzed'" (Mt 8:5–6).

CATHOLIC LISTENERS, THERE WAS a certain writer called Comestor, who commented in his discourse on the fifth chapter of the Book of Exodus, that when the Patriarch Moses was in Egypt, he had been renowned not only for the lustre of his excellent deeds and wondrous miracles, but also for the extraordinary beauty of his countenance. When he wandered along the public streets, his enemies took fright, yet his kindness and generosity had won him the grace and benevolence of all his people. The rays emanating from his kindly face encouraged and emboldened the country folk to flock to him, for they much preferred his presence to Pharaoh's deceptive whims and the hardships and miseries of the desert. Given that these graces were to be found in Moses the Patriarch, what then should we say about the Son of God, Christ our Saviour, who was the most wondrous of all human beings and fairest among the children of men? "You are more beautiful than the sons of men" (Ps 44:3). We may surely say that all kinds of people have been moved by His comeliness, His loving kindness, and the sweetness of His countenance. Observe how at His birth He drew towards Him the shepherds, and in the crib He attracted the Three Kings; in the flight to Egypt He caused the idols to fall to the ground; in His youth He discussed matters in the Temple and received the approval of the rabbis and teachers. Today we see Him as an adult, coming down the mountain followed by a large crowd of people who have no intention of leaving Him, for they were no doubt attracted by the friendliness of His features. As He was approaching the town of Capernaum, a centurion, who had possibly been convinced by the accounts of His miracles and attracted by His divine beauty, approached Him, begging that his paralyzed servant be healed, saying, "Lord, my servant lies at home paralyzed, suffering terribly." The centurion's request was heard, he was even praised, and his servant was healed. Our Saviour showed His mercy and omnipotence, the centurion showed his faith and humility. The lesson for all of us is that we need to show pity and compassion, mercy and empathy for our neighbours, as St Peter the Apostle teaches us when he exhorts us to "have compassion" (1 Pet 3). Have sympathy and compassion on your neighbours, share their misfortune and hardship, their illnesses and worries. Before I elaborate on this any further, let us first pray for the grace of the Holy Spirit through the intercession of the Blessed Virgin Mary, by presenting to her the angelic salutation,

Ave Maria

MARCILIUS FICINUS ONCE CLAIMED THAT THE PHILOSopher Plato would quote a proverb that said that a good and loyal friend is nothing more than a mirror.[1] In other words, a true friend is like a mirror which reflects the likeness, the constitution, and the complexion of the one he loves. For example, if he is happy, the other should also be happy; if he is sad, the other should also be sad; when one laughs, the other should also laugh and if one is sick, the other should also be sick. The centurion in today's Gospel was like this, for after he had been caressed by the sweet breeze of the Holy Spirit's powerful influence, he showed his love for his neighbour by empathising with him, keenly feeling the discomfort, pain and illness of his servant. And so, pale with sadness, he said to Our Saviour, "Lord, my servant lies at home paralyzed, suffering terribly." He cannot lift either his hand or leg and is suffering bitter pains. In this, he who was once a heathen showed himself to be a believer. He professed the Godhead of Jesus Christ, saying with assured humility, "Lord, I am not worthy that you should enter under my roof. But only say the

---

1 *Amicus est speculum.*

word, and he shall be healed" (Mt 8:8). Jesus praised him and granted him divine grace for this act of faith, thereby placing him among the Catholic believers. This no doubt echoes what the Prophet Jeremiah had wanted to make known when, through the spirit of prophecy, he foretold that the heathen would have to be converted to the true Faith. Speaking in the Person of Almighty God, he said, "See, I will gather them from the ends of the earth" (Jer 31:8). But how will this happen? Perhaps through force or violence, through wars and domination? No, says the Lord, "I will bring them back in mercy, and in prayer" (Jer 31:9). Catholic Listeners, do you not think that the following words might have been spoken to the centurion in today's Gospel? "I will bring them back in mercy, and I will lead them with consolation." See the extent of his love and mercy for his servant, see the compassion with which he comforts him, for to comfort a sick person means nothing more than having compassion for him. It was this compassion that led him to Our Saviour. And through this compassion the man became reckoned among the faithful and was bestowed with divine grace.

It was surely this great love that made his heart all the more fervent, giving courage to his soul by raising it to a glorious state. Among the various properties of love, there are two noble characteristics in particular that should be noted. The first is the property to bring joy to oneself and to be able to rejoice in the happiness and prosperity of another, and the second is to be able to bear the sadness of another, to show compassion for the troubles and misery of another. By sharing in both one and the other, a person will participate, so to speak, in both the good as well as the bad aspects of the person he loves. St Paul the Apostle speaks of the first of these aspects when he writes, "Love rejoices with the truth" (1 Cor 13:8). This was true of the shepherd who found his lost sheep, and the woman who found her lost coin. She even called her friends and neighbours together to rejoice with her. They both called out, "Rejoice with me, for I have found the sheep that was lost! Rejoice with me, for I have found the coin that I lost!" Take part in my joy! Even so, the truth of love shows itself clearer and fairer when a person shows pity and compassion for the misfortune of another, for this sharing seems to bring about a lessening in the other person's misfortune, trouble, and anxiety, making them easier to bear. The effect of this love on the centurion resulted in the compassionate act of seeking healing for his servant. There is a good example in this for all of us, Catholic Listeners, for it teaches us to show charity towards our servants and underlings when they are sick. We need to show compassion and concern for their health of soul and body. We should not act like so many indiscreet people who keep their servants at home as long as they are of good use and serve them well, but if they happen to become indisposed or fall ill, through God's will or perhaps as a result of their strenuous work-load, they send them away, saying that they will have nothing to do with sick people, and cannot be served by invalids. Charity is surely not a great price to pay, and this kind of behaviour is unworthy of a Christian person. For if an unbeliever, as in today's Gospel, can show such compassion for his servant that he felt compelled to approach Our Saviour and bother Him, so to speak, to seek healing for his servant, then how much more should a Catholic Christian show concern for the health of his servants? Almighty God had given man the commandment to love not just his friends, but also his enemies, "Love your enemies, do good to those who hate you" (Lk 6:27). And not without good reason, for we have all been created to attain the same glories of Heaven; we are all members of the same holy Catholic Church, which is the spiritual Body of Jesus Christ; we all have the same Father and the same Judge in Heaven.

The centurion in today's Gospel is to be praised when he says, "Lord, my servant lies at home paralyzed, suffering terribly," for see how quickly and how well this man had learnt to pray. This is not to be marvelled at, for the same heavenly Spirit that had poured into him such great love had also taught him to pray in such a way that he would obtain what he asked for. The man did not say, "Lord, give him strength that he may be restored to complete health," but in a few words he made the man's illness known and then left the cure to God's mercy and loving kindness. Seen from another side, even though his words were few, as were his demands, he nonetheless was asking much and there was great depth in what he did say, for they had an effect on the ears of Jesus Christ who heard of the miserable state in which the servant found himself, lying paralyzed alone and suffering much. Above all, the Lord was moved by the centurion's love and kindness, and the way he prayed with humility and concern for the health of his servant. These motives had the effect not only of moving Our Saviour, but also of spurring Him on, so to speak, to pity and compassion. How did He answer the man? "I shall come and make him well." Blessed Jesus, what does this mean, that you should come into the house of the centurion, even though he had not requested it? Observe, Catholic Listeners, the wondrous providence of Our Saviour. He knew well that the man would not have allowed it. He knew well that it was not necessary, nonetheless He answered him, "I shall come and make him well." This He said for two reasons, firstly, to test the centurion's submissiveness, and secondly, as an example to the perfidious Jewish people to demonstrate to them the wealth of faith and humility hidden in this pagan man.[2]

In the same way did God command the Patriarch Abraham in Genesis 22 to offer up his only son Isaac, in whom he had placed his hope to populate his people. God did this as an example to the people of the entire world that they should practice blind obedience and submissiveness when it comes to heeding God's commands. In a similar way did He test the patient Prophet Job, so that he might be to all people a mirror of meekness and patience. He tests us, too, every day, with troubles and worries, sickness and torments, either so that we may gain merit through our patience, or so that we might seek our refuge in God. For this very reason did He answer the centurion, "I shall come and make him well," so that he would answer both with humble reverence as well as a degree of embarrassed confusion, "Lord, I am not worthy that you should enter under my roof. But only say the word, and my servant shall be healed." These words were spoken in an obvious and public manner, so that both the Jews who were present as well as all those believers who would later hear this Gospel might be edified and led to salvation by the centurion's humility and strong faith. What is more, Our Saviour had above all offered His services to heal the servant through His personal presence in

---

2 The centurion was likely a Roman and therefore a pagan in the eyes of the Jews (Translator's note).

order to demonstrate the innate love and affection He holds for all people, as we read in another Scriptural passage, "My delights were to be with the children of men" (Prov 8:31). Of course, it is true as we read in the Gospel of John that when He was called upon to heal the royal official's son who was sick, He answered, "Go, your son will live" (Jn 4:50), but this in itself is mysterious, given that the man did not seem to have a particularly strong faith. Perhaps it was more to demonstrate that He is not impressed by a person's riches or wealth, and that He makes no distinction between people, but that He would favour a poor, downtrodden person over a rich one, in opposition to what the world teaches. This is why King David said, "The haughty He knows afar off, the lowly He looks upon in Heaven" (Ps 137:6). Almighty God can see well from afar off who are haughty and high-minded, proud and superb, yet the poor, the downtrodden, the simple and humble person He looks upon with kindness, both in Heaven as on earth, "But this is the one to whom I will look, to the humble and contrite in spirit, who trembles at my word" (Is 66:2).

Think then, Catholic Listeners, about how kind and gentle, how compassionate and merciful is your God. He disdains no one, no matter how wicked and reprobate; He despises no one, no matter how poor and needy, but He embraces everyone who returns to Him with sorrow and contrition. He presents His love, yes, His very self, to all people in the Most Blessed Sacrament of the Altar. When you were lost to sin, He did not send an angel or a pure person to ransom you, but the great God, the omnipotent Lord Himself came in person, and, so that you might always be mindful of His great love, He left as a witness His own Body and Soul and Godhead in the Most Blessed Sacrament of the Altar, so that It might strengthen your souls. Should you wish to share in this divine love by receiving the Most Blessed Body of Jesus Christ, after having first purified your conscience from all kinds of sin by making a sincere confession, then you should follow the example of the centurion by saying with deep humility, strong faith and ardent love, "Lord, I am not worthy that you should enter under my roof. But only say the word, and my servant shall be healed." 'O Lord! with one word you created the heavens and the whole world; Lord! with one word you made the blind see, the deaf hear, the lame walk and gave life to the dead; I am not worthy that you should come under my roof; I am not worthy to have you lodge in my home or in my soul; therefore, say but one word; be merciful to me, a poor sinner, and my servant shall be healed, my soul shall be made pure from every stain of sin.'

When Our Saviour heard the centurion's humble answer, he was amazed and astonished, and He said to those standing around Him, "Truly, I have not found anyone in Israel with such great faith" (Mt 8:10). But what reason do you have to be amazed, O Eternal Wisdom, for you know all things and nothing is hidden from your eyes? You already knew this pagan man's humility and faith before you offered him your gifts of kindness and grace. He acted surprised for the benefit of the Jews, who were present at that moment, so that they would be amazed at seeing such great faith and deep humility in a pagan man, which no doubt contributed to their shame, embarrassment, and confusion. Here Our Saviour was playing the role of a teacher instructing someone in a fine skill. The student then proclaimed what he has learnt with such solemnity and conviction, that even the Lord Himself was astonished. This occurs for no other reason than that the skills the student learnt should be observed to a greater degree and impressed more profoundly on the mind. In the same way did Christ Our Saviour use the centurion's excellent virtues, so that they should be impressed upon the hearts and minds of all those coming after him, yes even upon the hearts of all Catholic people to whom this Gospel would be announced; this is why the Lord was amazed at the man's deep faith. Even so, this astonishment was futile, for it was not enough to move the Jews, just as it is not enough to open the minds of many Catholic people. That is why Our Saviour was compelled to cry through the mouth of the Prophet Isaiah, "I reared children and brought them up, but they have rebelled against me. The ox knows its master, the donkey its owner's manger, but Israel does not know, my people do not understand" (Is 1:2–3). It is certainly a lamentable situation when strangers, foreigners and barbarians who are like lawless beasts without any knowledge of God, come from the furthest frontiers of the world with fervour and ready obedience (notwithstanding that they had been confounded with the darkness of error and disbelief) to embrace the truth and the knowledge of the holy Gospel in order to partake with all devotion and reverence of the holy Sacraments, and to invoke Almighty God with every attentiveness; whereas we Catholics who are given such great opportunities are so weak and lukewarm in the Faith. We think too lightly of attending the Holy Sacrifice of the Mass, we belittle the holy Sacrament of Confession, our belief in the Most Holy Sacrament of the Altar is weak, and we hardly consider the salvation of our souls. Should we, then, not say exactly the opposite in response to Our Saviour's words to us today, "I have not found anyone in Israel with even a little faith!" Never had there been weaker or scantier faith in the world.

Look, we have knowledge of Almighty God and of His only Son Jesus, the Saviour of the world, who suffered a bitter death out of love for us. We know He left us the holy Sacraments as means and treasures to enjoy His divine grace and subsequently His eternal glory; we know God's commandments and those of His holy Catholic Church. Yet despite God's excellent deeds towards us, and our explicit knowledge of them, the words St Paul the Apostle wrote to Titus about the Cretans can unfortunately also be said about many of us, "They profess that they know God: but in their works they deny him; being abominable, and incredulous, and to every good work reprobate" (Tit 1:16). Which nation or what people ever received clearer insight and explanation about things pertaining to eternal life, both Heaven and hell, as we Catholics? Apart from the Apostles, Evangelists, Prophets, and the holy Scriptures, we have priests and shepherds who illumine our minds and inflame our wills by proclaiming the Word of God to ensure that we will reach the glory of Heaven; yet, despite these opportunities and divine warnings, we pollute our souls with all kinds of sins: one with adultery, another with impurity; one with hatred, another with revenge; one with theft, another with cheating; one sleeps on Holy Days, another eats meat on Saturdays.[3] These people go about with polluted souls for

---

3 In some countries it was a custom of the faithful to practice abstinence from meat on Wednesdays and Saturdays, while Friday was a fast day. This practice probably originated in the monastic communities.

many days and even years without wanting to avail themselves of the holy Sacrament of Confession. This surely cannot be the practice of Catholic believers, but must be that of people who are obstinate, hard-headed, and perfidious.

Is it any wonder, then, that Our Saviour in today's Gospel said that many will come from the east and west and will feast with Abraham, Isaac, and Jacob in the Kingdom of Heaven, but that the heirs of that Kingdom (and here He meant Catholic Christians) would be thrown into the everlasting darkness? (see Mt 8:11). No, it is no wonder at all, seeing that our faith is feeble, our hope is weak, our love is lukewarm and our negligence is extremely great. And so we find Almighty God, who knows everything that will happen in the future, placing these words of lament in the mouth of the Prophet Jeremiah, "I have given my dear soul into the hands of her enemies. My inheritance has become to me like a lion in the forest. She roars at me; therefore, I hate her. Is my inheritance like a multi-coloured bird of prey to me? Are the other birds of prey all around her coming against her? Go, gather all the wild animals and bring them to devour it" (Jer 12:7–9). With these words Our Saviour is telling us, 'See, I have come from Heaven to earth to take on a human nature, in which I allowed Myself to be whipped, crowned and tormented, finally letting the cruel executioners nail me to a gibbet.' But what is the reason that you allowed all this to happen, O Jesus, Saviour of the world? 'To instruct sinners and to lead them to salvation; with my own Blood I washed the stains of their sins to bring them to the Kingdom of Heaven, to my eternal inheritance. Nevertheless, instead of having regard for the merit of my Blood that was spilled for them, they have turned against me like cruel lions, they rip apart my Heart, they renew my wounds, they trample my Precious Blood with their feet, they roar against me. How often do they swear and blaspheme against my blessed Name! How they use it in false oaths and slander! That is why I hated it. That is why I loathe them as I would loathe monsters from the hellish pit.' Do you not think, O sinner! that to your Saviour you might be like a multi-hued bird? See, how your lewdness has turned you yellow, your hatred and rage has made you red, you are white with jealousy and anger, green through dishonest thoughts and notions. In short, you are polluted with mortal sins from head to foot, and there is hardly one member that has not provoked the wrath of the Divine Majesty. Therefore, 'come, beasts of the earth, come spirits of hell, come, walk, fly, gather together,' says the Lord, 'and make yourselves ready to devour my inheritance, that is, the souls of the faithful sinners, those who were once my inheritance, those who once believed in me, but they did not observe their faith, they did not live by it. And so, I have judged them, rejected then, damned them to the eternal darkness.'

Lest this terrifying malediction should also befall us, Catholic Listeners, let us observe our time well, so that at the Last Judgement these hellish monsters will not take us by surprise, for they seek nothing more than our eternal loss. Let us concern ourselves with keeping the light of the true Faith burning brightly within us through love of God, through virtuous deeds and by the frequent reception of the holy Sacraments, so that by enjoying God's divine grace here on earth, we might share in the heavenly glory of the life to come. Who lives, etc.

On the Fourth Sunday after Epiphany

Quis est hic? Quia mare, et venti obediunt ei? — "What sort of man is this, that even the winds and the sea obey him?" (Mt 8:27).

ATHOLIC LISTENERS, THE renowned historian Plutarch writes in his life of Julius Caesar about a certain time when that Roman Emperor was at sea when a great storm, accompanied by furious lightning and thunder, blew up about him. So great was the wind, and so furious the waves that the ship on which he was sailing faced a real danger of running aground and being smashed to pieces. The ship took on so much water that it was just two inches short of sinking. The sailors quickly cut the ropes, struck the sails, lowered the mast, and dropped anchor; in short, they did everything they possibly could to save the ship. Half dazed and more dead than alive they started calling to each other "Alas! Help! Friends, we are going to drown!" Julius Caesar, who was of course present on the ship, seeing them so frightened, so defeated, so pale, and half dead, addressed them encouragingly with his masculine dapperness and imperial majesty, "Men, what are you afraid of? Be bold and fear not; you are carrying Caesar and Caesar's fortune in your boat."[1] Today St Matthew the Evangelist seems to present us with a similar adventure. We see Jesus, the Saviour of the world, entering a small ship and together with His disciples they sail out onto the Lake of Gennesaret. The water was calm and some of them were asleep, when suddenly a windstorm arose, so great that the boat was being swamped by the large waves stirred up by the furious wind and storm. His disciples were overcome with fear and they began to panic, crying out, "Lord, save us! We are perishing!" (Mt

1 Plutarch, The Life of Julius Caesar, ch. 38.

8:25). Waking up because of the clamour, He rebuked their lack of faith and trust, saying, "Why are you afraid, you of little faith?" (Mt 8:26). What He was saying was, 'What reason do you have to be anxious and frightened seeing that I am here with you, seeing that I am here in the ship. Did I not make the water and the sea? Do I not release the winds from my treasury?' And using His power and authority He commanded the sea and the wind, the storm and the thunder to be still.

The Blessed Virgin Mary is a veritable Star of the Sea, and by her intercession she assists us in the troubled sea of this world by protecting us against the winds, storms, and assaults of our enemies. In this way does she preserve all those sailing in the barque of the holy Catholic Church. In order that we may learn something from these words, let us call upon her to obtain for us the grace of the Holy Spirit by presenting to her the angelic salutation,

Ave Maria

IF THERE IS ANYONE HERE WHO HAS EVER EXPERIENCED the sea in its turbulent, foaming state, and has been tossed about by a howling storm, then I do not doubt that he would have wondered how it were possible that the furious waves, now rising high to the heavens, now plummeting down as if into an abyss, did not flood the entire earth, given their great power and cruel strength. Moreover, what is it about the sand and soil on the shore that they can break these fearsome waves and subdue the water's furious strength? What power is there in sand to be able to withstand such violence? What power is there in soil to be able to break these furious waves? Of itself, sand has minimal power of resistance, and soil has but little strength. It is through the command of Almighty God that the sea has been ordered not to extend beyond the limits and boundaries set by the dunes and the sand. The Wise Man clearly testifies to this when he says, "He set a law to the waters, that they should not pass their limits" (Prov 8:29). Likewise, the Prophet Job says that Almighty God gave the sea explicit orders, "Thus far shall you come, and no further" (Job 38:11). You waters of the sea, you may come thus far, but no further; you shall break your furious, seething waves against the dunes, against the shore, against the sand. Even though the sea has no ears, she understands the voice of God; even though she foments, she shows respect for her Creator; even though she is furious, she is obedient to Him; she is prevented from going beyond her boundaries by the hidden power of God's will.

The sea has neither intellect nor feelings, yet she fears and respects my commands, says Almighty God through the mouth of the Prophet Jeremiah. Should you then not fear me, my people? Should you not respect my Law, you people who have ears to hear and minds to understand? You will not listen to me, yet the waves fear me and the sea is obedient to my will. Will you be more deaf than the water or more obstinate than the sea? "Do you not fear me, who placed the sand as a boundary for the sea?" (Jer 5:22). And just as I placed boundaries for the sea, so I have set boundaries around the unbridled passions and affections of your hearts, namely, your avarice, concupiscence, gluttony, and wrath. Listen to my commandments and my laws. My word should be the boundaries and limits by which you must live. Did I not say: You shall not kill, you shall not commit adultery? Drunkards will not possess the Kingdom of Heaven. Love your neighbour as you love yourself. In short, my laws have placed limits on all your foolish passions; for example, your desires are curbed by justice, your pleasures by moderation, your anger by gentleness and your pride by humility. "Thus far shall you come, and no further." All this have I strengthened and confirmed by my word, protection, and threats. Yet the furious passions of sinners will often without fear or regret violate the boundaries of God's divine law and commandments. For instance, justice will be transgressed by fraud and theft, moderation by drunkenness and delights of the flesh, love by hatred and wrath by revenge, enmity, and slander. God merely placed some sand to break the sea's fury, and she obeyed Him. To us He has given many and varied laws and warnings to make us fear Him, and to restrain our wicked passions and affections, yet we seem not to care.

Indeed, not only the sea but also all other irrational creatures obey Almighty God without showing the least hint of stubbornness. Surely this should impel us to feel greatly ashamed of our disobedience and obstinacy. Not only do the sea and wind obey God's will and commands, as we see in today's Gospel, "The winds and the sea obey Him," but so also do Heaven, earth, the elements, and everything else the world contains, as King David writes in Psalm 118, "All things serve you" (Ps 118:91). And not without good reason, for according to the teachings of the Angelic Doctor, St Thomas, all workings of nature are directed by and subject to God's law. God also imprints on the whole of nature principles of their proper actions, "He has made a decree, and it shall not pass away" (Ps 148:6). In a similar way, the members of the body do not use intellect and reason, yet they obey reason and the intellect; for example, the eyes see, the hands work, the feet walk, and the entire body moves according to the desire of the intellect and the command of the will. Likewise, even though unintelligent creatures are incapable of understanding God's orders and commands, they still follow His law and direction. So it is by God's law that the heavens move, the planets are ruled, time is measured, night comes after day, winter follows summer, and all other natural things that happen throughout the world, as King David writes about in another psalm, "By your ordinance the day goes on; for all things serve you" (Ps 118:91). Therefore, the obedience of all creatures towards God's commands should be for us a reminder of the submissiveness we owe to Almighty God for having given us His law and commandments so that we can conduct our lives according to His holy will. All of nature and everything the world contains obeys God without murmur or contradiction; shall we, then, as Catholics, be the only ones to refuse Him our submission and obedience? Do we not make up the most important and noble part of the world, are we not rational creatures who have been endowed with reason and intelligence, enlightened with genuine truth, strengthened by divine grace, and called to God's heavenly glory? Shall we follow our unbridled passions instead of His divine directives? Shall we not, then, submit our wills to His law, under which all things come together and are united. According to St Chrysostom, it is the view of Sacred Scripture that by following the example of irrational creatures we may be inspired to do our duty well in those things that pertain to our salvation. It is no doubt to our great shame that they, who are devoid of intelligence, can do all things in such a disciplined and orderly manner. And we, who are intelligent beings, have such a wicked disposition. We infect our souls with sin and go against God's will and commands. This is why the Wise Man sends the sluggard to observe the ants, that he might learn from them diligence and industriousness. "Go to the ants, you lazy-bones, and learn wisdom" (Prov 6:6). Similarly, Christ sends us to the lilies of the field and the birds of the air to learn about divine providence, "Consider the lilies of the field, how they grow; they neither toil nor spin; yet I tell you, even Solomon in all his glory was not arrayed like one of these" (Mt 6:28–29). He sends us to the swallows and storks who know the times and seasons, so that by their example we might learn the time of our salvation, the season of its arrival, and about its inspiration and appearance. It is to our great shame that we need to be sent to the school of earth's creatures to learn obedience and submission to Almighty God's laws. "The winds and the sea obey him."

Do you want to hear the lesson on obedience the creatures give us? Even though some of them have neither mouth nor tongue with which to speak, they tell us each in their own way, 'Listen you people, you have been gifted with reason and intelligence. How is it that you do not demonstrate these gifts, why do you not seem to use them? Right reason clearly shows you that a lord and father of a household should be honoured, and each person living in the house must be subservient to him. No one can be so dull or stupid not to know that this is true.' Behold, Almighty God is the Lord, the Master, the Father of all things; the world is His house, irrational creatures are His slaves, we humans are His children made in His own image and called to inherit the glories of Heaven. As our Lord and Master, He gave us His commandments and holy law, so that we would keep them as a model on which to fashion our way of life. Nonetheless, unintelligent creatures are obedient and submissive to Him, whereas we are often obstinate and stubborn. They serve Him without having knowledge of His greatness. We know His endless majesty, His authority, and righteousness yet we think little of Him. Through our sins we even turn our backs on Him and on His commandments and grace. I would even venture to say in all honesty that we seem to use our intellects less than unintelligent creatures use their natural instincts. Indeed, how true are the words of the Prophet Isaiah, "The ox knows his owner, and the ass his master's crib: but Israel has not known me, and my people have not understood" (Is 1:3). This is the lesson, or admonition, we learn from the creatures. And what augments this even further is this: irrational creatures do not know what God has planned for them, yet they follow Him without contradiction. We Catholics, on the other hand, know very well God's designs for us, namely, that if we keep His divine commandments, He will raise us up and make us His friends and give us His grace; consequently, He will let us share in His eternal good and glory, which He has prepared for those who love Him. But despite this knowledge, we refuse to follow the divine law that guides us, and His light that leads us, and His grace that sweetly draws us close to Him. Fire knows not why God ordered it to burn, yet it regularly performs its task. O man! you know very well that God ordered you to love Him above all other things, that your heart should continually burn with love for Him, so that you may merit the joys of Heaven, yet you still refuse to love Him, you spurn the One who has placed before you the crown that is your reward for loving Him. The sea understands not why God has forbidden her to flow outside her boundaries, yet she obeys Him. You, on the other hand, know well that He has forbidden you to transgress His commandments, so that by not falling out of His favour, you would not fall into the eternal fires of hell. Nevertheless, without a hint of fear or respect or bother you quite easily break His laws. The sea is submissive to Him, despite not knowing Him, yet you who do know your Lord and the punishments He metes out for sin, continue to be stubborn and rebellious towards Him.

I pray you, Catholic Listeners, let us get to know and acknowledge the authority of those people, and even unintelligent things, who know and uphold His laws and commands. For stubbornness is the cause of all unhappiness, while on the contrary obedience is the cause of happiness. St Augustine was well aware of this, and that is why he wrote, "Nothing is more profitable for the soul than obedience; therefore, if it is profitable for a servant to obey his master, and a son to obey his father, and a wife her husband, then how much more profitable would it be for a soul to obey God?"[2] For God is the soul's Master through His authority, her Father through grace and her Bridegroom through love. Through disobedience a wife is driven out of the home, a son is deprived of his inheritance, a servant is

---

2 *Nihil tam expedit animae quam obedire; et si expedit servo ut obediat domino, filio ut obediat patri, uxori ut obediat viro; quanto magis animae ut obediat Deo?* St Augustine, Exposition on Psalm 70, Sermon 2.

punished, and a Christian soul is divested of all good and becomes filled with wickedness. Contrary to this, it is through obedience and servitude that a servant is rewarded, a son obtains his inheritance, the bride receives the heart of her bridegroom, and a soul attains the Kingdom of Heaven and the company of the angels. "Nothing is more profitable for the soul than obedience."

Indeed, we now know that it is profitable for irrational creatures to be obedient to Almighty God and to be submissive to His divine authority, for from this obedience arises their prosperity and conservation. Who can doubt that this is even more profitable for rational creatures, because for them there is nothing more harmful than following their own wills. On the other hand, there is nothing more blessed than to follow the will of Almighty God. St Augustine is quite clear about this when he declares, "Rational creatures are made in such a way, that their being subordinate to God is useful to them."[3] The opposite of this is that it is harmful for them to follow their own wills. Irrational creatures follow God's will without knowing Him, and they cannot follow their own wills, for they have no will, and therefore they can neither earn merit nor sin; subsequently, they can become neither holy nor damned. Only man, who is gifted with a free will, is capable of earning either eternal happiness or eternal misery, either God's friendship or enmity, either earning merit or falling into sin. By subjecting his own will to the will of God, man can earn the glory of Heaven. But if he follows his own illusions and will and acts contrary to God's law, he is only working towards his eternal damnation. Therefore, there is nothing more blessed than obedience, and nothing more damaging than disobedience by following one's own will. St Bernard rightly said, "Let self-will cease and there will be no hell."[4] For what is it that God punishes in sinners other than their own will? We would do well to imprint this verdict on our memory, remembering that each time we sin we undermine God's will by following our own; we then risk, as it were, following the devils and the damned.

Indeed, what a strange matter this is. You see, all things in the world, as I said just a moment ago, fulfil God's will; they seek the

3 *Creatura rationalis sic facta est, ut ei subditam esse sit utile.* St Augustine, The City of God, Book 14, ch. 12.
4 *Cesset voluntas propria, et infernus non erit.* St Bernard, Sermon 3 for Eastertide.

end for which they were created. The sinner alone follows his own illusions, that is, the inconstancy of his passions. He lives life as if it were a game of little consequence, as if he were created by chance and not by divine providence with the onus to work out the salvation of his soul. The Wise Man makes an appropriate comment on this, "They have counted their life a pastime" (Wis 15:12). Indeed, many people only care about gathering money and possessions, about lying and swindling, and all kinds of people seek their livelihood through cunning and deceit. "They have counted their life a pastime." It is certainly true that our life can be called a pastime. This was also the opinion of the old Philosophers, who considered everyone merely to be playing the role of a king, or of a prince, a burgher, merchant or husband. Do you know what this game is about? It is a prelude to eternity, either our eternal salvation or our eternal damnation. So, if we want to play our role by directing the prelude to our eternity towards a happy ending, we must keep in mind that it is not by accident that we were created and placed in the world; we were not put here to gather wealth or to enjoy the pleasures of the flesh, which only serve to pamper the body, but we were put here to serve God and to keep His commandments and those of the holy Catholic Church. Our purpose is to uphold justice, to preserve innocence, purity, and moderation, and above all to love God. Even so, the contrary usually happens: we forget the eternal good and we look to what is passing; we forget Heaven and focus our thoughts on the earth; we forget our soul and pamper the body. In the end, we neglect to love God by thinking only of loving ourselves. Ours is surely an unfettered love, a love that can only lead to us becoming lost for all eternity.

Can it be possible that we have forgotten the body's natural posture, which God has created in such a way that the head is at the top, thus pointing towards Heaven, so that we will always be mindful of our eternal home? Have we also forgotten our soul, which is immortal and non-perishable? How is it possible that we have forgotten the power of our faith, which raises us to God? Yes, how is it possible for us to have so easily forgotten God Himself, who daily calls to us and wakens us through His exterior words and inner whisperings? O man! Do you think so little of His sovereign divine authority, the authority of His commandments, which are not difficult to keep, and the thunder of His warnings? As He asks through the mouth of the Prophet Malachi, "If then I am a father, where is the honour due me? And if I am a master, where is the respect due me?" (Mal 1:6). It is I, says God, who as a Father have created you; it is I who ransomed you with my Blood after you had become lost; it is I, the Lord, who have given you laws and commandments by which to live your lives. It is I who rules the Heavens and orders the seasons and controls the wind and the sea. And it is I who commands every creature in the world. That is why I am adored by the angels and feared by devils and all things must bow before me, either out of love or out of force. How is it then that you, O sinful man, O worm of the earth, will refuse to respect me? Do you take pleasure in being rebellious and obstinate, in degrading my laws and commands? Would you rather follow your own will, which is fickle and deceitful, as opposed to my Word, which will last forever? Observe carefully that the devil has already tricked you once, and the scar of this deception will last for all eternity. Remember when he said to your first parents, "If you follow your own will, with its pleasures and lusts, 'you shall be like gods.'" But, O man! he deceived you, just as you deceive yourselves by following your own sensuality. In this manner, you will not become gods but devils who, if truth be said, had not been steadfast. If you follow that way, you will not be like gods, but like hellish demons. They refused to subject themselves to God's omnipotence, and so for all eternity they sigh under the weight of God's divine justice. Therefore, if you do not hasten to subject yourselves to the sweet yoke of my law, you shall for all eternity join the devil and his disobedient angels in being subjected to my severest punishments.

Seeing, then, Catholic Listeners, that all things must be submissive to Almighty God, as were the sea and wind in today's Gospel, so we, too, must bow our wills under His law so that He will not punish our obstinacy; and every time we offend His divine authority by sinning, we must invoke His help by crying out with the Apostles, "Lord, save us! We are perishing!" By your divine grace save us from the storm of temptation and the sea of sin, so that we may enjoy the restful calm of your eternal glory in the life to come. Who lives, etc.

On the Fifth Sunday after Epiphany

Simile factum est regnum caelorum homini, qui semi-navit bonum semen in agro suo — "The Kingdom of Heaven may be compared to a man who sowed good seed in his field" (Mt 13:24).

CATHOLIC LISTENERS, IN ANCIENT times the paintings of Apelles were held in such high esteem that no artist, no matter how gifted he might be, would dare put his hand or brush to any painting or portrait produced by the renowned Apelles. We would be considered audacious and impudent, yes even worthy of punishment, if we did not show the same honour and respect to the word of Jesus Christ our Saviour, for it is a product of His endless wisdom. It is because He is the eternal wisdom itself that He can explain the parable in today's Gospel so thoroughly and perfectly. It would, therefore, be a bold act to try to explain this parable in a different way. St Gregory commented on this very well when he said, "This parable has been explained by Truth itself; human frailty should not dare to expound on it."[1] We shall then simply just review the parable. A sower, says St Matthew, sowed good seed in his field, but during the night his enemy came and sowed weeds among the wheat. The servants saw that the wheat was starting to sprout, and they went to the master and said, 'Master, did you not sow good seed in your field? Where then did these weeds come from?' 'My enemy' said the Master 'has played this trick on me.' 'Would you like us to go gather them?' 'No,' he said, 'lest in gathering the weeds you uproot the wheat with them. Let both grow together until the harvest. I will then tell

---

[1] *Quam parabolam per semetipsam veritas exposuit; hanc discutere humana fragilitas non praesumat.* St Gregory the Great, On the Gospels. Homily 15.

the reapers to gather up the weeds to be burned, and then to gather the wheat to be stored in my barn.' This is, in short, the gist of the parable in today's Gospel. This parable was still unclear to Jesus' disciples, who begged Him to explain it further. "Explain to us the parable of the weeds of the field." From the very beginning of His coming He had taught in parables and explained their meaning. Long ago it was foretold of Him, "I will open my mouth in parables; I will utter what was hidden since the foundation of the world" (Mt 13:34). And so He did. Listen, He said, the one who sows good seed is the Son of Man; the field is the world; the good seed are those people who are favoured and predestined; the weeds are those wicked sinners who will be damned; the enemy who sowed the weeds is the devil; the time of harvest is the end of the world; the reapers are the angels whom the Son of Man shall send out on the Last Day to gather the wicked evildoers and throw them into the fires of hell. But the righteous will shine like the sun in my Father's kingdom. "He who has ears, let him hear" (Mt 13:43). This is how Our Saviour Himself explained it. But before explaining this further to you, let us first pray for the grace of the Holy Spirit through the intercession of the Blessed Virgin Mary by presenting to her the angelic greeting,

Ave Maria

THERE IS NO BETTER SAUCE TO ACCOMPANY OLIVES than the oil from the olives themselves, and there can be no better explanation of a text or manuscript than by the master or author who dictated it. Today, therefore, we shall not be burdened with examining the meaning of the parable in this Gospel, seeing that the author, Our Saviour, has already thoroughly explained it. We shall only expand on it somewhat, to imprint its meaning deeper on our hearts. Even though it is a short work, it loses none of its strength and value. So then, first of all, the field in which the sower sowed his seed is the world. "He sowed good seed in his field. The field is the world" (Mt 13:37–38). Since the beginning of time, the heavenly Father brought forth His Word, that is, His Son, and the Father and the Son together brought forth the Holy Spirit. Their Divine Being is one in nature and a Trinity in Persons. When the time had come, they wanted to outwardly announce the fruit of their love, "When the fullness of time had come, God sent forth His Son into the world" (Gal 4:4). So He created the whole world as a field in which to sow His good deeds, grace, and mercy. God therefore created this field through His omnipotence; He prepared it by His wisdom and cultivated it by His goodness, and in it He sowed the seed of His grace and generosity and abundant love.

Of these three Persons, who in particular was the sower of this field? It was Christ our Saviour, the Son of Man. The external works of the Blessed Trinity are inextricably linked and all three Persons act together, according to the saying of the scholars, *Opera Trinitatis ad extra, sunt indivisa* — "The external Trinitarian operations are undivided."[2] Furthermore, Sacred Scripture explicitly says that the creation, regulation, and administration of all things happens through the Divine Word, that is, through the Son of God who is eternal Wisdom. Thus we read in St Paul the Apostle, "In Him all things were created" (Col 1:16). And so we see that the Son of Man, the second Person of the Blessed Trinity who assumed our human nature, is the sower who sowed good seed in the field of the world. He is called the sower for a good reason, for He took on our nature and came into the world in order to labour and cultivate it with His own hands, thereby fulfilling the words the Prophet Jeremiah spoke of Him long ago, "He has been made like a stranger in the land, and almost like a wayfarer" (Jer 14:8). The Word of the Father has become like a farmer in the field, and like a wanderer, never resting, always working in the world. Rightly did He say that He had come as a labourer, for in Heaven He was a King, but on earth He was a labourer; in Heaven He was the Son of God, on earth He became the Son of Man; in Heaven He nourished the angels with the bread of heavenly delights, in the world He came to earn His bread with the sweat of His brow, and He prayed for the salvation of souls, "My food is to do the will of my Father" (Jn 4:34). He worked with such humility that He sweated water and blood. "His sweat became like great drops of blood falling down upon the ground" (Lk 22:44). Nonetheless, He cultivated the field of the world with hard labour, and sowed it with His Cross, watered it with

---

2   A phrase thought to have originated with St Augustine.

His sweat, fertilised it with His Blood, and sowed it with His grace and teachings. Yet this ungrateful worldly field has produced for Him nothing but the thorns, thistles and weeds of every kind of sin. How can this happen? Did the Son of God, who became the Son of Man in order to cultivate the field of the world, not sow good seed? Certainly He did. "He sowed good seed in his field."

So then, first of all, the good seed the Divine Sower scattered in His field indicates everything contained in the world, apart from sin. "All things were made through him, and without him was not anything made that was made" (Jn 1:3). But even more so, the good seed can be said to be the angels and humans, who are rational creatures created in God's image, and who have the capacity to enjoy God's presence for all eternity. God created the angels in Heaven and man on earth, so that he would grow and bring forth good fruits and virtuous deeds in obedience to God, thereby earning eternal glory and salvation. Furthermore, this good seed is divine grace, the Word of God, and the holy Sacraments. But returning to the theme of the Gospel, the good seeds are those good people who have been chosen and predestined and who produce good fruits by living according to the holy Sacraments, the Word of God and divine grace. "The good seed means the sons of the kingdom" (Mt 13:38). The world has never lacked the good seed of holy and righteous people. Behold, living under the law of nature there were Abel, Noah, Enoch, Abraham, and the other Patriarchs, under the written Law there were the Prophets Isaiah, Jeremiah, Ezekiel, Daniel, and many others; and now under the law of grace there are the Apostles, Martyrs, Doctors, Confessors, Virgins and many other righteous Catholic persons who carefully regulate their lives according to the law and Gospel of Jesus Christ. This is the good, holy seed that the world will never lack, even though in some quarters it is indeed very difficult to find. What is the reason for this? This is the question the servants asked in today's Gospel, "Sir, did you not sow good seed in your field? How then has it weeds?" Seeing that God only sows good seed in the world, where do all these weeds come from? For example, where does all the idolatry, witchcraft, heresy, sins, and faults found in the world come from, even among Catholics? 'An enemy, a hostile person,' says Our Saviour, 'has done this.' Insolent, shameless and false are the Reformed Brethren who dare to say that God is the author of wickedness, sin, and evil. Today Our Saviour tells us the exact opposite. He says He does not sow weeds, nor has He ever sown them. Even so, in his thirty-sixth Article, the blasphemous Martin Luther says, "God works wicked deeds in the sinner."[3] In a similar vein do we have the heretic John Calvin, who in his commentary on chapter eight of St Paul's Letter to the Romans says, "No less was Judas' betrayal a work of God, than the calling of Paul."[4] These are without a doubt blasphemies that should never again be heard, for they try to entirely destroy the Godhead. God can only be God if He does good. He cannot be good if He is effectively the author or cause of evil. King David is quite clear in saying, "You are not a God who delights in wickedness" (Ps 5:5). No, He is the Lord who forbids and punishes sin, as we read in many passages of Sacred Scripture and in the learned Tertullian, "God is not the author of sin, for He turns out to be its censurer and condemner."[5] God, then, is not the author of evil, nor is He the sower of weeds. The origin of sin is found in the wicked wills of creatures, and the origin of their wicked wills is their own anger, which often begins and is implemented by temptation from the devil, who works against right reason.

Those who have written about agriculture say that couch-grass[6] originally was a useful seed and a good grain, but later it degenerated into a weed, caused perhaps by either bad soil, air, or water. Whatever the case might be, the devil, who nowadays is so wicked and evil that today's Gospel calls him "the enemy," had once been a good angel. Almighty God had once created him good and just; but he changed, he sinned through his own will and wicked inclinations. "He did not remain in the truth."[7] He did not use his intellect well, nor did he stay alert. "An enemy came while they were asleep." But he fell asleep, and instead of turning towards God, he turned to his own self, and

---

3   *Deus operatur in impiis, mala opera.* The quote is found in Martin Luther, *De Servo Arbitrio,* 7, 113.

4   *Non minus fuit opus Dei, proditio Iudae; quam vocatio Pauli.* John Calvin, Acts of the Council of Trent with the Antidote, Canon 6.

5   *Deus non est delicti auctor, cuius est interdictor et condemnator.* Tertullian, Against Marcion, Book 2, ch. 9.

6   *Triticum repens.*

7   *In veritate non stetit.* St Augustine, The City of God, Book 11, ch.15.

while he slept, he was overcome by the weeds of self-love, pride, and ill-will. These did not make his God-given nature evil, but only his inclinations and will were affected, for he alone produced them. His nature, which Almighty God had created, remained good, but his will turned evil, for he himself had corrupted it. Thus he changed from a white angel into a black devil, and from brilliant light to murky darkness, from the celestial stars to the fires of hell, from wheat to weeds, and from a friend of God to an arch-enemy of both God and man. "An enemy has done this. The enemy is the devil." This was the beginning of the bad seed, that is, the wicked and unfettered will of the angel, who became a devil after falling from his place of eternal happiness. Seeing that he had fallen, and had no hope of climbing up again, he obstinately set himself up against God by trying to wage war against Him, His creatures, and all His works; and so he started corrupting and enticing whoever he could to enter his company. In Heaven he started sowing his bad seed among many other angels, and these joined him in their stubbornness and consequently they were banished into the deep abyss. "The dragon swept with him a third part of the stars" (Rev 12:4). But this did not satisfy him, and burning with unquenchable hatred and anger towards mankind, he sowed his bad seed in the earthly Paradise, and with devilish cunning he incited our first parents to transgress God's commandment not to eat of the forbidden fruit. Our first parents were sleepy, and their minds were not sufficiently alert for them to ponder who had given them the commandment and what punishment might be in store for them should they disobey. And so by their own will they listened to the devil and in wickedness and disobedience they plucked that fruit, thereby breaking God's commandment and bringing upon themselves death, misfortune, and misery. "An enemy came and over-sowed weeds." But through the death of Jesus Christ, God wanted to bring man back to the right path that leads to salvation, from which he had strayed by breaking God's commandments; this even further embittered and enraged the wicked enemy, who then continually set about sowing bad seed among the good, that is, setting sinners among the righteous, as King David wrote, "the pride of them that hate you ascend continually" (Ps 73:23). In this he was referring to the devils and damned spirits.

Even today the devil sows his weeds and bad seed in the field of the world, even within the domain of the Catholic Church, and in all of Christ's possessions. But, Catholic Listeners, what type of bad seed is he sowing? Both St Chrysostom and St Augustine claim these bad seeds are the heretics and other undesirables such as Politicians and Libertines[8] who live in this world as if there were no God in Heaven above. The weeds are those wicked Catholics who have given their lives over to adultery, impurity, thievery, injustice, gluttony, drunkenness, and other kinds of mortal sin. Those who persist in their wicked ways and die in such a state become the weeds of hell and children of the devil. They become seed that is damned but which, alas! to the devil's delight today still grows and flourishes due to man's negligence. What has caused this? This is caused by many people slumbering and sleeping because they are weak, dim, lazy, and careless when it comes to the matter of their salvation. They sin without thinking and they do not want to remember or put into practise what they have learned or heard preached to them. "While they were asleep, an enemy came." We can see this daily in some parts of Italy, where during the summer people are accidentally bitten by a viper, which is a kind of snake. The unfortunate victim falls into a deep sleep and dies while sleeping. In a similar way do the devil, sin, pleasure, the world and the flesh, make man sleepy; they bite him and cause an unfortunate sleep that brings eternal death, when he is least thinking about it. And when it is too late, when this drowsiness has passed, he realises there is nothing left for him but everlasting moaning and groaning. King David articulated this well when he said, "They have slept their sleep; and all the men of riches have found nothing in their hands" (Ps 75:6). Those worldly people who set their heart on pleasures, wealth, and possessions, have slept their sleep; but having woken they saw that everything was deception and vanity.

In one of his homilies, St Basil comments on the words of the Patriarch Moses, "It is written, 'take heed to yourself.' There is a certain

---

8 . Politicians and Libertines. In the 17th century politicians were regarded as people who acted in a manipulative and devious way, typically to gain personal advancement. Libertines were people devoid of most moral or sexual restraints, which they saw as unnecessary or undesirable. They typically ignored or spurned accepted morals and forms of behaviour established by the larger society.

animal called *dorras*,⁹ whose sight is so keen that it is able to see from afar every trick and cunning a hunter might use in trying to catch it. It is because of her keen sight that she is always alert, making it impossible for any hunter to snare her. God grant," continues St Basil, "that man were as alert and watchful for his eternal salvation as this creature is for its life. If only he used the same watchfulness and diligence not to fall into the devil's trap, and consequently into the fires of hell, as this creature uses not to fall into the hunter's snare."¹⁰ O man! if only you would keep open the eyes of your right reason, your intellect and your soul, for then you would become alert to the matters your faith proposes to you, and to the devil's cunning tricks. See how this sower of bad seed and wicked weeds who plucks courage from your sluggishness, will quickly flee, frightened off by your alertness and diligence. Resist the devil and he will flee from you. "While they were asleep an enemy came and over-sowed weeds."

The master's servants had heard from his mouth that he had sown good seed in his field, so when they saw the weeds they asked him, "Do you want us to pull them up?" But he answered, "No." Indeed, if Almighty God were as hasty as man is to mete out punishment and revenge, the world would have ended long ago. But Almighty God is patient, and He wants every person to become aware of his own sins. "I desire not the death of the wicked, but that the wicked turn from his way, and live" (Ez 33:11), God said through the mouth of His Prophet. Therefore, it is indeed true what St Augustine says, "Think not that wicked men are in this world for nothing, or that God does no good with them. Every wicked man lives, either to repent, or to exercise the righteous."¹¹ Which means that the wicked can become good because man can change his will, right up to the moment of his final breath. "The will is changeable unto death."¹² This is the reason why Almighty God is so patient with sinners, because there is always

---

9 A gazelle known as *Gazella dorcas*.
10 St Basil the Great, Homilies On Deuteronomy 15, Homily 3.
11 *Ne putetis gratis malos esse in hoc mundo, et nihil boni de illis agere Deum: omnis malus aut ideo vivit, ut corrigatur, aut ut per illum bonus exerceatur.* St Augustine, Exposition on Psalm 54.
12 *Voluntas est ambulatoria usque ad mortem.* From ancient Roman inheritance law.

the hope that they will repent whilst they are alive. I will say nothing about pulling up the wheat with the weeds. "Lest in gathering it up you also uproot the wheat." Look, if Almighty God had immediately eliminated our first father Adam after his sin, He would have in one blow also eliminated the good grain of penitence and other virtuous deeds performed by all his children that came after him, as well as all those they shall do in the future, until the end of the world. By eliminating Adam, God would have destroyed all the good seed of those predestined and chosen people who still need to fill the barns of the celestial Paradise. If God had immediately eliminated King David because of his adulterous relationship with Bathsheba, He would have destroyed the mirror of penitence that later illuminated the entire world. If He had immediately eliminated the sinful Magdalene, Matthew the tax collector, Paul the persecutor, and Peter the liar, then without a doubt He would have destroyed many examples of true repentance and conversion. He would have lost a secretary of His holy Gospel, a trumpet of the Word of God and the foundation stone of His Catholic Church. I also confirm what King David says, "If you, O Lord, should mark our guilt, Lord, who would survive?" (Ps 129:3). Clearly then, God is patient, forgiving, and merciful.

Catholic Listeners, it was to our great benefit that Almighty God did not hastily pull up the weeds. We had become those weeds because of our sins and wickedness, but because of our sorrow and contrition we can become clean wheat. Therefore, God waits patiently to see the fruits of penitence we will bring forth. But if nothing is forthcoming, we will be ashamed and embarrassed at the time of the summer harvest. But what is this harvest? The harvest, and the summer, is the Day of Judgement. For harvest time, or a little later, will be when the wheat and weeds will be separated, so on the last day there will be separation of those people who will be chosen, and those who will be rejected. "The harvest is the end of the age." The reapers will be the angels, the mowers will mow the grain and often also bind it up, especially when they mow the stalks with a scythe, as they do in the East and in Italy; Almighty God shall then use the angels' services to do the same work in the general harvest of the Day of Judgement. The ashes of the bodies will be gathered up by the angels, according to the Angelic Doctor, St Thomas.[13] It will be the angels who sound the trumpet to call all the dead to be judged, "For the trumpet will sound, the dead will be raised up" (1 Cor 15:52). They will separate the good from the wicked, and the weeds, that is, the sinners, shall be set to one side (the left, Sacred Scripture tells us) and bundled up and cast into the fiery furnace. What will they use to bundle them? Where will they find the ropes and chains with which to bind all those sinners? One does not have to go far to find ropes and chains. The ropes used to tie sinners will be their own sins. "The wicked are fast bound with the ropes of their own sins" (Prov 5:22). So listen well, Reformed Brethren! On the Day of Judgement your errors, lies and blasphemies shall bind you fast. Listen well, you audacious Catholics, for your adultery, lustfulness, thievery and injustices, gluttony and drunkenness, anger and revenge shall bind you fast. In short, the sins of all sinners will serve as chains and shackles; the pleasures and desires to which you are now attached will bind you fast to eternal suffering. "The cords of the wicked have encompassed me" (Ps 118:61). Almighty God will send His angels to extract from you the ropes that will bind you, and the fire that will torment you. Your stubbornness will bind you fast, your sins will ignite the hell into which you will be cast to burn for all eternity. "He will cast them into the furnace of fire." O unhappy weed! O unhappy sinner! What use was it to have been green and flowering in the world, and having given yourself to all kinds of pleasures and lusts, only to become dry and withered and thrown away to be burned, yet in burning you are not consumed by the flames? What use was your short time of merriment if it meant your being tormented for all eternity? "He shall cast them into the fiery furnace, where there will be weeping and gnashing of teeth" (Mt 13:42).

So then, Catholic Listeners, seeing that Almighty God sowed us as good seed in the field of the world, let us then grow and thrive as good seed, and not become weeds through sin and negligence. We must always keep in mind the end for which we were created. Do you want to think only about things that are passing and never about eternity? O, how the sighs, the laments and gnashing of teeth

---

13 . St Thomas Aquinas, On the First Epistle to the Corinthians, ch.15, 1007.

of those unfortunate, damned souls should constantly ring in our ears to move our hearts to contrition and repentance. Their groaning will bear no fruit; let us weep here, for our tears can still wash away our guilt, our sighs can still pay our debts. Let us then take heed that we become pure wheat, for only then will we be placed in the celestial barn of eternal happiness. Who lives, etc.

On the Sixth Sunday after Epiphany

Simile est regnum caelorum grano sinapis — "The kingdom of Heaven is like a mustard seed" (Mt 13:31).

CATHOLIC LISTENERS, THE LARGEST
and fairest things usually have a small beginning. It
seems that nature wants to hide her immense power
by bringing forth great and beautiful things from
small, humble beginnings. Pliny, therefore, was not
wrong when he said, "Nature can be found in her entirety nowhere
more than in her smallest creatures."[1] Thus great trees sprout from
small seeds; a mighty river springs from a small source; large animals
come from a small substance. The seeds of all things are encapsulated
in a bit of small stuff, and small material can contain great power.
Precious stones are worthy objects, and there is great value in only a
small quantity of them. Among all the seeds, the mustard seed must
be one of the smallest, yet in its smallness is contained such great
power and fertility that it will bring forth a plant which looks like a
tree, and that can outgrow all other plants in size. This is why Our
Saviour in today's Gospel compared the Kingdom of Heaven to a
mustard seed, for even though the Kingdom of Heaven now still
appears to be quite small to the world and its people, the day will
come when it will be great, beautiful, striking, and delightful. When
compared to Heaven the earth is only a small dot, and everything that
is now considered valuable and magnificent in the world shall become
vain and deceptive. Those people who have set their hearts on pleasures, lust, wealth and possessions, comfort and prosperity, will see
that they have been deceived, that everything is just smoke and fading

---

1 *Natura nusquam magis, quam in minimis tota est.* Pliny the Elder, Natural
History, Book 11, ch. 2.

vanity. That is why in the end the Wise Man, after experiencing joy, prosperity, pleasures of the flesh, and after he had possessed an abundance of furniture and house furnishings and animals and horses, had been forced to admit the truth, "Vanity of vanities, all is vanity" (Eccl 12:8). This is very close to the instruction Our Saviour gives us in today's Gospel, but before explaining this in broader terms, let us first pray for the grace of the Holy Spirit, through the intercession of the Blessed Virgin Mary, by presenting to her the angelic greeting,

Ave Maria

THE WORLD, TO OUR EYES, CAN SEEM A DELIGHTFUL place. Through our status of life, our honours, treasures, and riches, the world becomes elevated, much like a beautiful tree whose green, sweet branches are spread with pleasures and fleshly delights. By contrast, the Kingdom of Heaven seems small and insignificant because it cannot easily be seen by the world, and so it remains enclosed in the darkness and obscurity of the Faith. But the time will come when all this will change. "The world, and the desire for it, are passing away" (1 Jn 2:17). Like a tree, the world will pass, together with the flowers of its dignities, the greenness of its treasures and riches, and the leaves of its comforts and pleasures, by which many people are enticed and enchanted. The Kingdom of Heaven, that now might seem to us like a dream, shall raise itself from insignificance and dejection; and when we leave this world in God's love and untainted by sin, we will see its triumph and magnificence, provided that we be found worthy to enjoy it. However, the Kingdom of Heaven is not just the Church Triumphant and the glory awaiting us in Heaven on high, but it is also the Church Militant here on earth. We shall first examine how very small it was in the beginning, similar to a mustard seed, and how it has now become like a beautiful, tall tree. Then we shall show how the greatness and excellence of the coming glory of the Kingdom of Heaven, which is still hidden and small, shall be revealed through the beatific vision.

First of all then, the comparison of the Kingdom of Heaven to a mustard seed can be likened to the militant Catholic Church here on earth. So we read in Sacred Scripture, and in particular St Matthew's

Gospel, "The Son of Man will send His angels, and they will collect out of His kingdom all causes of sin" (Mt 13:41). Kingdom here means the Catholic Church. In the kingdom of the Saints, where eternal peace reigns, says St Gregory, there can be no causes of sin to be collected. We also see this in the parable of the Ten Virgins; there were five wise virgins and five foolish ones. If we compare this to the Kingdom of Heaven, then it is obvious that it cannot be understood as being the state of the Saints in Heaven, because no fools or reprobates can be found there, as portrayed by the foolish virgins. Instead, we understand this as being the gathering of the faithful in the Church Militant, where the grain and chaff, the good and wicked, the wheat and weeds, the wise and foolish, the chosen and rejected are all still mingled together until the angels separate them on the Day of Judgement. So we can be certain that when Sacred Scripture mentions the Kingdom of Heaven, it often means the Catholic Church Militant. As St Gregory says, "Often the sacred writings say that the Church is the Kingdom of Heaven here on earth."[2]

The dawn is considered to be the beginning of the day, even though it still contains some gloominess; so, too, the Catholic Church can be called the Kingdom of Heaven because she is the entrance and forecourt of the Celestial Kingdom. She can be likened to the breaking dawn of an eternal day, so to speak, even though some of the night still remains in the day, and even though the wicked are still mixed in with the good and the children of darkness with the children of light. Moreover, the seed contains all the power and integrity of the fruit, even though this has not yet been put into effect. It is like the grace of God, the seed of glory, that is given to us on earth, and which was prepared for us in Heaven. This grace contains in itself, in a certain manner, the Kingdom of Heaven, that is, both the glory and the Catholic Church. Furthermore, both the earthly and the heavenly Jerusalem belong to the same Kingdom, seeing these two cities both claim the same King, that is, Almighty God; they also follow the same law, which is His divine will, and they have the same subjects, that is, the people to whom the Divine King revealed Himself and

---

2 *Saepe in sacro eloquio regnum caelorum praesentis temporis Ecclesia dicitur.* St Gregory the Great, Homilies on the Gospels, Book 1, Homily 12.

made Himself known, for He bears to both the same love, given that He wants not a single one of them to be lost.

The Catholic Church, which is the place where we are now present, represents to us the Kingdom of Heaven, which is our final destination. In the beginning the Church was like a mustard seed, so she was very small in every way. She was small in her Founder, Christ our Saviour; she was small in her co-founders, the Apostles; she was small in her material goods, that is, her teachings and mysteries; she was small in her body and members, that is, the faithful people. The Founder of the Catholic Church even likened Himself to a worm of the earth, as we hear from the mouth of King David, "But I am a worm, and no man; the reproach of men, and the outcast of the people" (Ps 21:7). Her co-founders were considered scum of the earth, "We have become the garbage of the world" (1 Cor 4:13). Her material goods, which were nothing more than proclaiming the Cross and the One who was crucified on it, were a source of derision to the heathens, "Foolishness to the Gentiles" (1 Cor 1:22). In the beginning, her boundaries and limits did not extend beyond the small house in which the Blessed Virgin Mary and the Apostles were awaiting the coming of the Holy Spirit. The number of faithful that in the beginning made up the Church counted no more than one hundred and twenty persons in total. They were a poor, small, hidden group. Could there have been a more modest and more insignificant person than Jesus, the Founder of the Catholic Church? Listen, He was modest in His birth, being born in a stable, "for there was no room available for them." He was modest in His youth, being considered the son of a carpenter, and by remaining unknown in his foster-father's workshop. He was modest in His teaching, preaching nothing but humility. He was modest in His conversation, always fleeing from the world's honour and praise. Finally, He was modest in His death, dying a shameful death on the Cross. The modesty and humility that always accompanied Him in the world, both at His entrance into it, as well as His exit from it, were in fact the reason that the world did not want to know Him. "The world did not know Him" (Jn 1:10).

The Catholic Church, then, had a very modest Founder, but no less modest were the architects and builders who helped construct her, namely, the Apostles. Even though today we might take for granted the Church's qualities, status, teachings, eloquence, and prudence, we must keep in mind that she was started by common people; they were rough, poor, uneducated, simple men, and they were only twelve in total. But the doctrine they preached was grandiose, ostentatious, and pleasing to everyone. St Paul the Apostle himself testifies to this in somewhat similar words, "but we preach Christ crucified: a stumbling block to Jews and foolishness to Gentiles" (1 Cor 1:23). In other words, we do not preach the majesty of the gods, like Plato the Philosopher; we make no laws, nor do we give orders on the correct governance of a country, like Lycurgus; we do not argue or discourse about the ebb and flow of the sea, like Aristotle; all these sought nothing more than the world's vain glory and praise. But we preach that Jesus was crucified for man's salvation. We teach that man must deny himself and mortify his senses and reject whatever is transient. He must love his God above all other things and set his heart in firm hope on the everlasting good of Heaven.

What can I say about the modest expansion of this nascent Church and of the small number of faithful? At first she could not find a suitable location to establish herself. Jerusalem cast her out, the land of Judah drove her away, and she was persecuted by the heathens. She was odious to the senses, suspect to strangers, persecuted, and made to wander about here and there, attracting only a few poor, rejected people. St Paul the Apostle commented on this, "Not many of you were powerful, not many were of noble birth, but God chose what is foolish in the world to shame the wise; God chose what is low and despised in the world, even things that are not, to bring to nothing things that are" (1 Cor 1:26–28). See how modest the Church was in the beginning; she was like the mustard seed, the smallest among all the seeds. Just compare her modest state with the greatest of the states around her at that time. Compare Jesus with the emperors of Rome; compare the Apostles with the wise philosophers and eloquent orators; her teachings with worldly knowledge, her boundaries with the limits of the Roman Empire; her followers with the thousands of idol worshippers. Would you not say that she was like a speck of dust, or like an ant next to an elephant, or a spring compared to the sea, or a hillock compared to a great mountain? See how that small seed has become a beautiful, large tree that far surpasses all temporal greatness. "As far as cypresses are wont to do among the pliant viburnum."[3] See then how this Catholic Church, once so small and empty, has become so wide and broad, great and mighty. She became known through the generosity and nobleness of Jesus Christ; she expanded through the glory of the Apostles, and because of her magnificent doctrine she was received throughout the entire world. Now it is almost impossible to count the sheer number of her Catholic children, as King David had predicted, "Were I to count them, they would outnumber the grains of sand" (Ps 138:18).

Catholic Listeners, where has this miraculous growth come from if not from the hidden power contained in the mustard seed? This tiny seed was able to bring forth the mighty strength encapsulated within it. Jesus, the Founder and Foundation of the Catholic Church, is that mustard seed that sprouted out of the root of Jesse; it was born of the Blessed Virgin Mary, threshed on the Cross, and sown in the tomb. At His glorious Resurrection He rose from the dead, like a great, beautiful tree whose root tramples hell and whose top opens Heaven; its branches embrace the world and its leaves and fruit nourish all the peoples, "and the leaves of the tree are for the healing of the nations" (Rev 22:2). I do not say this of my own accord, but listen to what St Gregory says, "For He is Himself 'a grain of mustard seed', who, when He was planted in the burial place of the garden, rose up a great tree. For He was 'a grain', whereas He died, but 'a tree', whereas He rose again. 'A grain', through the abasement of the flesh, 'a tree', through the mightiness of His majesty."[4] The Apostles, too, according to Theophylactus, can be called mustard seeds, because from being very small they rose to great heights. Those who the world once

---

3 *Quantum lenta solent inter viburna cupressi.* Publius Virgilius Maro (Virgil), Bucolics, 1, 19–25. Virgil tries to show the superiority of Rome over the other cities. Rome, like a tall cypress tree, rises high over the pliant and spreading viburnum bush.

4 *Christus est granum sinapis, qui mortis sepultura plantatus arbor magna surrexit: granum namque fuit cum moreretur: arbor, cum resurgeret; granum per humilitatem carnis; arbor per potentiam maiestatis.* St Gregory the Great, Morals on the Book of Job, Book 19, ch. 3.

called scum of the earth have become princes. "You will make them princes over all the earth" (Ps 44:16). St Chrysostom says that kings and emperors considered it a great honour if they could be buried near the doors of the churches dedicated to the Apostles. "The kings have becomes the doorkeepers of the Fishermen."[5] Finally, St Jerome says the preaching of the Gospel can be likened to a mustard seed; the seed of the Gospel is tiny when compared to the splendid doctrines of men; it is enclosed in a little bit of stuff and is bitter to the taste; it does not at all seem desirable, yet when it is planted in the souls of believers it delivers a mystery that cannot be measured but must firmly be believed. And so the Catholic, evangelical Church spread quickly throughout the world, converting all nations and captivating even the most clever intellects. Theodoretus says[6] that twelve poor fishermen, lacking in education and eloquence, were able to convince all kinds of people, which is something the philosophers failed to do, despite all their teaching, their wisdom, knowledge, cleverness, and their eloquence. Thus the mustard seed of the Catholic Church had become a great, beautiful tree through the hidden powers of Jesus Christ, the Apostles and the teachings contained in the Gospels. "Which, when it grows becomes the largest of all shrubs." It rises high in authority and majesty over all the other states of the world, "and kings shall be your nurses" and she extends her branches throughout the world, "she stretched out her branches to the sea, and her boughs to the river."

The Catholic Church started off very small, yet in time grew to be so large that there is nothing on earth that can be compared to it. So, too, the Kingdom of Heaven that is promised us, and is in fact sown and planted in our hearts and souls, shall grow to such great proportions from the small seed it now appears to be, that it shall rise above all the temporal things of this world. I'm sure someone will say, "But where is this Kingdom of Heaven, the one you say is now small but will grow large?" I say that it is not necessary to traverse distant countries to find it. Just enter into your heart and your conscience, and you will find it. How? What are you saying? Shall I find the Kingdom of Heaven within me? Certainly, providing that you are

---

5 *Facti sunt reges ostiarii piscatorum.* St Chrysostom, Against the Jews, 9.
6 Theodoret of Cyrus, Cure of the Greek Maladies.

upright Christian Catholics, you will find it within you, if not as a fruit, then as a seed that will promise to bring forth the fruit. As Our Saviour tells us, "The Kingdom of God is within you" (Lk 17:21).[7] The Kingdom of God is within you, not in its perfection, but in its kernel, and as a shoot. Your heart, soul, and conscience make up the field in which the Kingdom is sown. The Word of God and the preached sermons are also sown there, but to be fruitful they require your consent and cooperation to be properly received. You have heard in today's Gospel how a man has taken this divine seed and sown it in his field. This is to teach us that Almighty God does not do everything by Himself, nor can everything be left to the pastors and priests to do, but that it is necessary for us to cooperate with them. We should therefore remember, maintain and set into action what we have been exhorted to do and what was taught us. Almighty God gives the seed of His Word, the priests till the field of our hearts, the teachers sow the seed, but if we do not get our hearts and souls ready to receive it, with God's grace, it will be sown in vain, and all preaching will have been useless. So then, Catholic Listeners, we must accept the seed of the Kingdom of Heaven with the hands of our conscience. For just as God sows it by His grace, and the priest by his diligence and zeal, so must we sow it in our hearts and souls through our good inclinations, through our Christian fervour and unswerving obedience. In the beginning it appeared very small, or we might better say, it appeared not to be there at all, for it was hidden in the shadows of the Faith, in the humility of the holy Gospel and in the humiliations of Jesus Christ. "Your life is hidden in Christ Jesus" (cf. Col 3:3). What could be more modest to outward appearances than the hope of a Catholic Christian person? For he walks towards a good he has never seen; he expects eternal reward from One who was nailed to a gibbet; his guarantees are just naked, simple words; the means he has are just a few Sacraments that to the senses seem nothing more than modest things; for example, some water at Baptism, some oil at Confirmation, three or four words of absolution in Confession. Nevertheless, through these modest things he can expect the greatest things to be found in the world, namely, the grace of God imparted through some

---

7   Other sources have "The kingdom of God is among you."

water, His Holy Spirit given through some oil, and the Cross with the crucified Jesus through which we receive eternal life. Indeed, it is the great modesty of this heavenly mustard seed that causes so many unbelievers and heretics to stumble, for they become exasperated at the humility of our mysteries, and they do not, or will not, understand the wisdom, the omnipotence, and the love of Almighty God.

Furthermore, do you see how nature uses a few simple means to help our faith and strengthen our hope, so that we might believe that a humble mustard seed could bring forth such a large tree? It is these same means that bring such confusion to unbelievers and comfort to believers. So we see how the modest mysteries of the Catholic Church can bring forth the great glory of the Kingdom of Heaven. If a person has never seen a small seed grow into a large plant, or a small kernel grow into a great tree, or a few small grains into a meadow, he would not believe it possible. We, on the other hand, see this happening daily in our fields and orchards, so we should expect the same to happen to our faith and hope, and we shall see that the seed of the Kingdom of Heaven that is so modestly hidden in the Christian mysteries and the holy Sacraments shall bring forth within us a beautiful tree of glory and immortality. Now some of you might say, "I do not see this glory, this good, this kingdom that was promised me." No wonder, because in the seed you see neither tree, branches, flowers, nor fruit. But the seed you see promises you a tree, which you do not yet see, and nature will not deceive you, but at the right time she will produce for you the tree, the flowers, and the fruit. In the same way should you believe and expect with firm hope that the Kingdom of Heaven, whose seed you now have in the holy Sacraments, shall at the right time not fail to produce fruits for you, provided you make yourself worthy to pluck them. "Like a tree that yields its fruit in due season" (Ps 1:3). Let us, therefore, trust more in God than in nature, more in His word than in a grain, more in His promise than in a small shoot. Even though what we possess of the Kingdom of Heaven is modest, we must keep in mind that it is just a grain, and a grain is usually small of body but great in potential strength; thus must we cultivate it by our love, by our fervent prayers, by the holy Sacraments and by virtuous deeds. This divine seed shall, without a doubt, grow strongly in our hearts, it shall rise by faith, it shall grow by hope, and it shall spread by love, thereby causing wonderful peace in our souls, which will be like a foretaste of heavenly peace, as St Paul the Apostle tells us, "The Kingdom of God is righteousness, joy and peace in the Holy Spirit" (Rom 14:17).

The person who wants to taste the strength of mustard must first grind or smash it to pieces; similarly, he who wants to taste the power of God's word and of the Catholic Faith must first carefully mull it over in his mind and meditate on it. Before long, he will notice the extent to which the great God, who owed us nothing, humbled Himself for our sake, even dying on the Cross for us. He will also notice God's great love, His endless mercy for the just, and His strict justice towards obstinate sinners. Eventually he will feel a hidden mighty strength that will move him to a holy fear of God; from his eyes and heart there shall be squeezed an upright sorrow and contrition for his sins. This contrition will be accompanied by a burning love for Almighty God, who will warm and inflame his heart. "In my meditation a fire shall flame out" (Ps 38:4). Indeed, he shall be shown what fire there is contained in just one small doctrinal point of the Catholic Faith. "Your word is exceedingly tried by fire" (Ps 118:140). Furthermore, when mustard is ground and mixed with vinegar it becomes an effective remedy against the bites of snakes and scorpions; in a similar way does the confirmation of the mysteries of our Faith, when mixed with the vinegar of penitence and applied to the interior wounds of our sins, provide spiritual relief and health. And finally, just as mustard gives a particular flavour to sauces and other dishes, so does observing the tenets of our Faith, and thinking about the Kingdom of Heaven, which we expect in the life to come, gives us a certain contentment of life, a relief of suffering, and an interior joy as we journey in our exile. So then, Catholic Listeners, notice how the Kingdom of Heaven was initially small, but in this present life it can grow large in the hearts of true Christians, where it produces the fruits of holy conversion and divine love. These are fruits, I say, that can weed out sins and bring spiritual comfort, which in sweetness and steadfastness far surpasses all temporal pleasures. "Which, when it grows becomes the largest of all shrubs."

But alas! very few people will taste the power of this divine seed. Very few will observe the truth of the Catholic Faith, and few will think about the Kingdom of Heaven that the Faith has sown within them. Our daily concerns often stifle the Word of God within us, and so we often do not think about loving Almighty God above all things, nor do we think about achieving Christian perfection. We dream about virtually nothing else than trying to get ahead in the world; we dream of prestige and honour, of money and possessions and of enjoying the pleasures of the world. We let ourselves be beguiled by the beautiful tree Nebuchadnezzar had seen in his dream, which meant nothing more than the vain glory of the world (see Dn 4). Yet there was a voice heard from the heavens, "cut down the tree and trim off its branches; strip off its leaves and scatter its fruit"; so too when we follow the vanity of the world, and think little about our salvation, Almighty God commands that we be cut down. He surprises us with death; and so He prunes the branches of our pleasures, the leaves of our lust, and the fruit of our temporal goods. The body is cast into the grave and the soul often ends up eternally lost. Yet despite all these warnings and experiences, we are not afraid, nor do we have misgivings, yet we are truly blind. The world misleads us, but it will one day pass like smoke; we are enchanted, yet we follow. We forget the true good for which we were created; we forget Heaven, which alone is steadfast, and we love the world that is passing. On our deathbed we cannot have both; we will leave this world, but we will have no part in the Kingdom of Heaven because we neglected to make a place for its seed in our soul while we were still in the world.

Catholic Listeners, let us then use our intelligence wisely. Let us spurn the world in which we will rot away and let us seek Heaven, which is where we will live for all eternity. Let us nurture the mustard seed of the Kingdom of Heaven planted in our souls by the Catholic Faith through the holy Sacraments, by keeping God's commandments and by doing good works. The seed will then certainly become a great tree reaching up to the glory of Heaven, where we will see God face to face for all eternity. Who lives, etc.

Authors and Sources

(The Romans numerals I, II, III, IV, V refer to the volumes where the sources may be found)

AMBROSE OF MILAN
Commentary on the Gospel according to Luke
(*Expositio evangelii secundum Lucam*)
    I Bk 1: 2 Sun Advent
        Bk 2: Christmas 2.
    II Bk 5: 5 Sun after Easter.
    III Bk 4: 24 Sun after Pent
        Bk 5: 15 Sun after Pent
        Bk 7: 14 Sun after Pent.
    IV Bl Godfrey
        Bk 2: Annunciation 2, Visitation 1.
    V Bk 4: St Michael Arch
        Bk 5: St Bartholomew
        Bk 10: St Matthew.

Exposition on the Psalms (*Explanatio psalmorum*)
    I Ps 118: 4 Sun Advent.
    II Ps 118: 5 Sun after Easter.
    III Ps 116: 23 Sun after Pent
        Ps 118: 5 Sun after Pent
        21 Sun after Pent.

On Flight from the World (*De fuga saeculi*)
    I 3 Sun Advent

On the Death of Theodosius (*De obitu Theodosi*)
    III 15 Sun after Pent

On the Mysteries (*De mysteriis*)
    II 1 Sun Lent

On the Christian Faith (*De fide ad Gratianum Augustum*)
    II Bk 1: Easter Sun 2

On the Life of Joseph (*De Ioseph Patriarcha*)
 II Easter Sun 2
On Naboth (*De Nabuthae Historia*)
 III 14 Sun after Pent
On the Birth of St John the Baptist
 (*De praerogativa eiusdem S. Ioannes Baptistae*)
 IV St Herman-Joseph
On Widows (*De viduis*)
 V St Martin
[uncertain] Homily on Saints Nazarius and Celsus
 (*Sermo de S. Nazario*)
 V St Martin

ANSELM OF CANTERBURY
Why God became Man (*Cur Deus homo*)
 I 6 Sun after Epiph
Meditation on Psalm 50 (*Meditatio super Miserere*)
 III 9 Sun after Pent
On the Conception of the Blessed Virgin Mary
 (*De conceptione Beatae Mariae Virginis*)
 IV Presentation BVM
Commentary on 1 Corinthians
 V All Souls
[uncertain] On the Excellence of the Blessed Virgin
 (*De excellentia gloriosissimae Viginis*)
 V Nativity BVM 1

ANTONINUS OF FLORENCE
Summa theologica moralis
 III Bk 3: Trinity Sun
 IV Bk 4: Visitation 1

APULEIUS (LUCIUS APULEIUS MADAURENSIS)
The Apologia
 IV St Nicholas

AQUINAS, THOMAS
 (*see* Thomas Aquinas)

ARISTOTLE
Lectures on Nature (Φυσικὴ ἀκρόασις) 4
    II   Easter Sun 1
Nichomachean Ethics (Ἠθικὰ Νικομάχεια)
    III 15 Sun after Pent
    IV St Thomas Ap

ARNOLD OF BONNEVAL (CARNOTENSIS)
In Praise of the Blessed Virgin Mary
  (*De laudibus Beatae Mariae Virginis*)
    II Easter Tues
    V Nativity BVM 2

ATHANASIUS OF ALEXANDRIA
Life of St Antony of Egypt (*Vita Antonii*)
    III 22 Sun after Pent
    IV Annunciation 2
Against the Arians (*Adversus Arianos*)
    IV Disc 3: St Peter's Chair
Defence to Constantius (*Apologiam ad Constantium*)
    V Dedication of church

AUGUSTINE OF HIPPO
Against Cresconius (*Contra Cresconium*)
    III 16 Sun after Pent
Against Faustus the Manichaean (*Contra Faustum Manichaeum*)
    II Easter Sun 2
City of God (*De civitate Dei*)
    I   Bk 11: 5 Sun after Epiph
         Bk 14: 4 Sun after Epiph
         Bk 16: 2 Sun Advent
    II Bk 18: Palm Sunday
         Bk 19: Easter Tues
         Bk 22: Easter Tues
    III Bk 11: 17 Sun after Pent
         Bk 12: Pent Tues
         Bk 22: 7 Sun after Pent
         Bk 22: 23 Sun after Pent
    IV Bk 11: St Matthias
    V Bk 20: All Souls

Confessions (*Confessiones*)
   I Bk 10: 1 Sun after Epiph
  II Bk 7: 1 Sun after Easter
      Bk 8: Passion 2
      Bk 10: 5 Sun Lent
 III Bk 3: 3 Sun after Pent, 20 Sun after Pent
      Bk 6: 7 Sun after Pent, 24 Sun after Pent
      Bk 8: 3 Sun after Pent, 8 Sun after Pent
      Bk 10: Pentecost Sun 1, 11 Sun after Pent
 IV Bk 1: St Herman-Joseph
      Bk 7: Corp Chr
  V Bk 1: St Norbert
      Bk 2: Conv St Aug
      Bk 3: Conv St Aug
      Bk 4: Conv St Aug
      Bk 5: Conv St Aug
      Bk 8: Conv St Aug
      Bk 4: St Catherine
      Bk 9: All Souls
      Bk 15: All Saints 1

Enchiridion (*Enchiridion de fide, spe et caritate*)
   I ch 26: 4 Sun Advent
  II ch 30: Palm Sunday
 III ch 76: 7 Sun after Pent

Exposition on the Psalms (*Enarrationes in psalmos*)
   I Ps 26: 3 Sun Advent
      Ps 54: 5 Sun after Epiph
      Ps 70: 4 Sun after Epiph
      Ps 84: 3 Sun Advent
      Ps 118: 4 Sun Advent
      Ps 131: 3 Sun Advent
  II Ps 34: 5 Sun Lent
      Ps 113: 5 Sun after Easter
      Ps 164: Easter Tues
 III Ps 4: 20 Sun after Pent
      Ps 30:10 Sun after Pent
      Ps 32: 7 Sun after Pent
      Ps 38: 22 Sun after Pent
      Ps 49: Pentecost Sun 1

Ps 61:19 Sun after Pent
Ps 118: 3 Sun after Pent
Ps 131: Corp Chr
IV Ps 54: Finding of Cross
Ps 86: St Matthias
Ps 118: Visitation 1
V Ps 1: St Matthew
Ps 36: All Saints 1
Ps 73: All Souls
Ps 93: All Saints 1
Ps 102: St Matthew

Letter 187 to Dardanus (*Epistola ad Dardanum*)
I Sunday in Oct Christmas
Letter 210 To Felicitas and Rusticus (*Ad Felicitati et Rustico*)
III 20 Sun after Pent
Letter 157 to Hilarius (*Epistola ad Hilario*)
II 5 Sun Lent
Letter 155 To Macedonius (*Ad Macedonium*)
III 17 Sun after Pent
On Catechizing the Uninstructed (*De catechizandis rudibus*)
I ch 4: 4 Sun Advent
II Palm Sunday
On Faith and Works (*De fide et operibus*)
IV St Thomas Ap
On the Perfection of Human Righteousness
(*De perfection iustitiae hominis*)
III 17 Sun after Pent
On Nature and Grace (*De natura et gratia*)
III 6 Sun after Pent
17 Sun after Pent
On Free Will (*De libero arbitrio*)
III ch 3: 2 Sun after Pent
IV ch 6: Conv St Paul
V ch 12: Conv St Aug, All Saints 1
On the Harmony of the Gospels (*De Consensu Evangeliorum*)
I Bk 2: Holy Innocents
On Holy Virginity (*De sancta virginitate*)
V Assumption 2

On the Catholic and Manichaean Ways of Life
(*De moribus Ecclesiae catholicae*)
   III ch 26: 12 Sun after Pent
On the Spirit and the Letter (*De spiritu et littera*)
   III Pentecost Sun 1
On True Religion (*De vera religione*)
   I ch 16: 4 Sun Advent
On the Trinity (*De Trinitate*)
   II Bk 13: 3 Sun after Easter
   III Bk 15: Trinity Sun
Rule of Saint Augustine (*Praeceptum*)
   II ch 1: Easter Tues
Sermons on the Old Testament (*De vetere testamento*)
   II Sermon 2: Passion 3
   III Sermon 9: 7 Sun after Pent
Sermons on the New Testament (*De verbis domini*)
   I Sermon 12: Christmas 2
   II Sermon 11: 5 Sun after Easter
   III Sermon 8: 10 Sun after Pent
      Sermon 61: 20 Sun after Pent
      Sermon 88: 20 Sun after Pent
   IV Sermon 37: St Andrew
      Sermon 69: St Thomas Ap
   V Sermon 55: All Saints 1
      Sermon 69: Assumption 2, St Bartholomew
Sermons on the Words of the Apostle (*De verbis apostoli*)
   I Sermon 171: 3 Sun Advent
   IV Sermon 175: Conv St Paul
   V Sermon 27: Assumption 2
      Sermon 172: All Souls
Sermons on the liturgical seasons (*Sermones de tempore*)
   II Sermon 119: Easter Sun 1
   III Sermon 4: 24 Sun after Pent
      Sermon 26: 16 Sun after Pent
   IV Sermon 157: St Peter's Chair
Sermons on the Ascension (*Sermo de Ascensione Domini*)
   II Sermon 1: Easter Sun 1
      Sermon 3: Ascension
   III Sermon 2:10 Sun after Pent

Sermon on the Lord's Sermon on the Mount
(*De sermone domini in monte*)
  II 3 Sun after Easter

Sermon to Catechumens on the Creed (*De symbolo ad catechumenos*)
  I Bk 4: 2 Sun Advent

Sermon 209 for the Feast of All Saints
  V All Saints 1

Sermon 319 for the Feast of Stephen the Martyr
(*In solemnitate Stephani martyris*)
  III 10 Sun after Pent

Sermon 338 for the Dedication of a Church
  III 22 Sun after Pent

Soliloquies (*Soliloquiorum libri duo*)
  I Bk 1: 2 Sun Advent, 2 Christmas
  III Bk 1:14 Sun after Pent, 24 Sun after Pent
  Book 2: 3 Sun after Pent

Tractates on the First Epistle of John
(*In epistolam Ioannis ad Parthos tractatus*)
  II Tract 5: 2 Sun after Easter
  III Tract 1: 12 Sun after Pent
  Tract 7: Pentecost Mon
  Tract 10: 12 Sun after Pent

Tractates on the Gospel of John (*In Ioannis evangelium tractatus*)
  I Tract 9: 2 Sun after Epiph
  Tract 24: 2 Sun after Epiph
  Tract 36: St John Ev
  Tract 113: 4 Sun Advent
  II Tract 26: 5 Sun Lent;
  III Tract 8: Corp Chr
  Tract 23: 14 Sun after Pent
  Tract 24: 16 Sun after Pent
  Tract 28: 12 Sun after Pent
  Tract 45: Pentecost Tues
  Tract 138: 17 Sun after Pent
  V Tract 34: All Saints 1
  Tract 49: Nativity BVM 1
  Tract 72: St Norbert

BASIL THE GREAT
Commentary on the Prophet Isaiah (*Commentariis in Isaiam*)
    I ch. 2: St Stephen
Homilies On Deuteronomy (*Commentariis in Deuteronomio*)
    I Homily 3: 5 Sun after Epiph
On Fasting (Περὶ Νηστείας)
    II Sermon 1: Ash Wednesday
        Sermon 2: Ash Wednesday
    III 6 Sun after Pent
The Six Days (Ἡ Ἑξαήμερος Δημιουργία)
    III Homily 2: Pentecost Sun 1

BARONIUS, CESARE CARDINAL
Ecclesiastical Annals (*Annales Ecclesiastici*)
    I Tome 1, 31: 3 Sun Advent
      Tome 1, 98: St John Ev
    II Tome 1, 34: Passion 2
    III Tome 3, 259: 8 Sun after Pent
      Tome 3, 302: 15 Sun after Pent
    IV Tome 1,31: Sts Philip & James
    V Tome 1, 60: St Michael Arch
      Tome 13, 775: Assumption 1
      Tome 16, 971: Assumption 1

BEDE, THE VENERABLE
Ecclesiastical History (*Historia ecclesiastica gentis Anglorum*)
    III Bk 1: Trinity Sun
On the Eleventh Sunday after Pentecost
    III 11 Sun after Pent
On the Gospel of Luke (*Commentarius in Lucam*)
    III 16 Sun after Pent
On the Gospel of John (*Expositio in S. Ioannis Evangelium*)
    IV Annunciation 2

BELLARMINE, ROBERT
On the Veneration of the Saints (*De cultu sanctorum*)
    III Bk 3: Trinity Sun

BERNARD OF CLAIRVAUX
Declamations (*Declamationes*)
   V Assumption 2
Letter 42, On the Office and Conduct of Bishops
   IV Sts Peter & Paul
Life of St Malachy (*Vita Sancti Malachiae*)
   I ch.7: 3 Sun Advent
   III ch.5: 12 Sun after Pent
   V ch.2: All Souls
Occasional Sermons (*De diversis*)
   II 5 Sun after Easter
On Consideration (*De consideratione*)
   III Bk 4: 16 Sun after Pent
On Loving God (*De diligendo Deo*)
   I ch. 2: 3 Sun Advent
      ch. 7: 3 Sun Advent
   II ch. 2: Palm Sunday
      ch. 3: Palm Sunday
   III ch. 2: 12 Sun after Pent
      ch. 5: 12 Sun after Pent
Sermon for the Feast of the Circumcision
   I New Year's Day
Sermon on the Holy Name of Jesus
   I New Year's Day
Sermons for Advent (*In adventu domini*)
   I Sermon 1: 4 Sun Advent
Sermons for Christmas (*In nativitate domini*)
   IV Sermon 1: Annunciation 1
      Sermon 3: St Joseph
Sermons for Lent on Psalm 90 (*Qui habitat*)
   V Sermon 7: St Catherine
      Sermon 17: All Saints 1
[uncertain] **Sermon for Maundy Thursday**
  (*Sermo de excellentia SS. Sacramenti et dignitate Sacerdotum*)
   III Corp Chr
Sermon on the Lord's Supper (*Sermo in coena domini*)
   III 23 Sun after Pent
Sermons for Eastertide (*Homilia in Pascha*)
   I Sermon 3: 4 Sun after Epiph

II   Sermon 1: Easter Sun 1

Sermon on the Lord's Ascension (*De ascensione domini*)
II   Sermon 2: Ascension
   Sermon 6: 4 Sun after Easter

Sermons for Pentecost
II   Sermon 3: 6 Sun after Easter

[uncertain] **Sermon on the Sevenfold Gifts of the Holy Spirit**
(*De septem donis S. Spiritus*)
III   5 Sun after Pent

Sermon for the Sixth Sunday after Pentecost
III   Sermon 1: 6 Sun after Pent
V   Sermon 3: St Martin

Sermons on the Annunciation (*De Annuntiatione B. Mariae Virginis*)
I   Sermon 1: Epiphany
II   Sermon 3: 5 Sun after Easter
III   Sermon 3: 10 Sun after Pent
IV   Sermon 1: Annunciation 1

Sermons on the Assumption (*De Assumptione B. Mariae Virginis*)
V   Sermon 4: Nativity BVM 2
   Sermon 5: Assumption 2

Sermon on the Sunday within the Octave of the Assumption
(*Sermo ex verbo Apocalypsis*)
V   Sermon 1: Assumption 2

Sermon on the Conversion of St Paul (*Sermo in conversione Sti Pauli*)
V   Conv St Aug

Sermons for the Feast of All Saints (*In festo omnium sanctorum*)
V   Sermon 2: All Saints 2

Sermon for the Feast of St Martin (*Sermo in festivitate sancti Martini*)
III   2 Sun after Pent
V   St Martin

Sermon on the Nativity of the Blessed Virgin Mary
(*Sermo in nativitate BVM*)
IV   Annunciation 2
V   Assumption 2

Sermons in Praise of the Blessed Virgin Mary
(*De laudibus beatae Mariae virginis*)
V   Sermon 2: Nativity BVM 1

Sermons for the Dedication of a Church (*In dedicatione ecclesiae*)
   V Sermon 2: Dedication of church
      Sermon 4: Dedication of church
Sermon on the Vigil of our Lord's Nativity
  (*Sermo in vigilia nativitatis Domini*)
     I Sermon 3: 1 Sun Advent
   III 8 Sun after Pent
   IV Sermon 13: Visitation 2
    V Assumption 1
Sermons on the Song of Songs (*Sermones super Cantica Canticorum*)
     I Sermon 15: 2 Sun Advent
       Sermon 20: 3 Sun Advent
       Sermon 30: 6 Sun after Epiph
       Sermon 33: Sun in Oct Christmas.
   II Sermon 11: Palm Sunday
       Sermon 16: 5 Sun after Easter
       Sermon 20: Palm Sunday
       Sermon 62: 5 Sun after Easter.
   III Sermon 14: 17 Sun after Pent
       Sermon 20: 12 Sun after Pent, 16 Sun after Pent
       Sermon 23: 17 Sun after Pent
       Sermon 27: 17 Sun after Pent
       Sermon 30: 3 Sun after Pent, 8 Sun after Pent
       Sermon 55: 24 Sun after Pent
       Sermon 61: 21 Sun after Pent
       Sermon 75: 20 Sun after Pent.
   IV Sermon 2: Annunciation 1
       Sermon 30: Sts Peter & Paul.
    V Sermon 11: All Saints 1
       Sermon 20: St Catherine
       Sermon 33: St Norbert.
Sermon on the Versatile Usefulness of God's Word
  (*De multiplici utilitate verbi Dei*)
   II Sermon 24: 4 Sun after Easter
[uncertain] **The Nature and dignity of divine love**
  (*De natura et dignitate divini amoris*)
   III 23 Sun after Pent
The Scale of Perfection (*Scala perfectionis*)
   II Book 1: 5 Sun after Easter

Treatise on the Passion of the Christ (*Tractatus de Passione Domini*)
 II Tract 3: Palm Sunday

BOETHIUS (ANICIUS MANLIUS SEVERINUS BOËTHIUS)
The Consolation of Philosophy (*De consolatione philosophiae*)
 V Book 3: All Saints 1

BONAVENTURE
Treatise of the Passion of the Lord (*Tractatus de Passione Domini*)
 III 6 Sun after Pent
The Sunday Sermons
 III Sermon 1: 13 Sun after Pent
   Sermon 21: 22 Sun after Pent
Commentary on St Matthew's Gospel
 (*Expositio evangelii secundum Matthaeum*)
 III Sermon 1: 14 Sun after Pent
Mirror of the Blessed Virgin Mary (*Speculum beatae Mariae virginis*)
 IV Imm Conc
 V Nativity BVM 1

BRIDGET OF SWEDEN
Revelations (*Revelationes coelestes*)
 V Assumption 2

CAESARIUS OF ARLES
Sermon 77 (*De genibus flectendis*)
 V St Bartholomew

CASSIODORUS
(FLAVIUS MAGNUS AURELIUS CASSIODORUS SENATOR)
Variae epistolae
 II Book 1: Ash Wednesday

CELSUS (AULUS CORNELIUS CELSUS)
On Medicine (*De medicina*)
 III 18 Sun after Pent

CICERO (MARCUS TULLIUS CICERO)
For Ligarius (*Pro Ligario*)
 I Book 6: St Stephen
For Marcellus (*Pro Marcello*)
 II Book 2: 4 Sun Lent

Letter to Brutus (*Orator ad Marcus Brutum*)
    I St John Evangelist
On the Nature of the Gods (*De natura deorum*)
    III Book I: Trinity Sun

CLEMENT OF ALEXANDRIA
The Stromata (Στρώματα)
    II Book 7: 5 Sun after Easter
    III 16 Sun after Pent
    IV Book 3: Sts Philip &James

CORNELIUS À LAPIDE
Commentary on Sacred Scripture (*Comentaria in scripturam sacram*)
    III Tome 2: Corp Chr
Commentary on the Pentateuch (*Commentaria in Pentateuchum Moysis*)
    III 2 Sun after Pent
Commentary on Matthew (*Commentaria in Matthaeum*)
    III 14 Sun after Pent

CYRIL OF ALEXANDRIA
On the Gospel According to John
    I Book 2: 2 Sun after Epiph
    III Book 1: Pentecost Sun 1
    IV Book 10: Sts Peter & Paul
Thesaurus on the Trinity (*Thesaurus de Trinitate*)
    IV Ch.16: St Peter's Chair

CYRIL OF JERUSALEM
Catechetical Lectures (Κατηχήσεις)
    III Lecture 16: Pentecost Sun 2
Procatechesis
    IV St Andrew

CYPRIAN OF CARTHAGE
On the Unity of the Catholic Church (*De catholicae Ecclesiae unitate*)
    III Treatise 1,9: 3 Sun Advent
Letter to Donatus (*Epistola ad Donatum*)
    III Epistle 1: 7 Sun after Pent
Letter to Nemesianus and Other Martyrs (*Ad Nemesianum et caeteros*)
    IV Epistle 76: St Andrew

Letter to the Roman Clergy
    IV   Epistle 3: St Peter's Chair

DE RIBERA, FRANCISCO
The Life of St Teresa of Jesus (*Vida de Santa Teresa de Jesús*)
    III   Corp Chr

DIONYSIUS (DENIS) THE AREOPAGITE
Ecclesiastical Hierarchy (*Ecclesiastica herarchia*)
    III   Pentecost Sun 1
    IV   St Matthias
    V   Dedication of church

EPIPHANIUS OF SALAMIS
Against Heresies (Πανάριον)
    I   Holy Innocents
    V   St Anne
Anchoratus (Ἀγκυρατός)
    II   Easter Sun 2

EUCHERIUS OF LYON
Homily for Pentecost
    III   Pentecost Tues
Letter to Valerian (*Epistola paraenetica ad Valerianum cognatum*)
    III   8 Sun after Pent
    V   St Catherine
Instruction to Salonius (*Institutionis ad Salonium*)
    V   Nativity BVM 1

EUSEBIUS OF CAESAREA
Life of Constantine (*Vita Constantini*)
    V   Dedication of church

EUTHYMIUS ZIGABENUS
Commentary on St Mark's Gospel
    III   Chapter 8: 20 Sun after Pent

FRANCIS DE SALES
Introduction to the Devout Life (*Introduction à la vie dévote*)
    III   5 Sun after Pent

FRANCIS SUAREZ
(*see* Suarez, Francis)

FULBERT OF CHARTRES
On the Annunciation (*De Annuntiatione Dominica*)
    I   Sermon 9: 2 Sun after Epiph

FULGENTIUS OF RUSPE
[uncertain] Homily in praise of Mary giving birth to the
    Saviour (*De laudibus Mariae ex partu Salvatoris*)
    V   Homily 36: Nativity BVM 1
[uncertain] Mythologies (*Mythologiae*)
    V   Book 1: All Souls

GALENUS, AELIUS
Commentaries on the Aphorisms of Hippocrates
    III   11 Sun after Pent

GÉNÉBRARD, GILBERT
Commentary on the Psalms (*Psalmi Davidis*)
    III   Ps 110: 8 Sun after Pent
         Ps 39: 16 Sun after Pent

GERMANUS OF CONSTANTINOPLE
Homily in Praise of the Virgin Mary's Belt
    (*De zona et fasciis Deiparae*)
    V   Nativity BVM 1

GERSON, JEAN
Treatises on the Magnificat (*Collectorium super Magnificat*)
    III   Tractate 9: Corp Chr

GERTRUDE THE GREAT
The Herald of Divine Love (*Legatus divinae pietatis*)
    I   Book 4: Christmas 2

GRATIAN (FLAVIUS GRATIANUS)
The Treatise on Laws (*Decretum Gratiani*)
    V   Part III: Dedication of church

GREGORY THE GREAT
Homilies on the Gospels (*Homiliae in Evangelia*).
    I   Homily 11: 1 Sun Advent
        Homily 12: 6 Sun after Epiph
        Homily 15: 5 Sun after Epiph, 6 Sun after Epiph
        Homily 25: New Year's Day
        Homily 29: 4 Sun Advent
        Homily 30: Christmas 1
    II   Homily 14: 1 Sun after Easter
        Homily 21: Ascension
        Homily 37: 3 Sun after Easter
   III Homily 29: 20 Sun after Pent
        Homily 33: 18 Sun after Pent
        Homily 34: 3 Sun after Pent
        Homily 38: 19 Sun after Pent
        Homily 39: 9 Sun after Pent
   IV Homily 13: St Herman-Joseph
        Homily 17: Finding of Cross
        Homily 26: St Thomas Ap
        Homily 34: Annunciation 1
        Homily 36: 2 Sun after Pent
    V   Homily 32: St Norbert
        Homily 39: Assumption 2
Moralia in Job (*Moralia*)
    I   Book 9: 2 Sun Advent
        Book 19: 2 Sun Advent, 6 Sun after Epiph
        Book 34: 1 Sun Advent
   III Book 5: 5 Sun after Pent
        Book 7: 12 Sun after Pent
        Book 17: 24 Sun after Pent
        Book 22: 10 Sun after Pent
        Book 23: 11 Sun after Pent
        Book 25: 21 Sun after Pent
        Book 26: 13 Sun after Pent
   IV Book 8: Sts Peter &Paul
        Book 28: Visitation 1
    V   Book 24: St Martin
The Dialogues (*Dialogi*)
    I   Book 2: 3 Sun Advent

III   Corp Chr
IV   Book 4: Visitation 2
 V   Book 3: Dedication of church
      All Souls
Commentary on Ezechiel (*Commentarius in Ezechielem Prophetam*)
III   Homily 10: 11 Sun after Pent
Commentary on 1 Kings (*Commentarium in libros I regum*)
IV   St Peter's Chair
Commentary on the Song of Songs (*Expositio super Cantica Canticorum*)
II   1 Sun after Easter
Letter to Gregoria (*Epistola a Gregoria*)
II   3 Sun after Easter

GREGORY NAZIANZEN
On Holy Baptism (*Oratione in S. Baptisma*)
II   Oration 40: Easter 2
On Love for the Poor (*De pauperum amore*)
III   Oration 14: 5 Sun after Pent
On Theology and the Appointment of Bishops
(*De theologia et constitutione episcoporum*)
 V   Oration 20: St Catherine
First Theological Oration (Oratio theological prima)
III   Oration 27: 16 Sun after Pent
On his sister Gorgonia (In laudem sororis suae Gorgoniae)
IV   Oration 8: St Joseph

GREGORY OF NYSSA
On the Beatitudes (*De beatitudinibus*)
 I   Oration 5: 1 Sun Advent
On Christian Profession (*De professione christiana*)
III   6 Sun after Pent
On the Soul and the Resurrection (*De anima et resurrectione*)
III   17 Sun after Pent
Homilies on the Song of Songs (*In Canticum Canticorum*)
IV   Homily 1: Sts Peter & Paul

HAYMO OF HALBERSTADT
Homily for the Seventh Sunday after Pentecost
III   Homily 118: 5 Sun after Pent
      Homily 129:16 Sun after Pent

On the Feast of St Andrew the Apostle (*In die S. Andreae Apostoli*)
    IV Homily 1: St Andrew

HEIRIC OF AUXERRE
Homilies for the Entire Year (*Homiliae per circulum anni*)
    III 10 Sun after Pentecost

HESIOD
Works and Days (*Operum et dierum*)
    I St John Ev

HILARY OF POITIERS
Commentary on St Matthew's Gospel
  (*Commentarius in Evangelium Matthaei*)
    I 1 Sun after Epiph
    IV Sts Peter & Paul
    V St Michael Arch, St Luke, St Catherine
Against Constantius (*Contra Constantium Augustum*)
    IV Sts Peter & Paul

HIPPOCRATES
Aphorisms (ἀφορισμός)
    III 18 Sun after Pent

HORACE (QUINTUS HORATIUS FLACCUS)
The Odes and Carmen Saeculare
    III Book 4: 24 Sun after Pent
    IV Book 3: St Nicholas
Epistles
    V Book 1: St Anne

HUGH OF SAINT-CHER
Commentary on the Psalms
    III 22 Sun after Pent

IDIOTA (RAYMUNDUS JORDANUS?)
Meditations on Divine Love (*Contemplationes de Amore Divino*)
    III 17 Sun after Pent
Contemplations of the Blessed Virgin Mary (*De contemplatione virginis*)
    V Prologue: Nativity BVM 1, Nativity BVM 2

IGNATIUS OF ANTIOCH (IGNATIUS MARTYR)
Epistle to the Ephesians (*Epistola ad Ephesios*)
    I   Epiphany Sun
Epistle to the Romans (*Epistola ad Romanos*)
    II Passion 1
    III Corp Chr
    IV Bl Godfrey

ISIDORE OF SEVILLE
On the Highest Good (*De Summo Bono*)
    II Book 3: 1 Sun Lent
    III 5 Sun after Pent

JEROME
Against the Pelagians (*Adversus Pelagianos*)
    II Book 2: 5 Sun Lent
Against Vigilantius (*Contra Vigilantium*)
    I   Book 1: 2 Sun after Epiph
    III Book 4: 23 Sun after Pent
Commentary on Daniel (*Commentarium in Danielem*)
    IV Annunciation 1
Commentary on Galatians
  (*Commentarii in Epistulam Pauli Apostoli Ad Galatas*)
    I   Book 3: St John Ev
Commentary on Habakkuk (*Commentarii in Habacuc*)
    IV St Peter's Chair
Commentary on Haggai (*Commentarius in prophetae Haggaei*)
    IV St Herman-Joseph
Commentary on St Matthew's Gospel
  (*Commentarii in evangelium Matthaei*)
    I   Book 1: St Stephen
    II Passion 2
    III 14 Sun after Pent, 16 Sun after Pent
        Book 26: 19 Sun after Pent
Homilies on Ezekiel (*Homilia in Ezechielem*)
    II Homily 33: 5 Sun Lent
Letter to Demetrias (*Ad Demetriadem*
    II Letter 130: Ash Wednesday
Letter to Eustochium (*Ad Eustochium*)
    I   Letter 22: St Stephen

Letter to Fabiola (*Ad Fabiolam*)
    III   Letter 64: 4 Sun after Pent
    IV   Letter 78: St Mark
Letter to Florentius (*Ad Florentium*)
    III   Letter 4: 24 Sun after Pent
Letter to Furia (*Ad Furiam*)
    II   Letter 54: Ash Wednesday
    III   6 Sun after Pent
Letter to Heliodorus (*Ad Heliodorum*)
    III   Letter 14: 24 Sun after Pent
Letter to Innocent (*Ad Innocentem*)
    III   Letter 1: 24 Sun after Pent
Letter to Laeta (*Ad Laetam*)
    IV   Letter 107: Finding of Cross
Letter to Marcella (*Ad Marcellam*)
    III   Letter 43: 22 Sun after Pent
Letter to Pammachius (*Ad Pammachiam*)
    V   Letter 66: All Souls
Life of Saint Hilarion (*Vita S. Hilarionis Eremytæ*)
    III   Pentecost Tues
The Interpretation of Hebrew Names (*De nominibus Hebraicis*)
    V   Nativity BVM 1

JOHN CALVIN
Acts of the Council of Trent with the Antidote
    (*Les Actes du Concile de Trent, avec le remède contre la poison*)
    I   5 Sun after Epiph

JOHN CASSIAN
The Conferences (*Collationes*)
    II   Conference 10: 5 Sun after Easter
On the Incarnation (*De incarnatione Christi*)
    IV   Book 3: Sts Peter & Paul

JOHN CHRYSOSTOM
Homilies Against the Jews (Κατὰ Ἰουδαίων)
    I   6 Sun after Epiph
Homilies for Pentecost (*Sermones in Pentecosten*)
    III   Sermon 1: Pentecost Sun 1

Homily on the Holy Martyrs (*De sanctis martyribus*)
    IV   Homily 1: St Andrew
    V   Homily 3: St Norbert, St Martin

Homilies on Hannah (*Sermones de Anna*)
    II 5 Sun after Easter

Homilies on the Acts of the Apostles (*In acta apostolorum*)
    IV   Homily 3: St Matthias

On Genesis (*Homiliae in Genesim*)
    II   Sermon 1: Ash Wednesday
    III Sermon 5: 4 Sun after Pent
           Sermon 28: 21 Sun after Pent
           Sermon 34: 5 Sun after Pent
    IV   Sermon 9: Sts Peter & Paul

On Penance (*De paenitentia*)
    II   Homily 3: 3 Sun Lent
    I   Homily 5: 1 Sun Advent

On the Cross and the Robber (*De cruce et latrone*)
    IV   Homily 4: Finding of Cross

On the Epistle to the Hebrews (*In epistolam ad Hebraeos*)
    II   Homily 24: Easter Sun 2

On the Epistle to the Romans (*In epistolam ad Romanos*)
    I   Homily 32: 2 Sun after Epiph
    III Homily 4: 8 Sun after Pent

On the Gospel of John (*In Ioannem*)
    I   Homily 29: 2 Sun Advent
    II   Homily 3: Passion 2
           Homily 45: Easter Sun 2
           Homily 83: Passion 2
    III Corp Chr
    IV   Homily 19: St Andrew

On the Gospel of Matthew (*In Matthaeum*)
    II   Homily 56: 2 Sun Lent
           Homily 70: 5 Sun after Easter
    III Homily 4: 22 Sun after Pent, 23 Sun after Pent
           Homily 21: 14 Sun after Pent
           Homily 28: 4 Sun after Pent
           Homily 83: Corp Chr
    IV   Homily 54: St Peter's Chair
           Homily 64: St Matthias

JOHN DAMASCENE
An Exact Exposition of the Orthodox Faith
(ἔκδοσις ακριβὲς της ορθοδόχου πίστεως)
    I   Book 3: Sunday in Oct Christmas
Oration on the Nativity of the Blessed Virgin Mary
(*Sermo in nativitate B. Mariae V.*)
    V   St Anne
Sermons on the Assumption (*De Assumptione*)
    V   Sermon 2: Nativity BVM 1

JOSEPHUS
Antiquities of the Jews (*Antiquitates Iudaicae*)
    I   Book 19: 4 Sun Advent
    II   Book 14: Passion 2
    III   Book 18: 22 Sun after Pent
The War of the Jews (*de Bello Iudaico*)
    II   Book 4: 2 Sun Lent
    V   Book 5: Dedication of church

JUVENAL (DECIMUS IUNIUS IUVENALIS)
The Satires
    III   Book 5 (satire XIV): 14 Sun after Pent

LACTANTIUS (LUCIUS CAECILIUS FIRMIANUS LACTANTIUS)
Divine institutes (*Institutions divinae*)
    III   15 Sun after Pent

LAËRTIUS, DIOGENES
Lives of the Eminent Philosophers
(Βίοι καὶ γνῶμαι τῶν ἐν φιλοσοφίᾳ εὐδοκιμησάντων)
    II   Book II: Easter Mon

LAURENCE JUSTINIAN
Treatise on Obedience (*de Obedientia*)
    I   Ch. 5: 3 Sun Advent
    III   12 Sun after Pent

LAURENTIUS SURIUS
(*see* Surius, Laurentius

MACROBIUS (MACROBIUS AMBROSIUS THEODOSIUS)
Saturnalia
>   III   21 Sun after Pent

MARTIN LUTHER
On the Bondage of the Will *(De Servo Arbitrio)*
>   I   5 Sun after Epiph

MAXIMUS OF TURIN
On having no fear of carnal foes *(De hostibus carnalibus non timendis)*
>   III   14 Sun after Pent
On the Nativity of the Lord VII *(Sermo De nativitate Domini)*
>   I   Sermon 13: Christmas 2
Sermon for all Martyrs *(De Sanctis martyribus)*
>   II   6 Sun after Easter

ORIGEN
Commentary on Jeremiah *(Commentarius in Ieremiam)*
>   IV   Homily 16: St Peter's Chair
Homilies on Exodus *(In Exodum)*
>   I   Homily 13: 1 Sun Advent
Homilies on Ezekiel *(Homiliae in Ezechielem)*
>   IV   Sts Peter & Paul
Homilies on Luke *(Homiliae in Lucam)*
>   II   Homily 25: 5 Sun Lent
>   IV   Homily 7: Visitation 1
Homilies on the Psalms *(Selectarum in Psalmos)*
>   III   Homily 2: 22 Sun after Pent

OVID (PUBLIUS OVIDIUS NASO)
Lamentations *(Tristia)*
>   II   Passion 1
Metamorphoses
>   IV   Book 1: Conv St Paul
>   Visitation 2
The Loves: the Doorkeeper *(Amores)*
>   II   Passion 2

PASCHASIUS RADBERTUS
Commentary on the Lamentations of Jeremiah
(*In lamentations Ieramiae Prophetae*)
   III   Book 2: 9 Sun after Pent
Commentary on St Matthew's Gospel
   III   Book 10: 22 Sun after Pent

PELAGIUS
Letter to Demetrias (*Epistola ad Demetriadem*)
   V   All Saints 1

PEREIRA, BENEDICT
De principiis
   III   Book 1, ch. 1: 8 Sun after Pent

PETER CHRYSOLOGUS
Sermon 25 On Renouncing the Things of this World
(*De terrenorum cura despicienda*)
   III   14 Sun after Pent
Sermon 29 On Avarice (*De avaritia*)
   III   16 Sun after Pent
Sermon 33 On the Twenty-third Sunday after Pentecost
   III   23 Sun after Pent
        Sermon 34: 23 Sun after Pent

PETER DAMIAN
Letter to Cencius (*Ad Cinthium Urbis Praefectus*)
   II   6 Sun after Easter
On the Birth of the Blessed Virgin Mary
(*In nativitate beatissimae virginis Mariae*)
   V   Homily 46: Nativity BVM 2
Sermon on St Luke the Evangelist
   V   Sermon 53: St Luke

PHILO JUDAEUS
 On the Embassy to Gaius (*De legatione ad Caium*)
   I   4 Sun Advent

PINDAR
The Victory Odes
   III   Book 1: 24 Sun after Pent

PLATO
Dialogues: Minos
    III Pentecost Sun 1

PLINY THE ELDER
Natural History (*Naturalis Historia*)
    I Book 11: 6 Sun after Epiph
    IV Book 37: Presentation BVM
    V St Norbert

PLUTARCH
Customs of the Spartans (*Instituta Laconica*)
    III 15 Sun after Pent
On the Love of Wealth (*De cupiditate*)
    III 16 Sun after Pent
Parallel Lives: The Life of Julius Caesar
    I 4 Sun after Epiph

PROCLUS OF CONSTANTINOPLE
Sermon on the Annunciation (*De annuntiatione*)
    IV Annunciation 1

PSEUDO-AMBROSE
On the Feast of Sts Nazarius and Celsus
    III 20 Sun after Pent, 23 Sun after Pent

PSEUDO-ATHANASIUS
On Virginity (*De virginitate*)
    II Ash Wednesday

PSEUDO-AUGUSTINE
Hypognosticon
    III Book 3: 13 Sun after Pent
On the Triple Abode (*De triplici* habitaculo)
    III Book 1: 2 Sun after Pent
On True and False Penance (*Liber de vera et falsa penitentia*)
    IV St Herman-Joseph
Questions on the Old and New Testaments
    (*Quaestiones Veteris et Novi Testamenti*)
    III 16 Sun after Pent, 18 Sun after Pent

Sermons on the Feast of the Holy Innocents (*Sermo de Innocentibus*)
    I   Holy Innocents
    III 9 Sun after Pent, 13 Sun after Pent
Sermons to the brothers in the hermitage (*Sermones ad fraters in eremo*)
    V   Sermon 31: St Matthew, Sermon 44: All
        Souls, Sermon 49: St Matthew

PSEUDO-AUGUSTINE (ALCHER OF CLAIRVAUX)
On the Spirit and the Soul (*De Spiritu et Anima*)
    I   6 Sun after Epiph
    III Pentecost 2

PSEUDO-AUGUSTINE (HIBERNICUS)
On the miraculous things in Sacred Scripture
  (*De mirabilibus Sacrae Scripturae*)
    I   Epiphany

PSEUDO-AUGUSTINE (QUODVULTDEUS)
Sermons on Barbaric Times II (*De tempore barbaric*)
    III 12 Sun after Pent

PSEUDO-BONAVENTURE (JOHAN OF CAULIBUS?)
Meditations on the Life of Christ (*Meditationes Vitae Christi*)
    IV Purification BVM

PSEUDO-CHRYSOSTOM
On St Matthew's Gospel — unfinished
  (*Opus imperfectum in Matthaeum*)
    III Homily 11: 5 Sun after Pent

PSEUDO-DIONYSIUS THE AREOPAGITE
On the Divine Names (*De divinis nominibus*)
    III Trinity Sun
    IV Sts Peter & Paul
    V   Conv St Aug
Ecclesiastical Hierarchy (*De eccclesiastica hierarchia*)
    III 17 Sun after Pent

PSEUDO-EPIPHANIUS
Homily In Praise of Holy Mary, Mother of God (*De laudibus Virginis*)
    V   St Anne

PSEUDO-IGNATIUS
Epistle to the Philippians (*Epistola ad Philippenses*)
    II   Ash Wednesday

PSEUDO-JEROME
Sermon on the Assumption (*Sermo de Assumptionis BMV*)
    IV   Annunciation 2

PUBLILIUS SYRUS
Sentences (*Sententiae*)
    I   Christmas 1
    V   St Norbert

QUINTILLIAN (MARCUS FABIUS QUINTILIANUS)
Institutes of Oratory (*Institutio Oratoria*)
    V   St Luke

QUINTUS CURTIUS RUFUS
History of Alexander the Great (*Historiae Alexandri Magni*)
    V   Book 4: Dedication of church

REMIGIUS (RÉMY) OF AUXERRE
Commentary on St Matthew
    V   ch.10: St Luke

RICHARD OF ST VICTOR
On the Song of Songs (*Explicatio in Cantica canticorum*).
    II   Part 2: 4 Sun after Easter

ROBERT BELLARMINE
    (*see* Bellarmine, Robert)

RUPERT OF DEUTZ
On the Divine Office (*Liber de divinis officiis*)
    IV   Annunciation 1
Commentary on Canticles (*Commentaria in canticum canticorum*)
    V   Book 6: Nativity BVM 1

SALVIANUS OF MARSEILLES
On the Government of God (*De gubernatione dei*)
    II   3 Sun after Easter

SENECA (LUCIUS ANNAEUS SENECA)
Moral letters to Lucilius (*Epistulae morales ad Lucilium*)
    IV Letter 84: Visitation 2
    II Letter 97: 5 Sun Lent

SUAREZ, FRANCIS
On the One and Triune God (*De Deo uno et trino*)
    III Pentecost Sun 1

SUETONIUS (GAIUS SUETONIUS TRANQUILLUS)
Life of Titus
    IV Book 8: St Nicholas

SULPICIUS SEVERUS
Letters to Eusebius (*Ad Eusebio*)
    V Letter 3: St Martin
Life of St Martin (*Vita Martini*)
    V St Martin

SURIUS, LAURENTIUS
The Life of St Thomas Aquinas (*Vita Sancti Thomae Aquinatis*)
    III 16 Sun after Pent

SYMMACHUS, POPE
Against Anastasius (*Adversus Anastasii*)
    III 24 Sun after Pent

TERTULLIAN
Address to the martyrs (*Ad martyres*)
    V All Saints 1
Against Marcion (*Adversus Marcionem*)
    I Book 2: 5 Sun after Epiph
       Book 4: 3 Sun Advent
    III Book 3: 14 Sun after Pent, 2 Sun after Pent
Against the Gnostics (*Liber contra Gnostici*)
    I ch. 8: 2 Sun Advent
On Fasting, against the materialistic (*De ieiunio adversus psychicos*)
    II Ash Wednesday
On Modesty (*Liber de Pudicitia*)
    III 3 Sun after Pent

On the Military Garland (*De corona militis*)
    V All Souls
On the Resurrection of the Flesh (*De Resurrectione Carnis*)
    I 1 Sun Advent
    II Easter 1

THEODORET OF CYRUS
A History of the Monks of the Desert (*Historia religiosa*)
    III Trinity Sun
Cure of the Greek Maladies (*De Graecarum Affectionum Curatio*)
    I 6 Sun after Epiph
    III 8 Sun after Pent

THEOPHYLACT OF OHRID
Explanation of St Matthew's Gospel
    III 21 Sun after Pent

THOMAS À KEMPIS
The Imitation of Christ (*De Imitatione Christi*)
    I Book 1, ch.1: 3 Sun Advent

THOMAS AQUINAS
Commentary on Aristotle's Posterior Analytics (*Posteriora Analytica*)
    II Book 1: 3 Sun after Easter
Commentary on St John
    III Pentecost Sun 1
Commentary on St Luke
    III 16 Sun after Pent
Commentary on the First Epistle to the Corinthians
  (*Super I ad Corinthios*)
    I 5 Sun after Epiph
    III 17 Sun after Pent
Commentary on the Four Gospels (*Catena aurea*)
    III 4 Sun after Pent
Commentary on St Matthew
    II 2 Sun Lent
    III 14 Sun after Pent
Commentary on St Paul's Letter to the Ephesians
    III 21 Sun after Pent
Commentary to the Sentences (*Scripta super libros Sententiarum*)
    II Book 1: 3 Sun after Easter

Summa Theologiae

   I   I, Q 73, A 3: New Year's Day
         I: II, Q 27, A 3: St John Ev
         I: II, Q 87, A 4, ad 3: 3 Sun Advent
         II: II, Q 124, A 3: St Stephen
         Suppl. III, Q 73, A 1, ad 1:1 Sun Advent
         III, Q 57, A 4: St Stephen
   II II: II, Q 87, A 16: 6 Sun after Easter
         III, Q 46, A 6: Passion 1
         III, Q 53, A 1: Easter Sun 1
         III, Q 53, A 2: Easter Sun 1
   III I, Q 43, A 3: Pentecost Sun 1
         I, Q 49, A. 2, Reply Obj. 3: 6 Sun after Pent
         I: II, Q 31, A 6: 17 Sun after Pent
         I: II, Q 32, A 3: 17 Sun after Pent
         II: II, Q 8, A 1: 8 Sun after Pent
         II: II, Q 23, A 6: 17 Sun after Pent
         II: II, Q 26, A 6: 12 Sun after Pent
         III, Q 1, A 3: 16 Sun after Pent
   IV I, Q 38, A 2: St Matthias
         II: II, Q 162, A 7, ad 3: Sts Peter & Paul
         III, Q 27, A 6: St Herman-Joseph
   V I: II, Q 113, A 9: St Norbert
         II: II, Q 8, A 1: St Catherine

THOMAS OF VILLANOVA

Sermons on the Nativity (*In Nativitatis Domini*)
   I Sermon 2: Christmas 2, 6 Sun after Epiph
Sunday Sermons (*Conciones in Dominicis totius anni*)
   II Ascension

VALERIUS MAXIMUS

Memorable doings and sayings
  (*Factorum et Dictorum Memorabilium Libri IX*)
   V Book 2: St Martin
   I Book 9: Holy Innocents

VEGETIUS (PUBLIUS FLAVIUS VEGETIUS RENATUS)

Concerning Military Matters (*De re militari*)
   II Book 3: Easter Tues

VINCENT FERRER
Sermon on the Trinity (*Sermo de sancta Trinitate*)
  III Sermon 2: Trinity Sun

VIRGIL (PUBLIUS VIRGILIUS MARO)
Bucolics (*Eclogae*)
  I Eclogue 1: 6 Sun after Epiph
The Georgicks (*Georgicorum*)
  III 17 Sun after Pent

WILLIAM OF PARIS
Divine rhetoric (*Rhetorica divina*)
  II 5 Sun after Easter

☩   ☩   ☩

LITURGICAL AND OTHER SOURCES

HYMNS
  III *O quam gloriosum*: 19 Sun after Pent
      Pange lingua: 9 Sun after Pent
      Veni Creator Spiritus: Pentecost Sun 1
  IV *Lauda mater ecclesia*: Conv St Paul
      Memento, salus Auctor: Annunciation 2
  V *Aeterne rerum conditor*: St Matthew
      Salve Regina: Nativity BVM 2
      Te Deum: Assumption 2

COUNCIL OF ADGE
  V Dedication of church

COUNCIL OF TRENT
On the Most Holy Eucharist (*De Sanctissimo Eucharistiae*)
  III Session 13: Corp Chr
On the Most Holy Sacraments of Penance and Extreme Unction
  (*De Poenitentiae et extremae Unctionis Sacramentis*)
  III Session 14: Pentecost 2

DIVINE OFFICE
  IV Christmas Day, Lauds, 2nd antiphon: St Joseph
      Circumcision, Vespers I, antiphon: Presentation
      Common of the BVM, Versicle: Imm Conc

St Andrew, Matins, lection 5: St Andrew
St Philip & St James, Matins, versicle: Sts. Philip & James
Nativity of BVM, Matins, responsory: Imm Conc
V   All Saints, Matins, responsory: All Saints 2
Common of the Dedication of a Church, Matins, responsory:
    Dedication of church
Common of Virgins, Vespers I, antiphon: Nativity BVM 2
Nativity of the BVM, Vespers II, Mag. antiphon: Nativity BVM
    1
Purification, Vespers I, antiphon: St Anne
St John the Baptist, Matins, hymn: All Saints 2
St Laurence, Matins, responsory: St Laurence
St Laurence, Matins, versicle: St Laurence
St Michael the Archangel, Matins, responsory: St Michael Arch
St Michael the Archangel's Apparition at Gargano, Matins,
    responsory: St Michael Arch
Little Office of the BVM (*Officium Parvum*) Assumption,
    Matins, antiphon: Assumption 1

ROMAN MISSAL

V   Feast of St Luke, collect: St Luke
From the liturgy of Ash Wednesday, verse: All Souls
Seventh Sunday after Pentecost, collect: Conv St Aug
Tenth Sunday after Pentecost, collect: Conv St Aug

ROMAN RITUAL

V   Rite of Baptism: Dedication of church

OTHER

I   Litany of the Saints: 1 Sun Advent
II Easter Proclamation (*Exsultet*): 4 Sun after Easter
Nicene Creed: 4 Sun after Easter
III *Dies Irae* Sequence: 3 Sun after Pent
O Sapientia. Antiphon for Advent: 6 Sun after Pen
Passio Sanctorum Viti, Modesti et Crescentiae: 5 Sun after Pent
Vita Godefridi Comitis Cappenbergensis 1124: 15 Sun after Pent
V   *Vita Norberti B* (12th cent): St Norbert

Biographical List of
Authors and Historical Figures
MENTIONED IN THE SERMONS

Abibus of Nekresi, Saint (d. 6th century) Helped spread Christianity in
Georgia. Bishop of Nekresi. Fought against Zoroastrianism. Stoned
to death by the Persians.

Aelius Galenus *See* Galen of Pergamon.

Alexander the Great (356 BC–323 BC) King of the ancient Greek kingdom of Macedon. Conducted numerous military campaigns throughout Asia and North Africa. Created one of the largest empires in
history, stretching from Greece to India. Considered one of history's
greatest and most successful military commanders.

Alexander Monachus (Alexander the Cypriot) (mid-6th century?)
Cypriot monk who wrote a treatise on the history of the early Church.

Alexander of Phrygia (mid-3rd century) Bishop of Hierapolis. His works
are now lost.

Alfonso Tostado Ribera de Madrigal (Tostatus Abulensis) (1400–1455)
Spanish theologian and exegete. Bishop of Avila.

Ambrose, Saint (c.340–397) Bishop of Milan. Doctor of the Church.
Staunchly opposed Arianism. Strongly influenced St Augustine of
Hippo.

Anaxagoras (510 BC–428 BC) Pre-Socratic Greek philosopher.

Andrea Alciato (1492–1550) Commonly known as Alciati. Italian jurist
and writer.

Angela of Foligno, Saint (1248–1309) Italian Franciscan Tertiary and
mystic.

Anicius Manlius Severinus Boëthius (477–524) Roman senator, consul,
philosopher.

Anselm of Canterbury, Saint (1033–1109) Italian Benedictine monk,
abbot, philosopher and theologian. Later consecrated as Archbishop
of Canterbury.

Antiochus IV Epiphanes (c.215 BC–164 BC) Hellenistic king of the Seleucid Empire.

Antoninus of Florence, Saint (1389–1459) Italian Dominican friar and theologian. Archbishop of Florence.

Antoninus Verus (Marcus Aurelius) Roman Emperor from AD 161–180.

Apelles of Kos (370 BC–306 BC) Greek painter.

Aquila Ponticus (Onkelos) 2nd century translator of the Old Testament into Greek.

Aristotle (384 BC–322 BC) Greek philosopher. Sometimes called the "Father of Western Philosophy."

Arminius, Jacobus (1560–1609) Dutch Reformer and Protestant. Founder of the Remonstrants.

Arnald Carnotensis (Arnold of Chartres) (1144–1156) Cistercian abbot of Bonneval and biographer of St Bernard of Clairvaux.

Arnold of Chartres *See* Arnald Carnotensis.

Athanasius, Saint (296–373) Patriarch of Alexandria. Doctor of the Church. Theologian and writer. Fought strenuously against Arianism.

Athenaeus of Naucratis (170–223). Greco-Egyptian rhetorician and grammarian. Author of the *Deipnosophistae* (Banquet of the Sophists).

Augustine, Saint (354–430) Bishop of Hippo. Doctor of the Church. Prolific spiritual writer. Author of a monastic Rule still followed today.

Aulus Cornelius Celsus *See* Celsus.

Aulus Gellius (c.120–180) Roman author and grammarian.

Averroës ('Abū l-Walīd Muḥammad bin 'Aḥmad bin Rušd) (1126–1198) Muslim Andalusian philosopher and thinker.

Baronius, Caesar Cardinal (Cesare Baronio) (1538–1607) Member of the Congregation of the Oratory and successor of St Philip Neri. Best known for his monumental work *Annales Ecclesiastici*.

Basil the Great, Saint (330–379) Bishop of Caesaria Mazaca. Theologian, spiritual writer and lover of the poor. One of the fathers of Eastern monasticism.

Bede the Venerable, Saint (672–735) Doctor of the Church. English Benedictine monk. Historian, theologian and scholar.

Bellarmine, Robert Cardinal, Saint (1542–1621) Doctor of the Church. Italian Jesuit Cardinal. Archbishop of Capua. Theologian and rector of the Roman College. Influential in the Counter-Reformation.

Bernard of Clairvaux, Saint (1090–1153) Doctor of the Church. French abbot and reformer of Benedictine monasticism, which led to the foundation of the Cistercian Order. Spiritual writer and promoter of *lectio divina*.

de Blois, Francois-Louis (1506–1566) Flemish Benedictine abbot and mystical writer.

Boëthius *See* Anicius Manlius Severinus Boëthius.

Bonaventure, Saint (1221–1274) Doctor of the Church. Was given the title "Seraphic Doctor". Cardinal Bishop of Albano. Italian Franciscan, theologian, philosopher.

Bridget (Birgitta) of Sweden, Saint (c.1303–1373) Mystic. Foundress of the Brigittine Order.

Bucer, Martin (1491–1551). German Protestant Reformer.

Bullinger, Heinrich (1504–1575) Swiss Protestant Reformer and successor of Zwingli.

Caesarius of Arles, Saint (470–542) Gallic Bishop of Arles and spiritual writer. Wrote the first monastic Rule for women. Fought against semi-Pelagianism.

Cajetan, Thomas Cardinal O.P. (Tommaso de Vio) (1469–1534) Italian philosopher, theologian and cardinal. Fought strenuously against the teachings of Martin Luther.

Cassiodorus. *See* Flavius Magnus Aurelius Cassiodorus Senator.

Celsus (Aulus Cornelius Celsus) (c.25 BC–c.AD 50) Greek philosopher and opponent of early Christianity.

Chrysostom *See* John Chrysostom, Saint.

Cicero (Marcus Tullius Cicero) (106 BC–43 BC) Roman philosopher, politician, lawyer, orator, consul.

Claudius Eusthenius (3rd century) Secretary to Emperor Diocletian and biographer.

Clement of Alexandria, Saint (Clemens Alexandrinus) (150–215) Hellenistic theologian.

Codrus (1091 BC–1070 BC) Last semi-mythical King of Athens. Exemplar of patriotism and self-sacrifice.

Cornelius Cornelii à Lapide (Cornelis Cornelissen van den Steen) (1567–1637) Flemish Jesuit priest. Spiritual writer and commentator on Sacred Scripture.

Crates of Thebes (c.365 BC–c.285 BC) Greek philosopher who gave away his wealth to embrace a life of poverty on the streets of Athens.

Cyprian, Saint (c.200–258) Bishop of Carthage. Prolific spiritual writer who opposed many heresies in the early Church.

Cyril of Alexandria, Saint (378–444) Patriarch of Alexandria. Doctor of the Church. Opponent of Nestorius.

Cyril of Jerusalem, Saint (313–386) Palestinian Bishop of Jerusalem. Wrote extensively on the instructions of catechumens and the liturgy.

Decimus Iunius Iuvenalis *See* Juvenal.

Demosthenes (384 BC–322 BC) Greek statesman and orator.

Denis the Carthusian (Dionysius van Rijkel) (1402–1471) Netherland-ish Carthusian monk, mystic and writer.

Diogenes (c.404 BC–323 BC) Greek philosopher and a founder of Cynic philosophy.

Diogenes Laërtius (c.180–240) Greek historian and biographer of Greek philosophers.

Dionysius the Areopagite, Saint (1st century AD) Convert of St Paul as mentioned in the Acts of the Apostles 17:34. Later became Bishop of Athens.

Dorotheus of Gaza, Saint (d. 565) Christian monk and abbot. Known for his spiritual instructions to monks.

Ebion Second century nebulous figure. No historical data. Gave rise to a school of thought which refuted Christ's divinity.

Eelko Liaukama, Blessed (1260–1322) Twelfth abbot of the Norbertine abbey of Lidlum (Friesland). Assassinated by his brethren when he protested their laxity of observance. Venerated as a martyr in the Norbertine Order.

Ephrem the Syrian, Saint (306–373) Syrian deacon, Doctor of the Church, theologian and hymnographer.

Epiphanius of Salamis, Saint (310–403) Bishop of Salamis. Strong defender of orthodoxy. Fought against many heresies.

Epipodius, Saint (d. 178) Layman. Martyred at Lyon together with his friend St Alexander.

Eucherius of Lyon, Saint (380–449) Bishop of Lyon and spiritual writer.

Eusebius of Emesa (Emissenus) (300–360) Bishop of Emesa (now Homs). Greek theologian, philosopher and scientist. Noted for his great learning and eloquence.

Euthymius the Great, Saint (377–473) Born in Armenia. Abbot, theologian and founder of many monastic communities throughout Palestine.

Eutyches (c.380–456) Greek archimandrite. Denounced at the Council of Chalcedon as a heretic.

Flavius Claudius Julianus *See* Julian the Apostate.

Flavius Magnus Aurelius Cassiodorus Senator (Cassiodorus) (c. 485–585) Roman statesman and writer. He later became a monk and founded a monastery in Calabria.

Francis de Sales, Saint (1567–1622) Bishop of Genoa, Italy. Mystical writer.

Francis of Paola, Saint (1416–1507) Italian mendicant and founder of the Order of Minims.

Francis Suarez (1548–1617) Spanish Jesuit priest, theologian and philosopher.

Francis Xavier, Saint (1506–1552) Spanish Jesuit missionary priest. Co-founder of the Society of Jesus (Jesuits).

Fulbert of Chartres (960–1028) Bishop of Chartres and spiritual writer.

Fulgentius of Ruspe, Saint (460–533) Bishop of Ruspe, abbot and theologian.

Gaius Cassius Longinus (87 BC–42 BC). Roman senator and jurist.

Gaius Fabricius Luscinus Monocularis (3rd cent. BC) Roman statesman and commander. Depicted as a virtuous example of austerity and poverty.

Gaius Mucius Scaevola (524 BC–480 BC) Roman youth famous for his bravery.

Gaius Plinius Secundus *See* Pliny the Elder.

Gaius Popillius Laenas (2nd cent. BC) Roman tribune in Caesar's army.

Gaius Suetonius Tranquillus (d. 122) Roman historian and biographer.

Galen of Pergamon (Aelius Galenus) (130–210) Greek physician, medical researcher, philosopher. [On the Feast of St Peter's Chair;

Génébrard, Gilbert (1535–1597) French Benedictine exegete and Orientalist.

George Cedrenus (Kedrenos) 11th century Byzantine historian and writer.

Germanus I, Saint (c.634–730) Patriarch of Constantinople.

Germanus of Auxerre, Saint (c.378–c.448) Gallic Bishop of Auxerre. Later went to Britain where he fought strenuously against paganism.

Gertrude the Great, Saint (1256–1302) German Benedictine nun, mystic, theologian.

Gnaeus Pompeius Magnus *See* Pompey.

Gomaris, Franciscus (1563–1641) Dutch Calvinist founder of the Gomarists. He upheld the theological position of Supralapsarianism.

Gregory the Great, Pope Saint (Pope Gregory I) (c.540–604) Doctor of the Church. Monastic. Spearheaded the mission to the Anglo-Saxons in England. Reformed the Roman liturgy. Theologian and spiritual writer.

Gregory Nazianzen, Saint (329–390) Doctor of the Church. Archbishop of Constantinople. Helped develop the theology of the doctrine on the Trinity. Spiritual writer.

Gregory of Nyssa, Saint (335–394) Greek bishop and theologian.

Gregory of Tours, Saint (538–594) Bishop of Tours and historian.

Haymo of Auxerre (d. c.865) Benedictine monk and author of exegetical commentaries. Defender of the real presence of Christ in the Eucharist.

Haymo of Halberstadt (778–835) German Benedictine monk. Bishop of Halberstadt. Prolific spiritual writer.

Hegesippus (c.110–180) Christian chronicler of the early Church. Possible Jewish convert. His works are entirely lost apart from some passages quoted by Eusebius.

Heiric of Auxerre (c.841–875?) Frankish Benedictine monk, theologian and writer.

Hermes Trismegistus Legendary pagan prophet, sage, teacher, magician and mystic of ancient times. Lived possibly in the time of Moses.

Herodotus (c.484 BC–c.425 BC) Greek historian, sometimes referred to as the "Father of History".

Hilary of Poitiers, Saint (c.310–367) Gallic bishop. Opposed Arianism. Author of many theological and exegetical works.

Hippocrates (c.460 BC–c.370 BC) Born in Kos. Greek physician. Known as the "Father of Medicine".

Horace (Quintus Horatius Flaccus) (65 BC–8 BC). Roman lyric poet.

Hugh of Saint-Cher (c.1200–1263) French Dominican cardinal and noted biblical commentator.

Idiota. *Nom de plume* of an ancient writer of the late 14th century whose identity remained unknown for centuries. Many identify him with Raymundus Jordanus, a French abbot and Augustinian canon regular, though some dispute this.

Ignatius of Antioch, Saint (c.50–108) Martyr. Bishop and early Christian theologian.

Irenaeus, Saint (c.130–c.202) Bishop of Lyon. Theologian. Fought against gnostic sects.

Isidore of Seville, Saint (560–636) Archbishop of Seville. Scholar, philosopher, writer.

Isidorus Clarius (Isidoro Chiari) (1495–1555) Italian Benedictine abbot and Bishop of Foligno. Noted commentator and translator of the Bible.

Jerome, Saint (347–420) Doctor of the Church. Priest, theologian, historian. Extensive spiritual writer, biblical commentator and translator of the Bible into Latin, known as the Vulgate.

Jesus ben Sira Hellenstic Jew of the 2nd century BC and author of the Book of the Wisdom of Sirach, also known as the Book of Ecclesiasticus.

Jesus (Joshua) son of Navi Entered the Promised Land. He later became the successor of Moses and wrote the Book of Joshua.

Johannes Thaulerus (c.1300–1361) German Dominican priest and mystic.

John Cassian, Saint (c.360–c.435) Founder of the Abbey of St Victor in southern Gaul. His monastic writings and principles profoundly influenced St Benedict of Norcia.

John Chrysostom, Saint (c.349–407) Doctor of the Church. Archbishop of Constantinople. Erudite preacher and prolific author. Reformed the Divine Liturgy.

John Damascene, Saint (c.675–749) Doctor of the Church. Byzantine monk and priest. Spiritual writer. Renowned for his sermons on the Assumption of the Blessed Virgin.

Joshua (Jesus) son of Josedech Jewish High Priest at the time of the prophet Zechariah (6ᵗʰ century BC).

Josephus *See* Titus Flavius Josephus.

Juan de Lugo y de Quiroga (1583–1660) Spanish Jesuit, Cardinal, and eminent theologian.

Julian the Apostate (Flavius Claudius Julianus) (330–363) Roman Emperor who tried to re-establish paganism throughout the Roman Empire.

Justus Lipsius (1547–1606) Flemish philologist, philosopher and humanist.

Juvenal (Decimus Iunius Iuvenalis) (c.60–135?) Roman poet and satirist.

Lactantius. *See* Lucius Caecilius Firmianus Lactantius.

Laurence Giustiniani (Justinian), Saint (1381–1456) Augustinian canon regular. Archbishop of Venice. Author of a number of ascetical and mystical works.

Leo the Great, Pope Saint (Pope Leo I) (c.400–461) Doctor of the Church. Influenced the Council of Chalcedon (451). Saved Rome from barbarian invaders, especially Attila the Hun.

Leonardus Lessius (Lenaert Leijs) (1554–1623) Jesuit Flemish moral theologian.

Libert Froidmont (Libertus Fromondus) (1587–1653) Flemish theologian and scientist. Educated by the Jesuits in Liège. Professor of Scripture at Louvain.

Lucius Annaeus Seneca (Seneca) (d. 65) Roman Stoic philosopher and statesman.

Lucius Caecilius Firmianus Lactantius (c.250–c.325) Early Christian author and adviser to the first Christian Roman emperor, Constantine.

Lucius Cornelius Sulla Felix (138 BC–78 BC) Roman general and statesman.

Lucius Mestrius Plutarchus *See* Plutarch.

Lucius Septimius Severus Augustus (145–211) Roman emperor.

Lucius Sergius Catilina (108 BC–62 BC) Roman senator and distinguished military commander.

Lycurgus of Sparta (800 BC–730 BC) Lawgiver. Reformed Spartan society according to the three virtues of equality, military fitness and austerity.

Macrobius Ambrosius Theodosius (c.370–430) Roman provincial whose writings influenced the thought of medieval Europe.

Manius Curius Dentatus (321 BC–270 BC) Consul and hero of the Roman Republic.

Marsilio Ficino (1433–1499) Italian priest, scholar, humanist philosopher and astrologer.

Marcion of Sinope (c.85–160) Follower of St Paul. Some early Christian Fathers denounced him as a heretic for preaching errant theology.

Marcus Annaeus Lucanus (39–65) Roman statesman and Latin poet.

Marcus Aurelius *See* Antoninus Verus.

Marcus Fabius Quintilianus (Quintillian) (35–100) Roman rhetorician.

Marcus Junius Brutus (85 BC–42 BC) Senator of the Roman Republic. Took a leading role in the assassination of Julius Caesar.

Marcus Tullius Cicero *See* Cicero.

Mary Magdalene de Pazzi, Saint (1566–1607) Italian Carmelite nun and mystic.

Maximus of Turin, Saint (d. c.465) Bishop of Turin. Theologian and author of numerous homilies, sermons and other spiritual writings.

Megasthenes (350 BC–290 BC) Greek ethnographer and explorer. Ambassador to India.

Nicephorus (1084–1090) Greek Patriarch of Antioch.

Numa Pompilius (753 BC–673 BC) Second king of Rome, succeeding Romulus.

Oecolampadius, Johannes (1483–1531) German Protestant Reformer.

Onkelos. *See* Aquila Ponticus.

Origen (c.184–c.253) Worked mainly in Alexandria. Early Christian theologian, scholar and ascetic. Prolific spiritual writer, apologist and exegete. His works influenced the early Church Fathers.

Ovid. *See* Publius Ovidius Naso.

Paschasius Radbertus (785–865) Frankish theologian and abbot of Corbie.

Pererius (Pereira), Benedict (1536–1610) Spanish Jesuit philosopher, theologian and exegete.

Peter Chrysologus, Saint (c.380–450) Doctor of the Church. Bishop of Ravenna. Renowned preacher.

Peter Damian, Saint (1007–1072?) Doctor of the Church. Italian Benedictine monk and cardinal-bishop of Ostia.

Petrus Comestor (1100–1178) French theological writer and university administrator.

Philo Judaeus (25 BC–AD 50) Hellenistic Jewish philosopher. Lived in Alexandria, Egypt.

Pindar (c.522 BC–c.443 BC) Ancient Greek lyric poet from Thebes.

Plato (c.429 BC–c.348 BC) Ancient Greek scholar whose thoughts had a profound influence on Western spirituality and philosophy.

Pliny the Elder (Gaius Plinius Secundus) (23–79) Roman author, naturalist and philosopher.

Plutarch (Lucius Mestrius Plutarchus) (c.46–c.120) Greek biographer, philosopher, moralist, magistrate.

Pompey (Gnaeus Pompeius Magnus) (106 BC–48 BC) Roman military and political leader.

Proclus of Constantinople, Saint (d. 446) Greek archbishop. Friend and disciple of St John Chrysostom. Noted for his writings on Mariology.

Procopius of Caesarea (c.500–c.570) Byzantine scholar, historian and legal adviser.

Pseudo-Athanasius A collection of treatises by unknown authors falsely attributed to St Athanasius of Alexandria.

Pseudo-Augustinus Hibernicus Anonymous 7th century Irish writer and philosopher.

Pseudo-Bonaventure The name given to the authors of a number of medieval devotional works believed at the time to be the work of St Bonaventure.

Pseudo-Dionysius the Areopagite Anonymous 6th century Syrian Christian theologian and philosopher who portrayed himself as the figure of Dionysius the Areopagite.

Publilius Syrus (85 BC–43 BC) Born in Syria. Former slave. Latin writer and author.

Publius Cornelius Tacitus (d. 117) Roman historian and senator. His most famous works are the *Annals* and *Histories* of the Roman Emperors.

Publius Cornelius Scipio Africanus (236 BC–183 BC) Roman general and consul.

Publius Flavius Vegetius Renatus. Late 4th century Roman writer, mainly known for his manual on military science.

Publius Ovidius Naso (43BC–AD18?). Roman poet.

Publius Servilius Casca Longus (84 BC–42 BC). Roman senator.

Publius Ventidius Bassus (1ˢᵗ century BC). Roman general and protégé of Julius Caesar.

Publius Virgilius Maro (Virgil) (70 BC–19 BC). Roman poet.

Quintillian *See* Marcus Fabius Quintilianus.

Quintus Curtius Rufus (1st century AD). Roman historian.

Quintus Horatius Flaccus *See* Horace.

Quintus Septimius Florens Tertullianus (Tertullian) (155–220) Prolific early Christian author from Carthage. Scholar, apologist, theologian. Known as the "Founder of Western Theology".

Quintus Sertorius (126 BC–72 BC) Roman statesman and general.

Remigius (Rémy) of Auxerre (841–908) Benedictine monk, teacher and commentator on scriptural and classical texts.

Richard of Middleton (c.1249–c.1308) Franciscan theologian and scholastic philosopher.

Richard of Saint Victor (d. 1173) Scottish Augustinian canon, philosopher and theologian. Later Prior of the Augustinian Abbey of Saint Victor in Paris.

Rupert of Deutz (1075–1129) Benedictine abbot, theologian, exegete and prolific writer on religious subjects.

Salianus, Jacobus (1557–1640) French Jesuit rhetorician, philosopher, theologian and biblical commentator.

Salvianus of Marseilles (5ᵗʰ cent.) Christian writer. Later he and his wife embraced monasticism.

Scipio. *See* Publius Cornelius Scipio Africanus.

Seleucus I Nicator (358 BC–281 BC) Greek infantry general who served under Alexander the Great. He established the Seleucid Empire.

Seneca *See* Lucius Annaeus Seneca.

Serapion the Sindonite, Saint (d. 356) Egyptian monk noted for the severity of his ascetic practices.

Simon Magus. Also known as Simon the Sorcerer. His confrontation with St Peter is recorded in the Acts of the Apostles 8:924.

Simonides of Ceos (556 BC–468 BC). Greek lyric poet.

Sixtus II, Pope Saint (d. 258) Martyred together with seven deacons under the Emperor Valerian.

Solon (638 BC–588 BC) Athenian statesman, lawmaker and poet.

Sophronius, Saint (560–638) Monk and theologian. Patriarch of Jerusalem.

Sulla. *See* Lucius Cornelius Sulla Felix.

Sulpicius Severus (363–425) French writer and biographer of St Martin of Tours. After the death of his wife he entered the monastic life.

Surius, Laurentius (1522–1578) German Carthusian hagiographer and Church historian.

Symeon the Metaphrast10th century Greek monk and hagiographer.

Tacitus *See* Publius Cornelius Tacitus.

Tertullian *See* Quintus Septimius Florens Tertullianus.

Theodoret of Cyrrhus (39–457) Bishop of Cyrrhus. Influential theologian and exegete.

Theodosius I Roman emperor from AD 379–395.

Theophylactus (1050–1107) Byzantine archbishop of Ohrid and biblical commentator.

Thermistocles (524 BC–459 BC) Athenian politician and general.

Thomas Aquinas, Saint (1225–1274) Doctor of the Church. Italian Dominican priest, philosopher, exegete and scholastic theologian. Holds the title "Doctor Angelicus". Known especially for one of his greatest works, the *Summa Theologiae*.

Thomas à Kempis (Thomas Hemerken) (1380–1471) Dutch canon regular, priest and devotional writer. Widely held to be the author of *The Imitation of Christ*. Follower of the *Devotio Moderna* movement.

Thomas of Villanova, Saint (1486–1555) Spanish Augustinian friar, later archbishop of Valencia. Noted preacher, ascetic and religious writer.

Thomas Surinus (Thomas O'Sheerin) (d.1673) Irish Franciscan priest, historian, editor and hagiographer. Later worked in Mechelen, Belgium.

Tiburtius, Saint (d.286) Christian martyr beheaded on the Via Labicana in Rome during the persecution of the Emperor Diocletian.

Timanthes of Cythnes (4th century BC) Renowned Greek painter.

Titus Flavius Josephus (d. AD 100) Roman-Jewish historian and scholar. His most important works were *The Jewish War* and *Antiquities of the Jews*.

Titus Flavius Caesar Vespasianus Augustus (Vespasian) (9–79) Roman Emperor.

Titus Lucretius Carus (99 BC–55 BC) Roman poet and philosopher.

Tommaso de Vio *See* Cajetan, Thomas Cardinal.

Tostatus Abulensis *See* Alfonso Tostado Ribera de Madrigal.

Valerius Maximus (14–37) Roman writer and author of historical anecdotes.

Venantius Fortunatus, Saint (c.530–c.600) Bishop of Poitiers and Latin poet.

Vincent Ferrer, Saint (1350–1490) Spanish Dominican priest. Missionary throughout Britain and Europe. Converter of many Jews.

Virgil *See* Publius Virgilius Maro.

Willem Hessels van Est (1542–1613) Dutch exegete. Hagiographer of the Martyrs of Gorcum.

William of Paris (William of Auvergne) (1180?–1249) Bishop of Paris. Scholastic theologian.

William of St-Thierry (1085–1148) Benedictine abbot and mystic. Later became a Cistercian monk.

Xenocrates of Chalcedon (396 BC–314 BC) Greek philosopher and mathematician.

ABOUT THE TRANSLATOR

FR. MARTIN ROESTENBURG, O. Praem., was born in Delft, The Netherlands, in 1957. While still a child his family migrated to Australia, where at 26 years of age he entered the novitiate of the Canons Regular of Prémontré, also known as Premonstratensians or Norbertines. He completed his bachelor's degree in theology at the Pontifical University of St Thomas Aquinas (Angelicum) in Rome. After his ordination in 1991, he returned to Rome where he completed a Licentiate in Sacred Liturgy at the Pontifical Athenaeum of St Anselm (Anselmiano). In 2010 he was invited back to Rome to assist at the Norbertine Generalate, where he currently serves as secretary to the Abbot General and as guest master. He is an Australian national. He is the translator of *Sister Rose: Her Life & Work* and *The Mass of Reparation* by Arthur Loth (Arouca Press, 2021).